J. J. M. Roberts

NAHUM, HABAKKUK, AND ZEPHANIAH

J. J. M. ROBERTS

NAHUM, HABAKKUK, AND ZEPHANIAH

A Commentary

Westminster/John Knox Press
Louisville, Kentucky

© 1991 J. J. M. Roberts

¹/₉₅

Book design by Ken Taylor

First edition

Published by Westminster/John Knox Press
Louisville, Kentucky

PRINTED IN THE UNITED STATES OF AMERICA

9 8 7 6 5 4 3 2 1

Library of Congress Cataloging-in-Publication Data
Roberts, J. J. M. (Jimmy Jack McBee), 1939–
    Nahum, Habakkuk, and Zephaniah : a commentary / J. J. M. Roberts. —
1st ed.
        p.   cm.
    Includes bibliographical references.
    ISBN 0-664-21937-3
    1. Bible. O.T. Nahum—Commentaries. 2. Bible. O.T. Habakkuk—
Commentaries. 3. Bible. O.T. Zephaniah—Commentaries.
I. Bible. O.T. Minor Prophets. English. Roberts. Selections.
1991. II. Title.
BS1625.3.R62 1991
224'.9—dc20   90-24082

c.1

CONTENTS

PREFACE

My work on this commentary began nine years ago, but almost all of the actual writing was done during the academic year 1988–89 while I was on sabbatical leave in Austin, Texas. This large block of time uninterrupted by teaching responsibilities and committee meetings allowed me the leisure to spend hours writing every day. I am very grateful, therefore, to Princeton Theological Seminary, whose very generous sabbatical policy gave me this research time free of financial worries. Without it, this long-delayed commentary would undoubtedly have taken even longer to produce. I am also grateful to the administration, staff, and faculty of Austin Presbyterian Seminary for welcoming me into their scholarly community, allowing me the use of their library, and providing me with convenient and inexpensive housing for the year. I cannot mention everyone at Austin Presbyterian who made our stay in Austin pleasant, but gratefulness demands that I single out Jack Stotts, the President; Robert Shelton, the Dean; Herman Harren, the Treasurer and Vice President for Business Affairs; as well as the two Old Testament faculty members, Prescott Williams and Andrew Dearman. Prescott is an old friend, but I had not met Andy before. He and his wife Kathy were our next door neighbors for a brief period, and throughout our stay in Austin they went out of their way to make us at home. Our new friendship with them and their family is one of the great blessings of our year there. The blessing was scholarly as well as social; Andy's solid scholarship and profound knowledge of the literature in the field made him a sympathetic but critical colleague against which to test my ideas.

I must also thank James Thompson and the faculty and staff of the Institute for Christian Studies in Austin for welcoming me into their delightful scholarly circle. In addition to providing weekly stimulation at their informal luncheons, they courageously allowed me to test my ideas on their constituency in their annual sermon seminar. I should also mention the leadership of both the University Avenue Church of Christ and the Westover Hills Church of Christ, who accepted us into their fellowship and made us a real part of both groups. A special word of thanks goes to our old friends Ed and Peggy Holley, who provided us with invaluable technical and practical help in setting up housekeeping and in furnishing my office and its computer system, and who also kept us sociable by sharing their circle of close friends with us.

I am also indebted to my colleagues and students at Princeton Theological Seminary for their contribution to this commentary. In addition to the students who worked through the Hebrew text of Nahum, Habakkuk, and Zephaniah with me, I should mention my colleague Patrick Miller, who encouraged me with his critical response to a preliminary essay on Habakkuk, and especially my younger colleague, Leong Seow, who took time from his busy schedule to read through several drafts of this manuscript. His critical eye and creative suggestions improved the commentary and saved me from some embarrassing blunders. I should also mention the contribution of a number of current students: Mark George, my research assistant, who helped me prepare the bibliographies; Kathryn De Witt, whose critique of the final revisions suggested some significant improvements; and Scott Starbuck, who provided invaluable computer and printing assistance. Mention should also be made of the Editorial Advisory Board of the Old Testament Library series and the editorial staff at Westminster/John Knox Press. Particular thanks go to David Petersen and Cynthia L. Thompson for their valuable suggestions for improving the manuscript. Despite the contributions of all these individuals, however, they are responsible neither for the opinions expressed in the text nor for any errors that may remain.

This list of those to whom my work on the prophets is indebted would be incomplete without mentioning my family. Without my parents, who taught me to love God's word, and my children, who taught me something of the complexity of parental love and thus influenced my understanding of the Bible's metaphorical language about God, this book would have been a very different book. But my greatest debt is to Genie, my wife and friend for over thirty years, whose support and encouragement have kept me at my scholarly work through good times and bad. For her grace and her beauty, which, even if as fleeting as Proverbs asserts (Prov. 31:30), has nonetheless made my life richer, but especially for her constancy as one who fears the Lord, this book is dedicated to her.

J.J.M.R.

Princeton, New Jersey
June 7, 1990

GENERAL INTRODUCTION

On Reading a Prophetic Book

The average contemporary reader of the Bible often has difficulty when he or she attempts to read a prophetic book with understanding. This is just as true of the devout Christian or religious Jew as it is of the secularist who has only an intellectual interest in the content of the Bible. For many readers, both religious and secular alike, the prophetic literature of the Bible has become a closed corpus, incomprehensible and therefore largely neglected except as a quarry from which to mine a few choice messianic nuggets or moral admonitions. A major reason for this difficulty is that modern readers are most at home with narrative literature or expositional writing, both of which normally develop a story line or an argument sequentially, chapter after chapter. This way of reading works well enough with the narrative literature in the Bible or with the Pauline letters but not with most prophetic books. The typical prophetic book consists of a collection of oracles given by the prophet at different times and occasions during the prophet's sometimes quite extended ministry.

In other words, if one were looking for a modern analogy to the ancient prophetic book, a collection of relatively short sermons by a particular minister would be a good analogy. When reading such a modern collection, one cannot assume that the sermons will be arranged in a particular, logical order. They might be arranged chronologically, they might be arranged topically, they might be arranged to produce some larger logical argument, or they might be arranged in a largely haphazard fashion. One cannot know until one has begun the actual reading, and by the nature of the genre, that reading must focus on the individual sermon as the fundamental unit for interpretation. As an original oral presentation on a discrete occasion or as a literary imitation of such an oral presentation, an individual sermon is complete in itself. Some historical information about the place and occasion of its delivery may help one to understand the sermon better, but one rarely needs to read several sermons in a collection in order to understand any one of them. In most cases, it makes no difference in what order one reads the sermons because the individual sermon is primary, not its placement in the book.

Sometimes, in fact, too much attention to the book as a whole may lead to misinterpretation of a particular sermon. Suppose, for instance, that a book contained a sermon on grace, and immediately following it in the book there was another sermon on the importance of good works. Suppose further that an inattentive reader accidentally turned two pages and thus skipped the end of the sermon on grace and the beginning of the one on works. If the vocabulary were similar, the reader might not notice that he or she had moved to a new literary unit. It would not be at all surprising if, having conflated grace and works, such a reader were puzzled or disturbed by elements of contradiction or inconsistency resulting from this mixing.

Moreover, if one were to write a commentary on a modern book of sermons, one might not find the sermons in the immediate vicinity of the sermon one was exegeting the most helpful for the exegetical task. If the book of sermons were arranged in chronological order, one might find that, for exegeting an early sermon on repentance, much later sermons on the same topic were more helpful than nearly contemporary sermons on other topics. On the other hand, if the sermons were arranged topically, one might find that an examination of all the sermons from the same general period scattered throughout the book shed more light on the particular concerns of a given sermon on faith than any of the other sermons on the same topic. In short, one cannot predict beforehand the best way to read such a book, except to say that the basic unit will normally be the individual sermon.

By analogy, in the typical prophetic book the basic unit of interpretation is the individual oracle. One of the main tasks of the reader is to recognize the beginning and ending of discrete oracles, because reading across oracle boundaries can produce the same confusion and conflict that reading across sermon boundaries causes. Moreover, in the interpretation of a discrete oracle, the oracles standing immediately on either side may contribute little or nothing to the elucidation of the oracle in question. Other oracles scattered chapters away may provide a better key for understanding a particular oracle than any oracle in the immediate vicinity.

This is an important observation, because it cuts against the grain of much contemporary literary and canonical criticism that, by concentrating on biblical *books,* fails to adequately distinguish between prophetic anthologies versus narrative literature. The claim is sometimes made that the sheer juxtaposition of literary units affects their meaning, whether or not such placement was intended to have such an effect; but this is a dubious claim. If a reader recognizes two literary units to be discrete, self-contained units, like two sermons in a book of sermons, two stories in a book of short stories, or an article and an advertisement in a magazine, the fact that these two units are contiguous will have little bearing on the reader's reading of either unit. A competent reader will seldom confuse the two. Moreover, even if two discrete units are mixed, as happens often enough in newspapers where the continuations of two separate articles sometimes get run together, the normal reader usually spots the mistake and edits out the intrusive material. It is only when the reader suspects that such juxtaposition of discrete units is intentional that the reader raises the question of what such juxtaposition means. Normally the juxtaposition of one sermon with another in a book of sermons only means that each sermon has to go somewhere and that it will fit there as well as it would fit somewhere else. The same is true in a typical book of prophetic oracles. It is only when the reader suspects that the particular juxtaposition of oracles in a prophetic collection reflects an intention to impose a higher level of meaning than the individual oracle itself presents that such juxtaposition becomes worthy of interpretation. In the typical prophetic book, such intentional attempts to create higher levels of meaning, particularly when an argument is developed sequentially across several contiguous oracles, are relatively rare.[1] They do occur, as we will see clearly in the book of Habakkuk, but most prophetic books, including Nahum and Zephaniah, show only slight evidence of similar concerns.

On Historical-Critical Scholarship

Nahum, Habakkuk, and Zephaniah are ancient books from a different time, place, and culture than our own, and they are written in a language unfamiliar to most modern readers. The average modern reader knows too little of the history, culture, literary conventions, and linguistic connotations of the vocabulary of these texts to read them with the same immediate comprehension that he or she would enjoy in reading a modern literary work. If one is to overcome that gap in understanding, it will require a significant reliance on the fruits of historical-critical scholarship.

Any attempt to understand an ancient text presupposes a sound textual and philological base, so this commentary pays close attention to issues of textual criticism and philology. Moreover, the character of Nahum, Habakkuk, and Zephaniah as prophetic literature requires that the commentary treat historical questions in some detail. As is generally true of prophetic literature, these books contain numerous passing allusions to historical events, and to understand the implications of these allusions one must learn more about their historical referents than the mere allusions themselves communicate. There are also allusions to other literary, religious, and mythic traditions, some of which require attention to extrabiblical Near

[1]Some contemporary scholars have attempted to demonstrate a coherent and thoroughgoing rationale behind the present arrangement of oracles in the various prophetic books, usually from a late, postexilic redactional context (on Isaiah, for example, see Marvin A. Sweeney, *Isaiah 1–4 and the Post-Exilic Understanding of the Isaianic Tradition* [BZAW 171; Berlin & New York: Walter de Gruyter, 1988] and the earlier literature cited there). In this writer's opinion, however, the intricate connections discovered in such redactional analyses tend to be artificial, contrived, and obvious only to the critic proposing the analysis.

Eastern parallels for full elucidation, so the commentary will also pay attention to questions of Near Eastern backgrounds. But historical-critical scholarship is more than philology, historical reconstruction, and comparative study. Any adequate reading of an ancient work requires some mastery of the literary conventions of the period and genre being studied. Thus issues of form criticism, rhetorical criticism, and redaction criticism are occasionally touched upon. Some may feel that the commentary has not been thoroughgoing enough in its devotion to one or another of these approaches, but I am convinced that devotion to "methods" too often produces a mechanical reading that gets in the way of the actual questions a text may raise or that one may wish to address to a text.[2] The prospects of obtaining a relatively satisfying answer to a question, given the sparsity of the available evidence, has also limited my treatment of certain issues. The treatment of the secondary redaction in Nahum and Zephaniah, for instance, is briefer than some might expect, not because of any doubt that such redaction took place, but because of serious doubts whether the evidence at hand allows us to accurately describe the redactional process, much less divine the rationale at work in its various stages.

On Previous Scholarship

Scholarship builds on the work of those who have gone before, and this commentary is no exception. The attentive reader will note a particular indebtedness to the great German exegete Wilhelm Rudolph. I have often differed from him, but I have always profited from his comments, which is why he is cited more often than any other commentator. Others are also cited, however, and many more have been consulted on every passage than are ever named. As a commentator, I decided early on in this work that the clarity of my own exposition was more important than bibliographic fullness in recording all the variant interpretations and their representatives for each passage. Those readers who regard this decision as flawed will perhaps accept the following selected bibliography of commentaries and exegetical studies on these books as partial amends. It is structured as a general bibliography on Nahum, Habakkuk, and Zephaniah taken together, followed by a specific bibliography on each of the three books.

---

[2]For a fine discussion of the various methods in biblical study, including both their advantages and their limitations, see John Barton, *Reading the Old Testament: Method in Biblical Study* (Philadelphia: Westminster Press, 1984).

ABBREVIATIONS

Biblical Books and Apocrypha

Dead Sea Scrolls

Mur	Wadi Murabba‘at texts
p	pesher (commentary)
Q	Qumran
1QpHab	*Pesher on Habakkuk* from Qumran Cave 1
4QpNah	*Pesher on Nahum* from Qumran Cave 4
1QIsaa	First copy of Isaiah from Qumran Cave 1

Texts and Versions

Arm	Armenian
Barb	Barberini Version of Greek of Habakkuk 3
LXX	Septuagint
MT	Masoretic text
S	Syriac (Peshiṭta)
Syh	Syroḥexaplaris
T	Targum
V	Vulgate

Greek Manuscripts

A	codex Alexandrinus
B	codex Vaticanus
Q	codex Marchalianus
S	codex Sinaiticus
V	codex Venetus
W	Washington papyrus
246	Greek minuscule, Rome, Vat., Gr. 1238
b	Rome, Chigi, R. vi 38 + Rome, Vat., Gr. 330
i	Paris, Bibl. Nat., Gr. 3
o	Paris, Bibl. Nat., Coislin 3
c^2	Moscow, Syn. Libr., Gr. 31
e^2	London, Brit. Mus., Royal 1 D. ii
g	Bâle, B. vi. 22

Grammatical and Other Abbreviations

*	reconstructed form
>	becomes

abs.	absolute
acc.	accusative
act.	active
c.	common
ca.	circa
ch(s).	chapter(s)
col(s).	column(s)
const.	construct
E	English
Ee	*Enuma elish*
f.	feminine
impf.	imperfect
inf.	infinitive
m.	masculine
mg.	marginal note
min.	minuscule
n.s.	new series
P	Priestly (source)
par.	paragraph
pl.	plural
PN	personal name
ptc.	participle
sg.	singular

Titles

AbrN	*Abr-Nahrain*
AfO	*Archiv für Orientforschung*
AHW	W. von Soden, *Akkadisches Handwörterbuch,* Wiesbaden, 1965–81
AJSL	*American Journal of Semitic Languages and Literature*
AOF	*Altorientalische Forschungen*
ANEP	J. B. Pritchard, *The Ancient Near East in Pictures,* Princeton, 1954
ANET	J. B. Pritchard, ed., *Ancient Near Eastern Texts,* Princeton, [2]1955, [3]1969
AOAT	Alter Orient und Altes Testament
ARM	Archives royales de Mari
ASTI	*Annual of the Swedish Theological Institute*
ATD	Das Alte Testament Deutsch
AugR	*Augustinianum,* Rome.
BASOR	*Bulletin of the American Schools of Oriental Research*
BBB	Bonner biblische Beiträge
BDB	F. Brown, S. R. Driver, and C. A. Briggs, *Hebrew and English Lexicon of the Old Testament,* Oxford, 1907
BeO	*Bibbia e oriente*
BHS	*Biblia hebraica stuttgartensia*
Bib	*Biblica*
BibFe	*Biblia y Fe*
BibNot	*Biblische Notizen*

BibRev	*Bible Review*
BK	*Bibel und Kirche*
BO	*Bibliotheca Orientalis*
BT	*The Bible Translator*
BZ	*Biblische Zeitschrift*
CAD	*The Assyrian Dictionary of the Oriental Institute of the University of Chicago*
CAT	Commentaire de l'Ancien Testament
CBQ	*Catholic Biblical Quarterly*
CMHE	F. M. Cross, *Canaanite Myth and Hebrew Epic,* Cambridge, Mass., 1973
ColcT	*Collectanea Theologica*
ComViat	*Communio Viatorum*
CTA	A. Herdner, *Corpus des tablettes en cunéiformes alphabétiques découvertes à Ras Shamra-Ugarit 1929–1939,* Paris, 1963
CurTM	*Currents in Theology and Mission*
DBAT	*Diehlheimer Blätter zum Alten Testament*
DISO	C.-F. Jean and J. Hoftijzer, *Dictionnaire des inscriptions sémitiques de l'ouest,* 1965
DJD	Discoveries in the Judean Desert
Dor	*Dor le Dor*
ErIsr	*Eretz Israel*
EstBib	*Estudios bíblicos*
EstE	*Estudios Eclesiásticos*
ETR	*Études théologiques et religieuses*
ExpTim	*Expository Times*
GKC	*Gesenius' Hebrew Grammar,* ed. E. Kautsch; 2nd English edition, ed. A. E. Cowley, Oxford, 1910
GraceTJ	*Grace Theological Journal*
HALAT	W. Baumgartner et al., *Hebräisches und aramäisches Lexikon zum Alten Testament,* Leiden, ^{2}1958; ^{3}1967–
HAT	Handbuch zum Alten Testament
HSM	Harvard Semitic Monographs
HTR	*Harvard Theological Review*
HUCA	*Hebrew Union College Annual*
ICC	International Critical Commentary
IDBSup	*Interpreter's Dictionary of the Bible,* Supplementary Volume, Nashville, 1976
IEJ	*Israel Exploration Journal*
Int	*Interpretation*
JANESCU	*Journal of the Ancient Near Eastern Society of Columbia University*
JAOS	*Journal of the American Oriental Society*
JBL	*Journal of Biblical Literature*
JNES	*Journal of Near Eastern Studies*
JNSL	*Journal of Northwest Semitic Languages*
JPSV	Jewish Publication Society Version (*Tanakh;* Philadelphia, 1985)

JQR	*Jewish Quarterly Review*
JRT	*Journal of Religious Thought*
JSOT	*Journal for the Study of the Old Testament*
JSOTS	Journal for the Study of the Old Testament–Supplement Series
JSS	*Journal of Semitic Studies*
JTS	*Journal of Theological Studies*
KAI	H. Donner and W. Röllig, *Kanaanäische und aramäische Inschriften,* Wiesbaden, ²1966–70
KAT	Kommentar zum Alten Testament
KJV	King James Version
Leš	*Lešonénu*
MRS	Mission de Ras Shamra
MScRel	*Mélanges de science religieuse*
MTZ	*Münchener theologische Zeitschrift*
MUSJ	*Mélanges de l'université Saint-Joseph*
Nederduitse GTT	*Nederduitse Gereformeerde Teologiese Tydskrif*
NedTTs	*Nederlands theologisch tijdschrift*
NT	New Testament
NTS	*New Testament Studies*
OIP	Oriental Institute Publications
Or	*Orientalia* (Rome)
OrChr	*Oriens christianus*
OT	Old Testament
OTS	*Oudtestamentische Studiën*
OTWSA	*Die Ou Testamentiese Werkgemeenskap Suid-Afrika*
POTT	D. J. Wiseman, ed., *Peoples of the Old Testament Times*
RA	*Revue d'assyriologie et d'archéologie orientale*
RAC	*Reallexikon für Antike und Christentum*
RB	*Revue biblique*
RHPR	*Revue d'histoire et de philosophie religieuses*
RivB	*Rivista biblica*
RSR	*Recherches de science religieuse*
RSV	Revised Standard Version
SBS	Stuttgarter Bibelstudien
SBT	Studies in Biblical Theology
SE	*Studia Evangelica: Texte und Untersuchungen zur Geschichte der altchristlichen Literatur*
Sef	*Sefarad*
ST	*Studia theologica*
TCS	Texts from Cuneiform Sources
TD	*Theology Digest*
TRE	*Theologische Realenzyklopädie*
TSK	*Theologische Studien und Kritiken*
ThWAT	G. J. Botterweck and H. Ringgren, eds., *Theologisches Wörterbuch zum Alten Testament,* Stuttgart, 1970–
TZ	*Theologische Zeitschrift*

UF	*Ugarit-Forschungen*
UT	C. H. Gordon, *Ugaritic Textbook,* Rome, 1965
VAB	Vorderasiatische Bibliothek
VT	*Vetus Testamentum*
VTS	Vetus Testamentum, Supplements
WMANT	Wissenschaftliche Monographien zum Alten und Neuen Testament
ZAW	*Zeitschrift für die alttestamentliche Wissenschaft*
ZDMG	*Zeitschrift der deutschen morgenländischen Gesellschaft*
ZLH	Franciscus Zorell, *Lexicon Hebraicum et Aramaicum Veteris Testamenti,* Rome, 1946–54
ZNW	*Zeitschrift für die neutestamentliche Wissenschaft*

SELECTED BIBLIOGRAPHY

General Bibliography on Nahum, Habakkuk, and Zephaniah

1. Commentaries.

Achtemeier, Elizabeth. *Nahum–Malachi.* Interpretation: A Bible Commentary for Teaching and Preaching. Atlanta: John Knox Press, 1986.

Bič, Miloš. *Trois prophètes dans un temps de ténèbres: Sophonie–Nahum–Habaquq.* Lectio Divina 48. Paris: Éditions du Cerf, 1968.

Calvin, John. *Commentaries on the Twelve Minor Prophets.* Trans. John Owen. I–V. Grand Rapids: Wm. B. Eerdmans Publishing Co., 1950.

Davidson, A. B., ed. *The Books of Nahum, Habakkuk and Zephaniah,* adapted to the text of the Revised Version with some supplementary notes, by H. C. O. Lanchester. Cambridge: Cambridge University Press, 1920.

Deissler, A., and M. Delcor. *Les Petits Prophètes.* La Sainte Bible, VIII. Paris: Letouzey & Ané, 1961.

Ehrlich, Arnold B. *Randglossen zur hebräischen Bibel.* V. Ezechiel und die kleinen Propheten. Leipzig: J. C. Hinrichs'sche Buchhandlung, 1912.

Elliger, Karl. *Das Buch der zwölf Kleinen Propheten: II. Die Propheten Nahum, Habakuk, Zephanja, Haggai, Sacharja, Maleachi.* ATD 25. Göttingen: Vandenhoeck & Ruprecht, 1959.

Holland, Martin. *Die Propheten Nahum, Habakuk und Zephanja.* Wuppertal: R. Brockhaus, 1986.

Hoonacker, A. van. *Les douze petits prophètes.* Paris: J. Gabalda, 1908.

Junker, Hubert. *Die zwölf kleinen Propheten: II. Hälfte: Nahum, Habakuk, Sophonias, Aggäus, Zacharias, Malachias.* Die Heilige Schrift des Alten Testaments VIII.3/2. Bonn: Peter Hanstein, 1938.

Keil, C. F. *Biblischer Commentar über die zwölf kleinen Propheten.* Leipzig: Dörfling & Franke, 1888.

Keller, Carl-A. "Nahoum–Habacuc–Sophonie," in René Vuilleumier and Carl-A. Keller, *Michée–Nahoum–Habacuc–Sophonie.* Commentaire de l'Ancien Testament 11b. Neuchâtel: Delachaux & Niestlé, 1971, 93–222.

Noetscher, Friedrich. *Zwölfprophetenbuch oder Kleine Propheten.* Echter–Bibel; Würzburg: Echter, 1948.

Nowack, Wilhelm. *Die kleinen Propheten, übersetzt und erklärt.* Göttingen: Vandenhoeck & Ruprecht, 1897.

Renaud, Bernard. *Michée, Sophonie, Nahum.* Paris: J. Gabalda, 1987.

Robinson, Theodore H., and Friedrich Horst. *Die zwölf kleinen Propheten.* HAT 14. Tübingen: J. C. B. Mohr (Paul Siebeck), 1964.

Rudolph, Wilhelm. *Micha–Nahum–Habakuk–Zephanja.* KAT 13/3. Gütersloh: Gütersloher Verlagshaus Gerd Mohn, 1975.

Sellin, Ernst. *Das Zwölfprophetenbuch,* II. KAT 12. Leipzig: Werner Scholl, 1930.

Szeles, Maria Eszenyei. *Wrath and Mercy: A Commentary on the Books of Habakkuk and Zephaniah.* Trans. George A. F. Knight. Grand Rapids: Wm. B. Eerdmans Pub. Co.; Edinburgh: Handsel Press, 1987.

Smith, J. M. Powis, William Hayes Ward, and Julius A. Bewer. *A Critical and Exegetical Commentary on Micah, Zephaniah, Nahum, Habakkuk, Obadiah and Joel.* ICC. Edinburgh: T. & T. Clark, 1911.

Smith, Ralph L. *Micah–Malachi.* Word Biblical Commentary 32. Waco, Tex.: Word Books, 1984.

Taylor, Charles L., Jr. "Nahum–Zephaniah: Introduction and Exegesis," *The Interpreter's Bible,* VI. Nashville: Abingdon Press, 1984, 953–1034.

Ungern-Sternberg, Rolf Freiherr von, and Helmut Lamparter. *Der Tag des Gerichtes Gottes: Habakuk, Zephanja, Jona, Nahum.* Die Botschaft des Alten Testaments 23/IV. Stuttgart: Calwer Verlag, 1960.

Van der Woude, A. S. *Habakuk-Zefanja.* De Prediking van het Oude Testament. Nijkerk: G. F. Callenbach, 1978.

———. *Jona, Nahum.* De Prediking van het Oude Testament. Nijkerk: G. F. Callenbach, 1978.

Wellhausen, J. *Die kleinen Propheten übersetzt und erklärt.* 4th ed. Berlin: Walter de Gruyter, 1963.

2. Monographs

Jeremias, Jörg. *Theophanie: Die Geschichte einer alttestamentlichen Gattung.* WMANT 10. Neukirchen: Neukirchener Verlag, 1965.

———. *Kultprophetie und Gerichtsverkündigung in der späten Königszeit Israels.* WMANT 35. Neukirchen: Neukirchener Verlag, 1970.

Selected Bibliography on Nahum

1. Commentaries

Cathcart, Kevin J. *Nahum in the Light of Northwest Semitic.* Rome: Biblical Institute Press, 1973.

Christensen, Duane L. "Nahum," in *Harper's Bible Commentary,* ed. James L. Mays. San Francisco: Harper & Row, 1988, 736–738.

Happel, Otto. *Das Buch des Propheten Nahum.* Würzburg: Gobel & Scherer, 1902.

Haupt, Paul. *The Book of Nahum: A New Metrical Translation with an Introduction, Restoration of the Hebrew Text and Explanatory and Critical Notes.* Baltimore: Johns Hopkins Press, 1907.

Kleinert, Paul. *The Book of Nahum.* Trans. and enlarged by Charles Elliott. New York: Charles Scribner, 1874.

Maier, Walter Arthur. *The Book of Nahum: A Commentary.* St. Louis: Concordia Publishing House, 1959.

2. Monographs

Christensen, D. L. *Transformations of the War Oracle in Old Testament Prophecy: Studies in the Oracles Against the Nations.* Missoula, Mont.: Scholars Press, 1975.

Haldar, Alfred. *Studies in the Book of Nahum.* Uppsala: Almqvist & Wiksell, 1947.

Reinke, Lorenz. *Zur Kritik der alteren Versionen des Propheten Nahum.* Münster: W. Niemann, 1867.

Schulz, Hermann. *Das Buch Nahum, Eine redaktionskritische Untersuchung.* Berlin and New York: Walter de Gruyter, 1973.

3. Articles or Chapters

Arnold, W. R. "The Composition of Nahum 1–2:3," *ZAW* 21 (1901): 225–265.

Becking, Bob. "Is het boek Nahum een literaire eenheid?" *NedTTs* 32 (1978): 107–124.

———. "Bee's Dating Formula and the Book of Nahum," *JSOT* 18 (1980): 100–104.

Bee, Ronald E. "An Empirical Dating Procedure for Old Testament Prophecy," *JSOT* 11 (1979): 23–35.

———. "Dating the Book of Nahum: A Response to the Article by Bob Becking," *JSOT* 18 (1980): 104.

Ben Yehuda, E. "Three Notes in Hebrew Lexicography. 3. Nahum 2.14," *JAOS* 37 (1917): 327.

Bewer, J. A. "Textkritische Bemerkungen zum A.T. Nah 1,10," in *Festschrift für Alfred Bertholet zum 80. Geburtstag,* ed. Walter Baumgartner et al. Tübingen: J. C. B. Mohr (Paul Siebeck), 1950, 68–69.

Cathcart, Kevin J. "Treaty-Curses and the Book of Nahum," *CBQ* 35 (1973): 179–181.

———. "More Philological Studies in Nahum," *Journal of Northwest Semitic Languages* 7 (1979): 1–12.

Christensen, Duane L. "The Acrostic of Nahum Reconsidered," *ZAW* 87 (1975): 17–30.

———. "The Acrostic of Nahum Once Again: A Prosodic Analysis of Nahum 1:1–10," *ZAW* 99 (1987): 409–414.

Dahood, M. "Causal Beth and the Root NKR in Nahum 3,4," *Bib* 52 (1971): 395–396.

Delcor, M. "Allusions à la déesse Ištar in Nahum 2,8?" *Bib* 58 (1977): 73–83.

Dietrich, M. and O. Loretz. "Zur ugaritischen Lexikographie (III)," *BO* 25 (1968): 100–101.

de Vries, S. J. "The Acrostic of Nahum in the Jerusalem Liturgy," *VT* 16 (1966): 476–481.

Döller, Johannes. " 'Ninive gleich einem Wasserteiche,' (Nah 2,9)," *BZ* VI (1908): 164–168.

Driver, G. R. "Studies in the Vocabulary of the Old Testament. III." *JTS* 32 (1931): 361–365.

———. "Farewell to Queen Huzzab," *JTS,* n.s. 15 (1964): 296–298.

Gaster, Theodor H. "Notes on the Minor Prophets," *JTS* 38 (1937): 163–165.

———. "Two Notes on Nahum: 1. Nahum 1,12. 2. Nahum 2,4," *JBL* 63 (1944): 51–52.

Glasson, T. F. "The Final Question—In Nahum and Jonah," *ET* 81 (1969–70): 54–55.

Görg, Manfred. "Eine formelhafte Metapher bei Joel und Nahum," *BibNot* 6 (1978): 12–14.

Gordon, R. R. "Loricate Locusts in the Targum to Nahum III 17 and Revelation IX 9," *VT* 33 (1983): 338–339.

Graham, W. C. "The Interpretation of Nahum 1:9–2:3," *AJSL* 44 (1927–28): 37–48.

Greenfield, J. C. "The Meaning of *tkwnh* [Nah 2, 10 + 2]," in *Biblical and Related Studies Presented to Samuel Iwry,* ed. A. Kort and S. Morschauser. Winona Lake, Ind.: Eisenbrauns, 1985, 81–85.

Gry, L. "Un épisode des derniers jours de Ninive (Nahum II, 8)," *RB,* n.s. 1 (1910): 398–403.

Gunkel, H. "Nahum 1," *ZAW* 13 (1893): 223–244.

Haupt, Paul. "Eine alttestamentliche Festliturgie für den Nikanortag," *ZDMG* 61 (1907): 275–297.

Held, Moshe. "Rhetorical Questions in Ugaritic and Biblical Hebrew," *ErIsr* 9 (1969): 71–79.

———. "Studies in Biblical Homonyms in the Light of Akkadian," *JANES* 3 (1971): 46–55.

Humbert, Paul. "Le problème du livre de Nahoum," *RHPR* 12 (1932): 1–15.

Jeppesen, Knud. "The verb *yā'ad* in Nahum 1,10 and Micah 6,9," *Bib* 65 (1984): 571–574.

Joüon, P. "Notes de critique textuelle, AT: Nahum 3,6," *MUSJ* 5 (1911–12): 485–586.

Kasser, R. "Un lexème copte oublié, TKHN a Khmimique (Nahum 3,19)," *Bulletin de la Société d'Égyptologie* 1 (1979): 23–25.

Keller, C. A. "Die theologische Bewältigung der geschichtlichen Wirklichkeit in der Prophetie Nahums," *VT* 22 (1972): 399–419.

Kselman, J. S. "*rb/kbd:* A New Hebrew-Akkadian Formulaic Pair," *VT* 29 (1979): 110–114.

Levenson, Jon D. "Textual and Semantic Notes on Nah. I 7–8," *VT* 25 (1975): 792–795.

Mihelic, Joseph L. "The Concept of God in the Book of Nahum," *Int* 2 (1948): 199–207.

Nestle, G. "Where Is the Birthplace of the Prophet Nahum to be Sought?" *Palestine Exploration Fund Quarterly Statement for 1879* (1879), 136–138.

———. "Miscellen: 5. Nah 2,4," *ZAW* 29 (1909): 154.

Peiser, F. E. "Miscellen: Nah 1,1," *ZAW* 17 (1897): 349.

Reider, J. "The Name Ashur in the Initials of a Difficult Phrase in the Bible," *JAOS* 58 (1938): 153–155.

———. "A New Ishtar Epithet in the Bible," *JNES* 8 (1949): 104–107.

Renaud, B. "La composition du livre de Nahum," *ZAW* 99 (1987): 198–219.

Ribera i Florit, Josep. "La versión aramaica del Profeta Nahum," *Anuario de Filologia* 6 (1980): 291–322.

Saggs, H. W. F. "Nahum and the Fall of Nineveh," *JTS,* n.s. 20 (1969): 220–225.

Schüngel, Paul H. "Noch einmal zu *qbṣw p'r wr* Jo 2,6 und Nah 2,11," *BibNot* 7 (1978): 29–31.

Seybold, Klaus. "Vormasoretische Randnotizen in Nahum 1," *ZAW* 101 (1989): 71–85.

Siegel, J. L. "*wᵉhuṣṣab gullᵉtāh hōʿªlātāh,* Nah. 2:8," *AJSL* 46 (1929–30): 139–140.

Soden, Wolfram von. "Hebräisch *NĀṬAR* I und II," *UF* 17 (1986): 412–414.

Tsumura, D. T. "Janus Parallelism in Nah 1:8," *JBL* 102 (1983): 109–111.

Van der Woude, A. S. "The Book of Nahum: A Letter Written in Exile," *OTS* 20 (1977): 108–126.

———. "Bemerkungen zu einigen umstrittenen Stellen im Zwolfprophetenbuch, NAHUM 1:8b–c," in *Mélanges bibliques et orientaux en l'honneur de M. Henri Cazelles,* ed. A. Caquot and M. Delcor. *AOAT* 212. Kevelaer: Butzon & Bercker; Neukirchen-Vluyn: Neukirchener Verlag, 1981, 493.

Van Doorslaer, J. "No Amon," *CBQ* 11 (1949): 280–295.

Van Wyk, W. C. "Allusions to 'Prehistory' and History in the Book of Nahum," in *De fructu oris sui: Essays in Honor of Adrianus Van Selms,* ed. I. H. Eybers et al. Leiden: E. J. Brill, 1971, 222–232.

Wildeboer, G. "Nahum 3,7," *ZAW* 22 (1902): 318–319.

Wolff, P. Maternus. "Nahum 1,5b," *BZ* XVI (1922–24): 92.
Yadin, Yigael. "Pescher Nahum (4Qp Nahum) erneut untersucht," *IEJ* 21 (1971): 1–12. Reprinted in *Qumran,* ed. Karl Erich Grözinger et al. Wege der Forschung 410. Darmstadt: Wissenschaftliche Buchgesellschaft, 1981, 167–184.

Selected Bibliography on Habakkuk

1. Commentaries

Duhm, Bernhard. *Das Buch Habakuk: Text, Übersetzung und Erklärung.* Tübingen: J. C. B. Mohr, 1906.

Happel, Otto. *Das Buch des Propheten Habackuk.* Würzburg: Andreas Gobel, 1900.

Lachmann, Johann. *Das Buch Habbakuk: Eine textkritische Studie.* Aussig: Selbstverlag des Verfassers, 1932.

2. Books and Monographs

Brownlee, William Hugh. *The Text of Habakkuk in the Ancient Commentary from Qumran.* Philadelphia: Society of Biblical Literature and Exegesis, 1959.

———. *The Midrash Pesher of Habakkuk.* Missoula, Mont.: Scholars Press, 1979.

Elliger, Karl. *Studien zum Habakuk-Kommentar vom Toten Meer.* Tübingen: J. C. B. Mohr (Paul Siebeck), 1953.

Feltes, Heinz. *Die Gattung des Habakukkommentars von Qumran (1QpHab): Eine Studie zum frühen jüdischen Midrasch.* Würzburg: Echter, 1986.

Gowan, Donald E. *The Triumph of Faith in Habakkuk.* Atlanta: John Knox Press, 1976.

Hiebert, Theodore. *God of My Victory: The Ancient Hymn in Habakkuk 3.* Harvard Semitic Monographs 38. Decatur, Ga.: Scholars Press, 1986.

Humbert, Paul. *Problèmes du Livre d'Habacuc.* Neuchâtel: University of Neuchâtel, 1944.

Jöcken, Peter. *Das Buch Habakuk: Darstellung der Geschichte seiner kritischen Erforschung mit einer eigenen Beurteilung.* Cologne and Bonn: Peter Hanstein, 1977.

Strobel, August. *Untersuchungen zum eschatologischen Verzögerungsproblem; auf Grund der spätjüdisch-urchristlichen Geschichte von Habakuk 2,2 ff.* Leiden: E. J. Brill, 1961.

3. Articles or Chapters

Albright, W. F. "The Psalm of Habakkuk," in *Studies in Old Testament Prophecy,* ed. H. H. Rowley. Edinburgh: T. & T. Clark, 1950, 1–18.

Arnold, W. R. "The Interpretation of *qrnym mydw lw,* Hab 3:4," *AJSL* 21 (1904–05): 167–172.

Baars, W. "A Witness to the Text of the Barberini Greek Version of Habakkuk 3," *VT* 15 (1965): 380–381.

Barré, Michael L. "Habakkuk 3:2: Translation in Context," *CBQ* 50 (1988): 184–197.

Barrick, W. Boyd. "The Meaning and Usage of RKB in Biblical Hebrew," *JBL* 101 (1982): 481–503.

Bévenot, Dom Hughes. "Le cantique d'Habacuc," *RB* 42 (1933): 499–525.

Bosshard, M. "Bemerkungen zum Text von Habakuk I 8," *VT* 19 (1969): 480–482.

Bousfield, G. "Resheph," *JTS* 31 (1930): 397–399.

Bratcher, Dennis R. "The Theological Message of Habakkuk: A Literary-Rhetorical Analysis." Diss., Union Theological Seminary, Richmond, 1984.

Brownlee, W. H. "The Placarded Revelation of Habakkuk," *JBL* 82 (1963): 319–325.

Budde, K. "Zu Habakuk 2,3ff." *ZAW* 9 (1889): 155–156.

———. "Problems of the Prophetic Literature. 2. Habakkuk," *Expositor* (1895-A): 372–385.

———. "Habakuk," *ZDMG* 84 (1930): 139–147.

Burkitt, F. C. "The Psalm of Habakkuk," *JTS* 16 (1915): 62–66.

Cannon, W. W. "The Integrity of Habakkuk cc. 1.2," *ZAW* 43 (1925): 62–90.

Carroll, R. P. "Eschatological Delay in Prophetic Tradition?" *ZAW* 94 (1982): 47–58.

Cassuto, U. "Chapter III of Habakkuk and the Ras Shamra Texts," *Biblical and Oriental Studies* 2 (1975): 3–15.

Cathcart, Kevin. "A New Proposal for Hab 1,17," *Bib* 65 (1984): 575–576.

Cavallin, H. C. C. " 'The Righteous Shall Live by Faith,' A Decisive Argument for the Traditional Interpretation," *ST* 32 (1978): 33–43.

Cirić, Iwan. "Zu Hab 1,9 *(mᵉgammat pᵉnêhem qādîmāh),*" *BZ* VI (1908): 169–171.

Coggins, R. "An Alternative Prophetic Tradition?" in *Israel's Prophetic Tradition: Essays in Honor of Peter Ackroyd,* ed. by Richard Coggins, Anthony Phillips, and Michael Knibb. Cambridge: Cambridge University Press, 1982, 77–94.

Coleman, S. "The Dialog of Habakkuk in Rabbinic Doctrine," *AbrN* 5 (1964–65): 57–85.

Condamin, Albert. "La forme chorale du Ch. III d'Habacuc," *RB* 8 (1899): 133–140.

Crenshaw, J. L. "*Wᵉdōrēk 'al-bām°tê 'āreṣ,*" *CBQ* 34 (1972): 39–53.

Dahood, M. "Two Yiphil Causatives in Habakkuk 3,13a," *Or* 48/2 (1979): 258–259.

———. "Hebrew *hapax legomena* in Eblaite [72 terms: . . . Hab 3,14 *pᵉrāzāw* . . .]," in *Il bilinguismo a Ebla: Atti del convegno internazionale (Napoli, 19–22 Aprile 1982).* Istituto universitario orientale, Departimento di studi asiatici, Series minor 22, 439–470.

Day, John. "New Light on the Mythological Background of the Allusion to Reshep in Habakkuk III 5," *VT* 29 (1979): 353–355.

———. "Echoes of Baal's Seven Thunders and Lightnings in Psalm XXIX and Hab 3,9 and the Identity of Seraphim in Isaiah VI," *VT* 29 (1979): 143–151.

Delcor, M. "La geste de Yahvé au temps de l'Exode et l'espérance du Psaumiste en Habacuc III," in *Miscellanea Biblica B. Ubach,* ed. Romualdo M. Diaz. Scripta et Documenta 1. Montisserrati, 1953, 287–352.

Derrett, J. D. M. " 'Running' in Paul: The Midrashic Potential of Hab 2,2," *Bib* 66 (1985): 560–567.

Diez-Macho, A. "El texto biblico del commentario de Habacuc de Qumran," in *Lex tua veritas: Festschrift für Hubert Junker zur Vollendung des siebzigsten Lebensjahres am 8. August 1961, dargeboten von Kollegen, Freunden, und Schülern,* ed. Heinrich Gross and Franz Mussner. Trier: Paulinus-Verlag, 1961, 59–64.

Driver, G. R. "Hebrew Notes," *ZAW* 52 (1934): 51–56.

———. "On Hab 3,7," *JBL* 62 (1943): 121.

———. "Difficult Words in the Hebrew Prophets," in *Studies in Old Testament Prophecy,* ed. H. H. Rowley. Edinburgh: T. & T. Clark, 1950, 52–72.

———. "On Hab 3,7," *JBL* 62 (1943): 121.

———."Hebrew Notes," *VT* 1 (1951): 241–250.

Eaton, J. H. "The Origin and Meaning of Habakkuk 3," *ZAW* 76 (1964): 144–171.

Elliger, Karl. "Das Ende der 'Abendwölfe' Zeph 3,3, Hab 1,8," in *Festschrift für Alfred Bertholet zum 80. Geburtstag,* ed. Walter Baumgartner et al. Tübingen: J. C. B. Mohr (Paul Siebeck), 1950, 158–175.

Emerton, J. A. "The Textual and Linguistic Problems of Habakkuk 2:4–5," *JTS* 28/1 (1977): 1–18.

Feuillet, A. "La citation d'Habacuc II.4 et les huit premiers chapitres de l'Épitre aux Romains," *NTS* 6 (1959–60): 52–80.

Fitzmyer, J. A. "Habakkuk 2:3–4 and the New Testament," in *De la Torah au Messie: Études d'exégèse et d'herméneutique bibliques offertes à Henri Cazelles pour ses 25 années d'enseignement à l'Institut Catholique de Paris (Octobre 1979),* ed. Maurice Carrez, Joseph Doré, and P. Grelot. Paris: Desclée de Brouwer, 1981, 447–455.

———. "Habakkuk 2:3–4 and the New Testament," in idem, *To Advance the Gospel: New Testament Essays.* New York: Crossroad, 1981, 236–246.

Fohrer, G. "Das 'Gebet des Propheten Habakuk' (Hab 3,1–16)," in *Mélanges bibliques et orientaux en l'honneur de M. Mathias Delcor,* ed. A. Caquot et al. AOAT 215. Kevelaer: Butzon & Bercker; Neukirchen-Vluyn: Neukirchener Verlag, 1985, 159–167.

Gaster, T. H. "On Hab 3,4," *JBL* 62 (1943): 345–346.

Good, E. M. "The Barberini Greek Version of Habakkuk ch. 3," *VT* 9 (1959): 11–30.

Gosse, Bernard. "Le 'Moi' prophétique de l'oracle contre Babylone d'Isaïe XXI, 1–10," *RB* 93 (1986): 70–84, esp. pp. 76–78, "La reprise en Is. XXI, 1–10 de Hab II, 1ss."

Graham, W. C. "A Note on Habakkuk 2:4–5," *AJSL* 42 (1925–26): 128–129.

Gruenthaner, M. J. "Chaldeans or Macedonians? A Recent Theory on the Prophecy of Habakkuk," *Bib* 8 (1927): 129–160, 257–289.

Holt, J. M. "So He May Run Who Reads It," *JBL* 83 (1964): 298–302.

In der Smitten, W. T. "Habakuk 2,4 als prophetische Definition des Gerechten," in *Bausteine biblischer Theologie: Festgabe für G. Johannes Botterweck zum 60. Geburtstag dargebracht von seinen Schülern,* ed. Heinz-Josef Fabry. BBB 50. Cologne and Bonn: Peter Hanstein, 1977, 291–300.

Irwin, W. A. "The Psalm of Habakkuk," *JNES* 1 (1942): 10–40.
———. "The Mythological Background of Habakkuk, Chapter 3," *JNES* 15 (1956): 47–50.
Janzen, J. Gerald. "Habakkuk 2:2–4 in the Light of Recent Philological Advances," *HTR* 73 (1980): 53–78.
———. "Eschatological Symbol and Existence in Habakkuk," *CBQ* 44 (1982): 394–414.
Jöcken, P. "War Habakuk ein Kultprophet?" in *Bausteine biblischer Theologie: Festgabe für G. Johannes Botterweck zum 60. Geburtstag dargebracht von seinen Schülern,* ed. Heinz-Josef Fabry. BBB 50. Cologne and Bonn: Peter Hanstein, 1977, 319–332.
Johnson, M. D. "The Paralysis of Torah in Habakkuk i 4," *VT* 35 (1985): 257–266.
Jung, Peter. "HAB 2,5 *katoinōmenos* ODER *katoiomenos?*" *Bib* 32 (1951): 564–566.
Keller, Carl-A. "Die Eigenart der Prophetie Habakuks," *ZAW* 85 (1973): 156–167.
Kelly, Fred T. "The Strophic Structure of Habakkuk," *AJSL* 18 (1901–02): 94–119.
Klein, Joel T. "Habakkuk 3:13—a Problematic Verse," *Dor* 13 (1984): 105–110.
Kmoskó, M. "Zu Hab 1,9 *(mgmt pnyhm qdymh),*" *BZ* VIII (1910): 135–137.
Koch, Dietrich-Alex. "Der Text von Hab 2,4b in der Septuaginta und im Neuen Testament," *ZNW* 76 (1985): 68–85.
Koenig, J. "Zum Verständnis von Habakuk 2,4–5," *ZDMG* Sup. 1/1 (1968): 291–295.
Kutler, Laurence. "A 'Strong' Case for Hebrew *mar,*" *UF* 16 (1984): 111–118.
Loewenstamm, Samuel. "*yāpîaḥ, yāpiaḥ, yāpēaḥ,*" *Leš* 26 (1962–63): 205–208.
Marcos, N. F. "El texto Barberini de Habacuc III reconsiderado," *Sef* 36 (1976): 3–36.
Margolis, Max L. "The Character of the Anonymous Greek Version of Habakkuk, Chapter 3," *AJSL* 24 (1907–08): 76–85.
Margulis, Baruch. "The Psalm of Habakkuk: A Reconstruction and Interpretation," *ZAW* 82 (1970): 409–442.
Moody, R. M. "The Habakkuk Quotation in Romans 1,17," *ExpTim* 92 (1980–81): 205–208.
Mowinckel, Sigmund. "Zum Psalm des Habakuk," *TZ* 9 (1953): 1–23.
Nestle, E. "Miscellen: 3. Das Lied Habakkuks und der Psalter," *ZAW* 20 (1900): 167–168.
Nielsen, Eduard. "The Righteous and the Wicked in Habaqquq," *ST* (1952): 54–78.
Otto, Eckhart. "Die Stellung der Wehe-Worte in der Verkündigung des Propheten Habakuk," *ZAW* 89 (1977): 73–107.
———. "Habakuk/Habakukbuch," *TRE* 14 (1985): 300–306.
———. "Die Theologie des Buches Habakuk," *VT* 35 (1985): 274–295.
Parmentier, Roger. "Livre du prophète Habaquq," *ComViat* 22 (1979): 205–222.
Peckham, Brian. "The Vision of Habakkuk," *CBQ* 48 (1986): 617–636.
Propp, William H. "The Skin of Moses' Face—Transfigured or Disfigured?" *CBQ* 49 (1987): 375–376.
———. "Did Moses Have Horns?" *BibRev* 4/1 (1988): 30–37.

Rast, Walter E. "Habakkuk and Justification by Faith," *CurTM* 10 (1983): 169–175.

Roberts, J. J. M. "Habakkuk," *The Books of the Bible.* Vol. I: *The Old Testament/The Hebrew Bible,* ed. Bernhard W. Anderson. New York: Charles Scribner's Sons, 1989, 391–396.

Robertson, O. Palmer. " 'The Justified (by Faith) Shall Live by His Steadfast Trust'—Habakkuk 2:4," *Presbyterion* 9 (1983): 52–71.

Sasson, Jack M. "Bovine Symbolism in Exodus," *VT* 18 (1968): 380–387.

Schmidt, Hans. "Ein Psalm im Buche Habakuk," *ZAW* 62 (1950): 52–63.

Schreiner, Stefan. "Erwägungen zum Text vom Hab 2,4–5," *ZAW* 86 (1974): 538–542.

Scott, J. M. "A New Approach to Habakkuk ii 4–5a," *VT* 35 (1985): 330–340.

Smith, J. P. M. "Some Textual Suggestions: ii. Hab 2:17," *AJSL* 37 (1920–21): 239.

Southwell, P. J. M. "A Note on Habakkuk 2:4," *JTS,* n.s. 19 (1968): 614–617.

Stade, B. "Miscellen: 3. Habakuk," *ZAW* 4 (1884): 154–159.

Staerk, W. "Zu Habakuk 1,5–11, Geschichte oder Mythos?" *ZAW* 51 (1933): 1–28.

Stenzel, M. "Habakuk 2, 1–4.5a," *Bib* 33 (1952): 506–510.

———. "Zum Vulgatatext des Canticum Habacuc," in *Colligere Fragmenta: Festschrift Alban Dold zum 70. Geburtstag am 7.7.1952,* ed. B. Fischer and V. Fjala. Beuron in Hohenzollern: Beuroner Kunstverlag, 1952, 25–33.

———. "Habakkuk ii 15–16," *VT* 3 (1953): 97–99.

Stephens, Ferris J. "The Babylonian Dragon Myth in Habakkuk 3," *JBL* 43 (1924): 290–293.

Strobel, August. "Habakuk," *RAC* 13/98 (1984): 203–226.

Thackery, H. St. J. "Primitive Lectionary Notes in the Psalm of Habakkuk," *JTS* 12 (1911): 191–213.

Tsumura, D. T. "Hab 2,2 in the Light of Akkadian Legal Practice," *ZAW* 94 (1982): 294–295.

———. "An Exegetical Consideration on Hab 2:4a," *Tojō* 15 (1985): 1–26.

Tuttle, G. "Wisdom and Habakkuk," *SBT* 3 (1973): 3–14.

Van Daalen, D. H. "The *'emunah/pistis* of Hab 2:4 and Romans 1:17," *SE* 7, Texte und Untersuchungen 126 (1982): 523–527.

Van der Wal, A. J. O. "*LŌ' NĀMŪT* in Habakkuk 1:12: A Suggestion," *VT* 38 (1988): 480–483.

Van der Woude, A. S. "Der Gerecht wird durch seine Treue leben. Erwägungen zu Habakuk 2:4–5," SBS (1966): 367–375.

———. "Habakuk 2,4," *ZAW* 82 (1970): 281–282.

———. "Bemerkungen zu einigen umstrittenen Stellen im Zwölfprophetenbuch, HABAKUK 2:1–4," in *Mélanges bibliques et orientaux en l'honneur de M. Henri Cazelles,* ed. A. Caquot and M. Delcor. *AOAT* 212. Kevelaer: Butzon & Bercker; Neukirchen-Vluyn: Neukirchener Verlag, 1981, 494–496.

Walker, H. H. "The Literary Structure of the Book of Habakkuk," *JBL* 53 (1934): 355–370.

Whitley, C. F. "A Note on Habakuk 2,15," *JQR* 66 (1975–76): 143–147.

Ziegler, J. "Konjektur oder überlieferte Leseart? Zu Hab 2,5, [*Katoinōmenos*] *katoiomenos,*" *Bib* 33 (1952): 366–370.

Selected Bibliography on Zephaniah

1. Commentaries

Deddens, K. *Zefanja's profetiean.* Goes: Oosterbaan & Le Cointre, 1973.

Kuhner, Heinrich Oskar. *Zephanja.* Zurich: Zwingli-Verlag, 1943.

Reinke, Lorenz. *Der Prophet Zephanja: Einleitung, Grundtext und Übersetzung nebst einem vollständigen philologisch-kritischen und historischen Commentar.* Münster: W. Niemann, 1868.

Sabottka, Liudger. *Zephanja: Versuch einer Neuübersetzung mit philologischem Kommentar.* Biblica et Orientalia 25. Rome: Biblical Institute Press, 1972.

2. Books and Monographs

Ball, Ivan Jay, Jr. *A Rhetorical Study of Zephaniah.* Berkeley, Calif.: Bibal Press, 1988.

Edler, Rainer. *Das Kerygma des Propheten Zefanja.* Freiburg im Breisgau: Herder, 1984.

Gerleman, Gillis. *Zephanja: textkritisch und literarisch Untersucht.* Lund: C. W. K. Gleerup, 1942.

House, Paul R. *Zephaniah: A Prophetic Drama.* JSOTS 69. Sheffield: Almond Press, 1988.

Hunter, A. V. *Seek the Lord! A Study of the Meaning and Function of the Exhortations in Amos, Hosea, Isaiah, Micah, and Zephaniah.* Baltimore: St. Mary's Seminary and University, 1982.

Irsigler, Hubert. *Gottesgericht und Jahwetag: Die Komposition Zef 1,1–2,3, untersucht auf der Grundlage der Literarkritik des Zefanjabuches.* Münchener Universitätsschriften: Arbeiten zu Text und Sprache im Alten Testament 3. St. Ottilien: EOS Verlag, 1977.

Kapelrud, Arvid S. *The Message of the Prophet Zephaniah.* Oslo: Universitetsforlaget, 1975.

Krinetzki, Günter. *Zefanjastudien: Motiv- und Traditionskritik + Kompositions- und Redaktionskritik.* Regensburger Studien zur Theologie 7. Frankfurt am Main: P. Lang, 1977.

Langohr, Guy. *Le livre de Sophonie et la critique d'authenticité.* Analecta Lovaniensia Biblica et Orientalia V/17. Louvain: Éditions Peeters, 1967; = Ephemerides Theologicae Lovanienses 52 (1976), 1–27.

Lippl, Joseph. *Das Buch des Propheten Sophonias.* Freiburg im Breisgau: Herder, 1910.

Seybold, Klaus. *Satirische Prophetie: Studien zum Buch Zefanja.* Stuttgarter Bibelstudien 120. Stuttgart: Katholisches Bibelwerk, 1985.

Zandstra, Sidney. *The Witness of the Vulgate, Peshitta and Septuagint to the Text of Zephaniah.* New York: Columbia University Press, 1909.

3. Articles and Chapters

Anderson, George W. "The Idea of the Remnant in the Book of Zephaniah," *ASTI* 11 (1978): 11–14.

Asurmendi, Jesús M. "Sofonías y Jerusalén, análisis estilistico," *Escritos de Biblia y Oriente* (1981): 153–169.

Bacher, W. "Zu Zephanja 2,4," *ZAW* 11 (1891): 185–187.

Bachmann, J. "Zur Textkritik des Propheten Zephania," *TSK* 67 (1894): 641–655.

Bennett, W. H. "Sir J. G. Frazer on 'Those that leap over (or on) the threshold.' (Zeph. 1, 9)," *ET* 30 (1918–19): 379–380.

Bewer, J. A. "Textual Suggestions on Isa 2,6; 66,3; Zeph 2,2.5," *JBL* 27 (1908): 164–166.

Botterweck, G. J. "Gott und Mensch in den alttestamentlichen Löwenbildern," in *Wort, Lied und Gottesspruch: Beiträge zu Psalmen und Propheten: Festschrift für J. Ziegler,* ed. Josef Schreiner. Forschung zur Bibel 2. Würzburg: Echter, 1972, 117–128.

———. "*z^{e}'ēb,*" *ThWAT* II (1977): 586–594.

Budde, K. "Die Bücher Habakkuk und Sephanja," *TSK* 66 (1893): 383–399.

Calès, Jean. "L'authenticité de Sophonie, II, 11 et son contexte primitif," *RSR* (1920): 355–357.

Cathcart, Kevin J. "*bōšet* in Zephaniah 3:5," *JNSL* 12 (1984): 35–39.

Cazelles, H. "Sophonie, Jéremie et les Scythes en Palestine," *RB* 74 (1967): 24–44.

———. "Zephaniah, Jeremiah, and the Scythians in Palestine," in *A Prophet to the Nations: Essays in Jeremiah Studies,* ed. Leo Perdue and Brian W. Kovacs. Winona Lake, Ind.: Eisenbrauns, 1984, 129–149.

Childs, B. S. "The Enemy from the North and the Chaos Tradition," in *A Prophet to the Nations: Essays in Jeremiah Studies,* ed. Leo Perdue and Brian W. Kovacs. Winona Lake, Ind.: Eisenbrauns, 1984, 151–161.

Christensen, Duane L. "Zephaniah 2:4–15: A Theological Basis for Josiah's Program of Political Expansion," *CBQ* 46 (1984): 669–682.

Clark, David. "Wine on the Lees (Zeph 1.12 & Jer 48.11)," *BT* 32 (1981): 241–243.

———. "Of Birds and Beasts: Zephaniah 2.14," *BT* 34 (1983): 243–246.

De Roche, M. "Zephaniah 1,2–3: The 'Sweeping' of Creation," *VT* 30 (1980): 104–109.

Diebner, Bernd J. "Bemerkungen zum Text des sahidischen und des achmimischen Fragments der sog. Zephanja–Apokalypse," *DBAT* 14 (1979): 54–60.

———. "Die Söhne des Priesters Jo(a)than; Anspielung auf ein Stück verlorener Heiliger Schrift [Ri 9, 2 Kgs 15,30; . . . Zephanja–Apokalypse 3,6]," *DBAT* 16 (1982): 40–49.

Donner, H. "Die Schwellenhüpfer: Beobachtungen zu Zephanja 1,8f.," *JSS* 15 (1970): 42–55.

Edens, A. "A Study of the Book of Zephaniah as to the Date, Extent and Significance of the Genuine Writings, with a Translation." Ph.D. diss., Vanderbilt University, 1954.

Efros, I. "Textual Notes on the Hebrew Bible. 2–6." *JAOS* 45 (1925): 153–154.

Elliger, Karl. "Das Ende der 'Abendwölfe' Zeph 3,3 Hab 1,8," in *Festschrift für Alfred Bertholet zum 80. Geburtstag,* ed. Walter Baumgartner et al. Tübingen: J. C. B. Mohr (Paul Siebeck), 1950, 158–175.

Fagnani, C. P. "The Structure of the Text of the Book of Zephaniah," in *Old Testament and Semitic Studies in Memory of William Rainey Harper,* vol. 2, ed. R. F. Harper et al. Chicago: University of Chicago Press, 1908, 259–278.

Fensham, F. C. "A Possible Origin of the Concept of the Day of the Lord," *OTWSA* 10 (1967): 90–97.

———. "The Poetic Form of the Hymn of the Lord in Zephanjah," *OTWSA* 13/14 (1970/71): 9–14.

Florit, D. E. "Sofonia, Geremia e la cronaca di Gadd," *Bib* 15 (1934): 8–31.

Gaster, T. H. "Two Textual Emendations. Zephaniah iii.17," *ET* 78 (1966–67): 267.

Gordis, Robert. "A Rising Tide of Misery: A Note on a Note on Zephaniah II, 4," *VT* 37 (1987): 487–490.

Gray, J. "A Metaphor from Building in Zephaniah II 1," *VT* 3 (1953): 404–407.

Greenfield, J. C. "A Hapax Legomenon, *mimšaq ḥarûl,*" in *Studies in Judaica, Karaitica, and Islamica Presented to Leon Nemoy on His 80th Birthday,* ed. Sheldon R. Brunswick. Ramat-Gan: Bar-Ilan University Press, 1982, 79–85.

Grill, F. "Der Schlachttag Jahwes," *BZ* 2 (1958): 278–283.

Haupt, P. "The Prototype of the Dies Irae," *JBL* 38 (1919): 142–151.

———. "Pelican and Bittern," *JBL* 39 (1920): 158–161.

———. "*Qaš,* straw, and *qăšt,* bow," *JBL* 39 (1920): 161–163.

Heintz, J. G. "*Ūmūšū qerbū,*" *VT* 21 (1971): 528–540.

Heller, J. "Zephanjas Ahnenreihe (Eine redaktionsgeschichtliche Bemerkung zu Zeph. I)," *VT* 21 (1971): 102–104.

Hesse, Franz. "Wurzelt die prophetische Gerichtsrede im israelitische Kult?" *ZAW* 65 (1953): 45–53.

Humbert, Paul. " 'Étendre la main' (Note de lexicographie hébraïque)," *VT* 12 (1962): 383–395.

Hyatt, J. P. "The Date and Background of Zephaniah," *JNES* 7 (1948): 25–29.

Ihromi. "Die Häufung der Verben des Jubelns in Zephaniah III 14f, 16–18: *rnn, rw', śmḥ, 'lz, śwś* and *gîl,*" *VT* 33 (1983): 106–110.

Irsigler, Hubert. "Äquivalenz in Poesie: Die kontextuellen Synonyme *ṣa'aqā–yalalā–šibr gadu(w)l* in Zef 1,10 c.d.e," *BZ,* n.s. 22 (1978): 221–235.

Jeppesen, K. "Zephaniah I 5b," *VT* 31 (1981): 372–373.

Jongeling, B. "Jeux de mots en Sophonie III 1 et 3?" *VT* 21 (1971): 541–547.

Kapelrud, A. S. "Eschatology in Micah and Zephaniah," in *De la Tôrah au Messie, Études d'exégèse et d'herméneutique bibliques offertes à Henri CAZELLES pour ses 25 années d'enseignement à l'Institut Catholique de Paris (Octobre 1979),* ed. Maurice Carrez et al. Paris: Desclée de Brouwer, 1981, 255–262.

Kselman, John S. "A Note on Jeremiah 49:20 and Zephaniah 2:6–7," *CBQ* 32 (1970): 579–581.

Kulp, Johannes. "Der Hymnus Dies irae, dies illa," *Monatschrift für Gottesdienst und kirchliche Kunst* 38 (1933): 256–263.
Langohr, Guy. "Rédaction et composition du livre de Sophonie," *Muséon* 89 (1976): 51–73.
Lohfink, Norbert. "Gottesvolk als Lerngemeinschaft," *BK* 39 (1984): 90–100.
———. "Zefanja und das Israel der Armen," *BK* 39 (1984): 100–108.
———. "Zephaniah and the Church of the Poor," *TD* 32 (1985): 113–118.
Loretz, O. "Kleinere Beiträge: Weitere ugaritisch-hebräische Parallelen," *BZ* 3 (1959): 292–294.
———. "Textologie des Zephanja-Buches," *UF* 5 (1973): 219–228.
Mayer, R. "Zur Bildersprache der alttestamentlichen Propheten," *MTZ* 1 (1950): 55–65.
Mendecki, Norbert. "Das Ende der Schmach und die Erhöhung Israels in Zef 3,18–20," *ColcT* 53/4 (1983): 53–59.
Olivier, J. P. J. "A Possible Interpretation of the Word *ṣiyyâ* in Zeph 2,13," *JNSL* 8 (1980): 95–97.
Olmo Lete, G. del. "El libro de Sofonías y la filología semítica nor-occidental (A propósito de L. Sabottka, Zephanja)," *EstBib* 32 (1973): 291–303.
Ribera Florit, Josep. "La versión aramaica del Profeta Sofonías," *EstBib* 40 (1982): 127–158.
Rice, G. "The African Roots of the Prophet Zephanja," *JRT* 36 (1979–80): 21–31.
Rimbach, James A. "Those Lively Prophets—Zephaniah Ben-Cushi," *CurTM* 7 (1980): 239–242.
Rose, M. "'Atheismus' als Wohlstandserscheinung? (Zephanja 1,12)," *TZ* 37 (1981): 193–208.
Scharbert, J. "Zefanja und die Reform des Joschija," in *Künder des Wortes: Beiträge zur Theologie der Propheten, J. Schreiner zum 60. Geburtstag,* ed. L. Ruppert et al. Würzburg: Echter, 1982, 237–253.
Schwally, F. "Das Buch Sefanjâ: Eine historisch-kritische Untersuchung," *ZAW* 10 (1890): 165–240.
Seybold, Klaus. "Text und Textauslegung in Zef 2,1–3," *BibNot* 25 (1984): 49–54.
———. "Die Verwendung der Bildmotive in der Prophetie Zefanjas," in *Beiträge zur prophetischen Bildsprachen in Israel und Assyrien,* ed. Helga Weippert et al. Freiburg, Switzerland: Universitätsverlag; Göttingen: Vandenhoeck & Ruprecht, 1985, 30–54.
Smith, Louise Pettibone, and Ernest R. Lacheman. "The Authorship of the Book of Zephaniah," *JNES* 9 (1950): 137–142.
Spieckermann, Hermann. "Dies Irae: Der alttestamentliche Befund und seine Vorgeschichte," *VT* 39 (1989): 194–208.
Stenzel, M. "Zum Verständnis von Zeph. III 3b," *VT* 1 (1951): 303–305.
Thomas, D. W. "A Pun on the Name of Ashdod in Zeph. 2.4," *ET* 74 (1962–63): 63.
Tsevat, M. "Some Biblical Notes—(Zeph 3.17ff)," *HUCA* 24 (1952–53): 111–112.
Van der Woude, A. S. "Bemerkungen zu einigen umstrittenen Stellen im Zwölfprophetenbuch, ZEPHANJA 3:3b," in *Mélanges bibliques et orientaux en l'honneur*

de M. Henri Cazelles, ed. A. Caquot and M. Delcor. *AOAT* 212. Kevelaer: Butzon & Bercker; Neukirchen-Vluyn: Neukirchener Verlag, 1981, 496.

———. "Predikte Zefanja een wereldgericht?" *NedTTs* 20 (1965–66): 1–16.

Vogt, Ernst. "Das Wachstum des alten Stadtgebietes von Jerusalem," *Bib* 48 (1967): 337–358.

Williams, D. L. "The Date of Zephaniah," *JBL* 82 (1963): 77–88.

Zaleman, L. "*Di Siva,* Desert, Dessert [Zph 3,3; Hab 1,8 *z*^{e}*'ēbê 'ereb* 'wolves of evening/steppe/hunger/(best) ravening,' like *'ōrēb*]," *ET* 91 (1979): 311.

———. "Ambiguity and Assonance at Zephaniah ii 4," *VT* 36 (1986): 365–371.

Nahum

Nahum

INTRODUCTION

The book of Nahum is unified by the theme of Yahweh's impending judgment on Assyria, the Assyrian king, and his capital city Nineveh. Despite several different types of oracles and a wide range of metaphors and stylistic devices, this basic theme runs through all the oracles in the short book. It begins, following a short superscription (1:1), with an abbreviated acrostic hymn celebrating Yahweh as an awesome God who takes implacable vengeance on his enemies (1:2–8). The prophet uses this hymn to challenge the Judeans' lack of confidence in Yahweh's ability to deliver them from their unnamed Assyrian oppressor (1:9). He argues that, despite all the appearances to the contrary, Yahweh is about to totally destroy the Assyrian oppressor (1:10–2:1 [1:10–15E]). The second oracle, fictitiously addressed to the Assyrian ruler (2:2 [1]), warns him that a mighty enemy is coming up to besiege him (2:2, 4 [1, 3]), and the rest of the oracle portrays that siege and its aftermath (2:4–11 [3–10]), ending with a taunt over the fate of the Assyrian king, his land, and his capital (2:12–14 [11–13]). This is followed by an elaborate *hôy*-oracle against Nineveh, a city of bloodshed and oppression, which is about to get a justly deserved taste of bloodshed and oppression herself (3:1–17). Then the book ends with an oracle addressed to the Assyrian king assuring him that Assyria is finished, that there is no recovery from its collapse (3:18–19). There are a number of textual problems in the book, but the only clear gloss is the awkwardly placed comment in 2:3 [2].

Outline

I. Superscription (1:1)

II. Oracle of reassurance to Judah (1:2–2:1) [1:2–1:15]
- A. The acrostic (1:2–8)
- B. The challenge to Judah (1:9)
- C. Reassurance that Assyria will fall (1:10–2:1) [1:10–1:15]

III. Oracle threatening the Assyrian king (2:2–14) [2:1–13]
- A. A powerful enemy threatens Assyria (2:2, 4) [2:1, 3]
- B. A visionary portrayal of the siege of Nineveh (2:5–11) [2:4–10]
- C. Yahweh taunts the Assyrian king (2:12–14) [2:11–13]

IV. *Hôy*-oracle against Nineveh (3:1–17)
- A. Nineveh characterized as a city of blood (3:1)

B. Its fall portrayed (3:2–3)
C. Nineveh as the humiliated harlot (3:4–7)
D. Comparison to Thebes, whose fate she will share (3:8–11)
E. The certainty of her fate conveyed by different metaphors (3:12–17)

V. Oracle against the king of Assyria (3:18–19)
A. His people scattered without leaders (3:18)
B. Happily for others, the situation incurable (3:19)

Date

Since the superscription gives no information on the time of Nahum's prophetic activity, any judgment on the date of the book or of the individual oracles contained in the book is totally dependent on the internal clues found in the oracles themselves. A *terminus a quo* is provided by the mention of the fall of Thebes (663 B.C.) as a past historical event (3:8), and a *terminus ad quem* is provided by the fall of Nineveh (612 B.C.), since Nahum's need to reassure his Judean audience that Yahweh really will destroy Assyria would hardly be necessary after that event. This concern to reassure Judah of Yahweh's ability and will to destroy Nineveh runs throughout the book; it is the motivation for the use of the acrostic and for the citation of the example of Thebes, and it is made quite explicit in 1:9–2:1 [1:9–15]. Thus the period of Nahum's prophetic activity against Assyria must fall somewhere between 663–612 B.C., and the evidence that establishes these outside dates suggests an earlier date rather than a later one. Thebes soon recovered its independence from Assyria, and, by 616 B.C., if not earlier, Egypt had become Assyria's ally; the later one goes within the time frame for Nahum's prophecy, the less compelling the example of Thebes would become. Moreover, the need to reassure Judah that Yahweh would destroy Assyria would be more intense earlier in this time frame, when the Assyrian power was still at full strength. After the abdication of Ashurbanipal ca. 635 B.C., when factional disputes broke out within Assyria as to the succession to the throne, Assyrian power would hardly have seemed so absolute, and once Babylon successfully revolted from Assyria ca. 625 B.C., the fall of Assyria would not have seemed totally implausible. Josiah's reform followed within a few years of this development (622 B.C.), and there is good reason to believe that one of the motivating factors behind it was a desire to throw off the Assyrian yoke.

Within the earlier period of this time frame, there is a wide range of possibilities. Rudolph dates Nahum's activity to the middle of the seventh century, during the reign of Manasseh, and, in answer to the objection that this faithful Assyrian vassal would not have permitted such oracles against his overlord, Rudolph argues that Nahum's oracles were presented only in writing, in a book (*sēper,* 1:1) circulated among his support group (pp. 143–144). It is extremely doubtful, however, whether the word *sēper* will bear the weight Rudolph's interpretation places upon it. Nor is it necessary to adopt the hypothesis that makes Nahum a secretive, writing prophet in order to defend Rudolph's dating. The Assyrian empire was shaken by the revolt of Babylon under Ashurbanipal's brother Shamash-shum-ukkin in 652–648 B.C., and, during this period, Manasseh may have been less than totally loyal to Assyria, since the Chronicler records an Assyrian expedition against him that brought him bound to the Assyrian king at Babylon (2 Chron. 33:11). If Nahum's activity dated to that period, he may have been a major support to Manasseh's brief revolt against Assyria. It is also possible to date Nahum's work slightly later, following Manasseh's reign, either in the reign of Amon (642–640 B.C.) or early in the reign of Josiah (640–609 B.C.), though it is difficult to be very precise. I would prefer a date between 640 and 630 B.C.

The Prophet and His Message

Little is known about the prophet Nahum apart from his hometown, and even its location is disputed. His preserved oracles all deal with God's imminent destruction of Nineveh. One could explain this feature of the book of Nahum as accidental, as due to a topical collection of all his oracles on this particular subject. However, though they may have been given over a long period of time, it seems more likely that these oracles all stem from a relatively short period of time when the fate of Assyria was the dominant concern of this prophet. This does not necessarily mean, however, that the prophet's ministry was short or that his theology was restricted to the contents of this small collection. His book simply preserves Nahum's comments on this one issue, and one should be hesitant to criticize the range of Nahum's theology on this limited basis. The prophet may not emphasize Judah's sin in these oracles or call his people to repentance, but he is aware that what has befallen Judah has been due to Yahweh's punishment (1:12). His task, however, at least in these oracles, is not to call Judah to account for sin, but to reassure Judah that Yahweh has seen his people's affliction and that he is about to take vengeance on Judah's cruel and unjust oppressor. At the heart of his message is a recognition of Yahweh as a God of justice who will not let injustice and oppression go unpunished. The awesome terror of God's avenging power is both frightening and reassuring to the oppressed. It is frightening, because it is a reminder that Yahweh is a God with whom one cannot trifle, but it is also reassuring, because it affirms that the oppressor will not have the last word. Deliverance will come, for soon Yahweh will repay the oppressor in full for his evil deeds.

COMMENTARY

1. The Superscription: 1:1

1:1 The oracle concerning Nineveh. The book of the vision of Nahum the Elkoshite.

Commentary

The superscription provides a minimum of useful information for the interpretation of the book. It designates the contents of the book as "the oracle concerning Nineveh." *Maśśā'* is a technical term for a prophetic oracle which underscores the divine origin of the message. Though it is apparently connected to the idiom *nāśā'* + a word designating either voice or a spoken message (*nāśā' dābār/qînāh,* "to lift up a word/lamentation" [Amos 5:1]; *nāśā' māšāl,* "to lift up a saying" [Hab. 2:6; Num. 23:7, 18; 24:3, 15]; *nāśā' qôl,* "to lift up the voice" [Cathcart, *Nahum,* 36]), and thus has a distinct meaning from *maśśā',* "burden," the fact that they are homonyms created an ambiguity that was open to exploitation (see Jer. 23:33–40) or misunderstanding (note V's translation of the prophetic term with *onus,* "burden"). Despite Jeremiah's unhappiness with the prophetic use of the term in his day, *maśśā'* was widely used prior to and after his time to designate the prophetic word (Isa. 13:1; 15:1; 17:1; 19:1; 21:1, 11, 13; 22:1; 23:1; 30:6; Zech. 9:1; 12:1; Mal. 1:1; cf. Prov. 31:1). Though it is most often used in connection with oracles against a foreign power, its use is not limited to such oracles, and its usage provides no criterion for judging whether oracles so designated were the work of professional cult prophets.

An oracle of judgment concerning Nineveh would be a positive word to Judah, however. Nineveh (Akkadian *Ninuwa, Ninua, Ninâ*), located on the east bank of the Tigris at the site marked by the mounds Nebi Yunus and Quyunjiq opposite Mosul, was made the royal capital of the Assyrian empire by Sennacherib (705–681 B.C.). From Sennacherib's devastating campaign against Judah in 701 B.C. down to the revolt of Babylon against Ashurbanipal (reigned c. 668–627 B.C.) under his brother Shamash-shum-ukkin in 652–648 B.C., Assyria's domination of Judah was harsh and relatively thorough. Babylon's revolt may have suggested the beginning of the end for Assyria, and Manasseh may have been drawn into it (2 Chron. 33:10–13), but Assyria appears to have reasserted its control over Palestine at least until 635 B.C., when Assyria's internal troubles began to give the new Judean king, Josiah, greater freedom of action. On the other hand, Nineveh was utterly destroyed by the Medes and Babylonians in 612 B.C., so an oracle against the city could hardly date more than a few months after that event, at the latest.

The word *sēper,* though translated conventionally as "book," only means "written document." It can refer to a document inscribed or written on a stone stela, an ostracon, a scroll, loose sheets of papyrus, or any other suitable material. Thus the term gives no clue as to where this prophecy was first recorded in writing. The superscription further specifies this *sēper* as the written document containing the *ḥ*ᵃ*zôn,* "vision," of Nahum the Elkoshite. *Ḥāzôn* is derived from the verb *ḥāzāh,* "to see" (cf. Isa. 1:1; 13:1; Hab. 1:1), and originally designated the manner of reception of the divine revelation, but it may have come to mean little more than "prophecy" (see Delbert R. Hillers, *Micah* [Hermeneia; Fortress Press, 1983], 13). The verb *ḥāzāh* is certainly used in contexts where the emphasis lies more on the prophet's communication of the message than on his or her reception of it (Isa. 30:10; Zech. 10:2; Lam. 2:14).

The prophet's name, *Naḥûm,* is from the root *nḥm,* which also occurs in the biblical names Nehemiah, Nahamani (Neh. 7:7), Tanhumeth (Jer. 40:8), and Menahem (Cathcart, *Nahum,* 37). *Nḥm* is well attested on seals and seal impressions from the seventh and sixth centuries B.C. (see Nahman Avigad, *Hebrew Bullae from the Time of Jeremiah: Remnants of a Burnt Archive* [Jerusalem: Israel Exploration Society, 1986], nos. 77, 121, 153, 176, 202; Ruth Hestrin and Michel Dayagi-Mendels, *Inscribed Seals* [Jerusalem: Israel Museum, 1979], no. 17); the vocalization of the name as *Naḥûm* is supported by the Elephantine *Nḥwm* (Bezalel Porten and Jonas C. Greenfield, *Jews of Elephantine and Arameans at Syene: Aramaic Texts with Translation* [Jerusalem, 1974], 64, 66, 72). The name may be analyzed on the analogy of such names as *ḥannûn* or *raḥûm* as meaning "comfort," or it may be analyzed as a shortened form of *nḥmyh* (Nehemiah), "Yahweh has comforted" (Rudolph, 148; Martin Noth, *Die israelitischen Personennamen im Rahmen der gemeinsemitischen Namengebung* [Stuttgart: W. Kohlhammer, 1928], 175; Jeaneane D. Fowler, *Theophoric Personal Names in Ancient Hebrew: A Comparative Study* [JSOTS 49; Sheffield: JSOT Press, 1988], 107, 351). Despite the meaning of the name, however, any connection between it and the prophet's message is probably coincidental (so also Cathcart, *Nahum,* 37–38). Nahum is characterized as "the Elkoshite," a gentilic that indicates that the prophet was from the village or clan of Elkosh. Unfortunately this name occurs nowhere else in the Bible, so its location remains uncertain. Neither Jerome's location of it in the Galilee nor the much later tradition locating it near Nineveh has much to commend it (Rudolph, 148–149). The place name *'lqwš* may contain the Edomite divine name *Qauš,* "*Qauš/Qôš*-is-God," and if so, one should look for a site in the south of Judah near the border with Edom (Rudolph, 149).

2. The Acrostic and God's Promise of Deliverance: 1:2–2:1 [1:2–15E]

א 1:2 Yahweh is a jealous and avenging God,[1]
Yahweh is vengeful and lord of a violent temper,[2]
Yahweh takes vengeance against his foes,
He rages[3] against his enemies.
3 Yahweh is slow to anger but great in power,
And Yahweh will certainly not acquit (the guilty).
ב In the whirlwind[4] and in the storm is his path,
And the clouds are the dust of his feet.
ג 4 He rebukes the sea and dries it up,
And all the rivers he parches dry.
ד Bashan and Carmel languish,[5]
And the buds of Lebanon wither.
ה 5 The mountains quake before him,
And the hills melt.[6]
ו The earth heaves[7] before him,
The world and all who inhabit it.
ז 6 Who can stand before his indignation?[8]
And who can endure the heat of his anger?
ח His wrath is poured out like fire,[9]
And the rock cliffs are shattered by him.
ט 7 Yahweh is good to those who wait for him,[10]
A place of refuge[11] on the day of affliction.
י ⟨Yahweh⟩[12] knows those who take refuge in him,
8 And in the sweeping flood ⟨ ⟩.[13]
כ He totally annihilates the opposition,[14]
And his enemies he pursues into darkness.[15]
9 Why do you meditate[16] against Yahweh?
He is about to wreak total annihilation.
Hostility[17] will not arise twice.
10 Though a thicket of entangled thorns,[18]
And soaked with their liquor,[19]
They will be devoured like very dry stubble.
11 From you has departed
The one who plotted evil against Yahweh,
Who counseled wickedness.
12 Thus says Yahweh,
Even if they are strong and just so numerous,[20]
Just so they will be cut down and pass away.[21]
I afflicted you, but I will not afflict you again.[22]

13 And now I will break his yoke[23] from upon you,
And your bonds I will snap apart.
14 And Yahweh has commanded concerning you:
Seed will not be sown from your name again.
From the house of your gods I will cut off
The carved and molten images.
I will prepare your grave because you are worthless.[24]
2:1 [1:15E]
Look! On the mountains
Are the feet of the herald,
Who proclaims peace:
"Celebrate your festivals, O Judah!
Fulfill your vows!
For he will not cross over you again,
The scoundrel[25] is totally cut off."

Textual Notes

[1]The word translated God here is not the normal word *'ᵉlōhîm* but the word *'ēl,* which can be used as the proper name for the Canaanite deity El.

[2]The first element in the idiom *ba'al ḥēmāh,* "a lord/possessor of wrath," is identical with the proper name Baal, the epithet normally used to designate the Canaanite deity Hadad. Cathcart plausibly suggests a conscious play on the divine names El and Baal in these two lines (*Nahum,* 40), but the idiom itself has no necessary connection to the divine name. It is used synonymously with *'îš 'ap,* "a man of anger" (Prov. 29:22), and merely designates a person who possesses a violent temper, a hot- or quick-tempered individual. Other synonymous expressions are *ba'al 'ap,* "a lord/possessor of anger" (Prov. 22:24; Sir. 8:16), and *'îš ḥēmôt,* "a man of wrath" (Prov. 22:24).

[3]LXX's *exairōn,* "he lifts up, takes away," is either a loose translation or presupposes a Hebrew reading *nōṭēl.* The Hebrew verb used here, *nāṭar* II, should be distinguished from *nāṭar* I, "to guard, keep." *Nāṭar* II is cognate with Akkadian *nadāru,* "to rage," and refers to a violently raging or seething anger. (See Driver, *JTS* 32 [1931]: 361–363; D. Winton Thomas, in *Record and Revelation,* ed. H. Wheeler Robinson [Oxford: Clarendon Press, 1938], 394; M. Held, *ErIsr* 9 [1969]: 73 n. 19; *JANES* 3 [1971]: 46–55; and Cathcart, *Nahum,* 42–44; cf. the less convincing derivation of W. von Soden, *UF* 17 [1986]: 412–414.)

[4]LXX's *en synteleiai,* "in completion," presupposes the faulty reading *bᵉsôp* for *bᵉsûpāh* (Rudolph, 151).

[5]Reading *dālᵉlû* or the singular *dālal* for MT's *'umlal,* "wither." MT repeats the same verb in both lines, a very unusual feature for Hebrew parallelism, and one needs a verb beginning with *daleth* for the continuation of the acrostic. See Isa. 19:6 for the use of *dālal* in a related context. One might also consider the reading *dā'ēb* with a related meaning (Rudolph, 151), though orthographically it is less likely. The versions translate the two verb forms differently, but it is unclear whether that represents a difference in their Hebrew Vorlage. The Wadi Murabba'āt scroll has *'mll* in both places (DJD II, 197).

[6]LXX has "the hills were shaken (*esaleuthēsan*)," and this more general meaning cannot be ruled out (*HALAT* [3rd ed.]), 526), but the more specific meaning "melt" is suggested by the role of liquids in producing this effect (Amos 9:13; Ps. 65:11 [10]) and by the similar use of *nāmēs,* "to melt," in other theophanic texts (Micah 1:4; Ps. 97:5; cf. Cathcart, *Nahum,* 52).

[7]The verb form *wattiśśā'* from the root *nāśā',* "to lift, raise, carry," is used intransitively here and literally means "and (the earth) rises up," but it refers to the heaving motion associated with earthquakes. Note the similar use of *'ālāh,* "to go up," in a related theophanic text (Amos 9:5; cf. Jer. 46:7–8). This interpretation of the form is supported by the renderings of LXX, V, and S. An intransitive use of *nāśā'* is rare, however (Hab. 1:3; Ps. 89:10 [9]), and this has led scholars to seek other interpretations. T translated the form with *wḥrwbt,* "and (the earth) became desolate," a translation that suggests the reading *wattiššā',* the niphal of *šā'āh,* "to crash into ruins." Cathcart accepts this reading, though he mistakenly identifies the form as a qal (p. 53). Rudolph rejects both these renderings on the basis that neither provides a suitable predicate for the inhabitants in the following line. He assumes an ellipsis of *qôl* in the idiom *nāśā' qôl,* "to lift the voice," and translates, "the earth cries out before him" (p. 150). Rudolph's objection is not compelling, however; any upward heaving of the earth in an earthquake would certainly be experienced as well by its inhabitants.

[8]To maintain the acrostic, one should slightly emend the order of the text from *lipnê za'mô mî ya'ᵃmôd,* "Before his indignation, who can stand?" to *za'mô mî ya'ᵃmôd lᵉpānāyw,* "His indignation, who can stand before it?" The corruption into the present form of the text reflects the tendency in textual transmission for unusual word order in poetic texts to be reverted back to more common patterns over the course of time.

[9]LXX's *archas,* "authorities," is apparently due to the misreading of *k'š,* "like fire," as *r'š,* "head."

[10]LXX's *tois hypomenousin auton,* "to those who wait upon him," can hardly be a translation of MT's *lᵉmā'ôz,* "to/as a place of refuge." In Lam. 3:25 LXX uses the same expression to translate *lᵉqōwāw,* "to those

who wait upon him," and Isa. 64:3 [4] suggests that it could also translate *limḥakkāyw.* It is likely that the original text of Nahum 1:7 had *ṭôb yhwh limḥakkāyw mā'ôz b*e*yôm ṣārāh,* but that MT lost *mḥkyw* by haplography due to homoioarchton while the Hebrew Vorlage of LXX lost the following *m'wz* for the same reason. Restoring both words completes the verse and allows one to restore the *yodh* line more appropriately (cf. Rudolph, 152).

[11]See the preceding note.

[12]To recontruct the *yodh* line, the copulative on *wyd',* "and he knows," must be dropped. The length of the opening line would be closer to the norm if one also restored the divine name *yhwh.* The present text might be explained on the basis of the haplography going back to the preexilic orthography: *yhw yd'* → ⟨*yh*⟩*w yd'* → *wyd'.*

[13]The *yodh* line would be missing its answering line if one took *wbšṭp 'br* with v. 8 as MT and the versions do. To read it with the preceding line, however, requires either that one drop the copulative, "Yahweh knows those who take refuge in him in the sweeping flood," or that one assume an element has dropped out of the line (cf. Rudolph, 152). The first alternative produces a poetic structure anomalous in this poem, so the second alternative is preferable, but the possibilities are too numerous to permit a convincing restoration. One could think of a variety of verb forms from a variety of verbs, e.g., *ya'*a*zōr,* "he helps (them)" (Rudolph, 152), or one could think of a number of nominal expressions, e.g., *sēter hû',* "he is a shelter."

[14]The MT reads *m*e*qômāh,* "her place," but the context offers no antecedent for the feminine suffix, and "place" provides a poor parallel for "his enemies" in the next line. LXX's *tous epēgeiromenous,* "the opponents," implies that LXX read a plural participle from the root *qwm.* Suggested corrections included *qāmāyw,* "his foes," *b*e*qāmāyw,* "against his foes," and *miqqāmēhû,* "from his foes" (Cathcart, *Nahum,* 57–58; Cathcart's vocalization *miqqômēhû* is incorrect; it cannot be supported by the vocalization of the hithpolel in Ps. 59:2 [1]). Rudolph, following several other scholars, assumes an abstract noun from the root *qwm* with the same pointing as the MT reading minus the mappiq: *m*e*qômāh,* "opposition" (Rudolph, 152). One may accept the reading with a slight correction of the vocalization. The normal pattern for forming abstract nouns from middle-*waw* verbs would produce *m*e*qûmāh,* a form that could also be represented by the same consonantal text as MT.

[15]LXX takes darkness as the subject: "darkness pursues his enemies." This is a possible reading of the Hebrew text, but the parallel line supports the analysis of *ḥošek,* "darkness," as an adverbial accusative rather than as the subject of the verb.

[16]Literally, "What are you thinking with regard to Yahweh." The idiom *ḥaššēb 'el* can be used with the accusative complement *ra',* "evil," in the sense of "to plot against" (Hos. 7:15), but without such a complement, the verb simply means "to meditate, reflect on, consider" (Pss. 73:16; 77:6 [5]). The context suggests that this reflection on Yahweh was negative in character, but it does not necessarily imply an active, hostile plotting against God (see the commentary below).

[17]The noun *ṣārāh* is an abstract noun, "hostility," that can be used concretely as a substitute or synonym for "adversary, enemy" (*CTA* 2.4[68].9; 3['NT].3.34; 3['NT].4.48, 50; cf. Ex. 23:22; Pss. 54:9 [7]; 138:7; see Cathcart, 59–60).

[18]This line is difficult to translate because of the problematic use of the preposition *'ad* in the MT, "For/though (*kî*) unto/like (*'ad*) entangled thorns . . . ." The meaning "like" has been suggested on the basis of a very few passages (BDB, 724). LXX does not help, because it apparently read *'d ysdm,* "down to their foundation." The translation given above presupposes a concessive understanding of *kî* and the reading *kî ⟨y⟩a'ar sîrîm sᵉbūkîm.* Even if God's enemies present a formidable, unapproachable front like a thicket of interwoven thorns, God's destruction of them is still certain. The same thought could be found without the emendation if *'ad* can legitimately be assigned the meaning "like": Though (they) are like interwoven thorns . . . ."

[19]This line is even more difficult, because the root *sb',* which is associated with the excessive consumption of alcoholic beverages, does not seem to fit the context. LXX translates this line with a phrase that implies a Hebrew text very similar to that found in the preceding line: *kai hōs smilax periplekomenē,* "and like an entangled bindweed . . . ." This translation has led critics to emend the text in an attempt to find a better parallel to the preceding line, but none of the suggestions have been convincing. The other versions reflect the MT, and that raises the possibility that the LXX translation is, in fact, an alternate translation of the preceding line, and that our line is simply not represented in the LXX. In light of this strong possibility, one should not dismiss the MT lightly. The translation given above presupposes only the slight emendation from *ûkᵉsob'ām,* "and like their liquor," to *ûbᵉsob'ām,* "and with their liquor." One could also consider the emendation to *ûkᵉsōbᵉ'īm,* "and like drunkards they are well-liquored." A double metaphor is involved in these two lines. Though God's enemies present a formidable front like a thicket of interwoven thorns, and though their warriors are stout, well-provisioned, and well-liquored (cf. Nahum 1:12)—this is not a dried-up thicket, but a green one—they will still be devoured like dried-out stubble.

[20]The first *wᵉkēn* refers back to the thicket of interwoven thorns

mentioned in v. 10. Even if the enemy is just as numerous as the thorns in such a thicket and as healthy as well-provisioned warriors, they will still be destroyed. LXX's peculiar reading of this line as *katarchōn hydatōn pollōn,* "a ruler of many waters," is based on the misreading of a possibly damaged Hebrew Vorlage as *mšl mym rbym.* S has a related reading, "upon the heads of many waters," but neither of these readings fits syntactically in the context or offers any improvement over the MT.

[21]The second *w^{e}kēn* refers back to the destruction of the dry stubble mentioned in v. 10. Just as dry stubble is devoured, so the Assyrians will be cut off and pass away. One should probably redivide the Hebrew to make the verb "pass away" plural: *wʿbr wʿnytk* > *wʿbrw ʿnytk.* LXX renders *wkn ngzw wʿbrw* with a single verb, "and thus they will be sundered," but S does not follow LXX in this, and it hardly represents a different, much less superior, Hebrew Vorlage.

[22]LXX's strange rendering, "and your report will not be heard again," is apparently based on a misreading of the Hebrew root *ʿnh* II, "to oppress," as if it were *ʿnh* I, "to answer."

[23]LXX and V read *maṭṭēhû,* "his staff," but this reading does not provide as good a parallel with "your bonds." S supports MT.

[24]LXX adopts the other sense of *qll* and translates the word as "because you are swift." This appears to have influenced S's translation of the line as "And I will quickly make it (presumably referring back to the pagan temple) your grave."

[25]The LXX reading *eis palaiōsin,* "in dilapidation," apparently read a preposition *b^{e}* before the *blyʿl* of the MT. It either understood *blyʿl* in the sense of Hebrew *bly, blw,* or *blh,* or it simply read one of these forms, since LXX uses the verbal root *palaioō* as its standard translation for the Hebrew root *bālāh,* "to grow old, wear out." Hebrew *b^{e}lîyaʿal* is a noun that is usually found in construct with a preceding noun: *bn(y) blyʿl,* "son(s) of *B.*" (Deut. 13:14; Judg. 19:22; 20:13; 1 Sam. 2:12; 10:27; 25:17; 1 Kings 21:10, 13; 2 Chron. 13:7), *bt blyʿl,* "daughter of *B.*" (1 Sam. 1:16), *'dm/'yš/'nšy (h)blyʿl,* "man/men of *B.*" (1 Sam. 25:25; 30:22; 2 Sam. 16:7; 20:1; 1 Kings 21:13; Prov. 6:12; 16:27), *dbr blyʿl,* "word of *B.*" (Pss. 41:9 [8]; 101:3; cf. the apparent adjectival use in Deut. 15:9), *nḥly blyʿl,* "the wadis of *B.*" (2 Sam. 22:5; Ps. 18:5 [4]), *yʿṣ blyʿl,* "counselor of *B.*" (Nahum 1:11), and *ʿd blyʿl,* "witness of *B.*" (Prov. 19:28). Apart from Nahum 2:1 [1:15], it occurs only twice used absolutely (2 Sam. 23:6; Job 34:18). This suggests that the Hebrew Vorlage behind LXX may have originally had *b⟨n⟩ blyʿl,* which was then misread as the noun + the preposition *b.* In the intertestamental literature, Qumran, and NT literature, *Belial/r* is sometimes personified as the name of a demon or of Satan himself (*HALAT,* 128), which explains V's treatment of the word as a proper name, but there is no clear evidence for this usage

in the OT. The nearest approximation to this usage in the OT is the use of the compound term *nḥly bly'l,* "the wadis of Destruction," used in parallel with *mšbry/ḥbly mwt,* "the breakers/cords of Death," as a designation for the Netherworld (2 Sam. 22:5; Ps. 18:5 [4]). Normally the noun, which appears to be a composite of *bᵉlî,* "without," + **ya'al,* "usefulness, profit," means "worthlessness, unworthiness," and as a nominalized adjective "a good-for-nothing, scoundrel" (*HALAT,* 128; cf. the rival etymology and discussion in Nicholas J. Tromp, *Primitive Conceptions of Death and the Nether World in the Old Testament* [Chicago: Loyola University Press, 1969], pp. 125–128). For the sake of balance between the two parallel lines it is best to take the first line as having an unexpressed subject and to take *bly'l* as the subject of the second line. For the use of *kullōh,* "all of him/it," to emphasize a preceding noun in the same line, see Jer. 48:31; Ezek. 11:15; 20:40; 36:10; Hos. 13:2.

Commentary

Nahum 1:2–2:1 [1:15] is composed of several disparate elements that have been fashioned together to form a coherent literary whole. It begins with a partial acrostic that characterizes Yahweh as a God of fierce judgment (1:2–8). The acrostic extends only through the letter *kaph,* and textual corruption has marred the acrostic at a couple of points, but for the most part the acrostic is clear. With the exception of the initial letter *aleph,* the opening word of the first line of each couplet begins with the succeeding letter of the Hebrew alphabet. The initial letter *aleph* is followed, not by a single couplet, but by three couplets, an expansion that seems to give added emphasis to the opening of the acrostic. The acrostic is followed by a warning not to meditate against Yahweh, for he is about to make a complete end of the opposition against him (1:9). Verses 10–13 elaborate that threat with a promise to Judah or Jerusalem that Yahweh will destroy her oppressor regardless of how strong and invincible the oppressor may appear. In the next verse (1:14), Yahweh turns from Judah to address the oppressor with the same threat of judgment, but in 2:1 [1:15] the announcement of salvation is again proclaimed to Judah. The unit clearly ends at 2:1 [1:15], since 2:2 [2:1] introduces a new oracle against Assyria.

It is likely that the prophet simply adapted part of a preexisting acrostic familiar to him from the cultic hymnody. Though Nahum is probably not the original composer of this hymnic text, its powerful portrayal of Yahweh as the avenging divine warrior fitted the prophet's purpose admirably. It was easily adaptable as a compelling introduction to Nahum's announcement of judgment on Assyria, and that is the way in which the prophet appears to have used the acrostic. Contrary to the opinions expressed by some commentators, there is no reason to dismiss the acrostic as a secondary addition to the prophetic book.

The other elements in the unit may have had their own prior history, but their current arrangement in the text has sacrificed that prior history to their present literary function. They are all so short, taken independently, that it is difficult to believe they ever existed as single, individual oracles, though a weak case might be made for 2:1 [1:15].

[1:2] The opening verse of the acrostic has been expanded, probably by the prophet himself, who used other hymnic lines, perhaps some of them from the latter half of the same original acrostic, in this expansion. One effect of this expansion is to underscore the characterization of Yahweh as a God of vengeance. Three times Yahweh is characterized with the participle *nōqēm,* "avenging, vengeful, takes vengeance." George E. Mendenhall in his study of the root *nqm* has tried to find a better English translation for the root in order to eliminate all the negative implications often associated with the English word vengeance (*The Tenth Generation* [Baltimore: Johns Hopkins University Press, 1973], 69–104), but in my opinion the attempt has been a failure. While the root does not imply an illegal punitive abuse of power, it does imply harsh punitive retribution in retaliation for wrongs committed against one. Human attempts to avenge wrongdoings may run the risk of the illegal abuse of power, of "taking the law into one's own hands," though scripture acknowledges the legitimate role of constituted authority in exercising this function (Rom. 13:4), but no such limitation rests on the divine sovereign, whose rule is the source of the law. Yahweh's retributive punishment of evildoers is legal by definition, and Nahum's emphasis on Yahweh's vengeance is a way of underscoring that God will not let injustice win out. The rule of Yahweh will not allow the oppressors to go unpunished. One should beware of any bogus morality that dismisses vengeance as both inappropriate to humans and unworthy of God. Such a view simply betrays a glaring absence of the most elementary sense of justice. While the desire to see vengeance done can be twisted and corrupted like any other human desire, it arises out of a sense of justice, and vengeance cannot be discarded without discarding the concern for justice as well.

Yahweh's vengeance is closely associated with both his jealousy or zeal and his anger. The statement that Yahweh is a jealous God *('ēl qannô')* is a statement about God's self-respect; he will not be treated as merely one among many nor will he allow his demands to be ignored; he is God, and he will be acknowledged as God or else (Ex. 20:5; 34:14; Deut. 4:24; 5:9; 6:15; Josh. 24:19). The motif of his anger is a closely related concept. One cannot offend God with impunity. He has a violent temper, so it is extremely dangerous to cross him. Once his enemies have enraged him, their fate is sealed. God will take vengeance on them in the heat of his rage.

Such language about God is metaphorical, of course, and it must be held in tension with other biblical metaphors that stress God's love, his care for his people, and his accessibility. Without such paradoxical tension, one could misread this portrait of Yahweh as that of an irrational divine bully. On the other hand, without this frightening side of the paradox, one could misread the portrait of the loving God as that of a passionless, doting, and undemanding dispenser of cheap grace. The God of the cross remains an awe-inspiring, devouring fire (Deut. 4:24; Heb. 10:26–31; 12:29). One cannot treat him lightly. God's love is an expression of strength, not weakness.

[**3**] The last two lines of v. 2 may derive from the *nun* couplet of the original acrostic, but the first couplet of v. 3 appears to have been inserted into the acrostic from a different source. Slightly variant forms of the same confessional characterization of Yahweh are found in a number of passages (Ex. 34:6–7; Num. 14:18; Joel 2:13; Jonah 4:2; Pss. 86:15; 103:8; 145:8; Neh. 9:17). In most of these passages the emphasis is upon God's mercy, his slowness to anger, and his willingness to forgive. Nahum's emphasis, however, is quite different. While he acknowledges this traditional confession about the nature of Yahweh, he shapes the statement to support his own borrowed portrait of Yahweh as an enraged God of harsh vengeance. In contrast to all the other occurrences of this confessional statement, where Yahweh's slowness to anger is expanded by the statement *wᵉrab ḥesed* or *ûgᵉdôl ḥāsed,* "and great in loving kindness," Nahum has *ûgᵉdôl kōaḥ,* "but great in strength." This shifts the thought from God's merciful willingness to forgive back to God's majesty, and the shift is completed by the following statement that Nahum shares with Ex. 34:7 and Num. 14:18: "And Yahweh will certainly not acquit the guilty." Contrary to what some might think (Jonah 4:2), God's traditional graciousness and willingness to forgive would not allow his enemies to escape their deserved judgment.

The last couplet in v. 3 resumes the acrostic with a portrayal of Yahweh as a storm god who comes wrapped in thunderclouds. This is typical theophanic language derived from the earlier portrayals of Near Eastern storm gods and widely used in the Old Testament to portray God's coming in judgment (cf. the discussion on Habakkuk 3).

[**4**] This theophanic imagery is continued in v. 4 with the motif of Yahweh rebuking the sea and drying up the rivers. The parallelism between sea and rivers goes back to the Canaanite myth, where Prince Sea and Judge River serve as parallel designations for the cosmic enemy of Baal, the storm god. Moreover, Yahweh's rebuke of the sea is often found in contexts where this mythological background seems clear (2 Sam. 22:16 = Ps. 18:16 [15]; Isa. 17:13; 50:2; Ps. 104:7). The motif is used once in reference to the exodus event (Ps. 106:9), but this usage merely adapts the mythological language to apply it to a historical event. There is no clear reference to the exodus in Nahum's use of this mythological language.

The wilting of nature also has a mythological background. It appears as a motif in Mesopotamian theophanies (see Thomas W. Mann, *Divine Presence and Guidance in Israelite Traditions: The Typology of Exaltation* [Baltimore and London: Johns Hopkins University Press, 1977], 30), and it sometimes appears along with other convulsions in nature in descriptions of Yahweh's theophanic march as the divine warrior. It is often directly related to Yahweh's thundering rebuke, to his voice or word of judgment (Amos 1:2; Isa. 19:1–10; 24:3–6; Jer. 4:23–28). At other times the wilting of nature is less directly attributed to Yahweh's action and is portrayed merely as nature's response to human sinfulness (Isa. 33:9; Jer. 12:4, 10–11; 23:10; Hos. 4:2–3). Drought was typically understood as divine judgment on those affected by it (Jer. 14:1–7; Amos 4:7–8), but it could be understood more radically as one of the phenomena marking a complete return to chaos (Jer. 4:23–28), the destruction of God's enemies, as in the primeval flood or in the expected Day of Yahweh (see Zeph. 1:2–3, 18). Bashan, the northern trans-Jordanian plateau; Carmel, the mountain range that extends to the northwest along the southern edge of the Esdraelon Valley in Israel until it juts into the Mediterranean just south of Haifa and the Bay of Acco; and Lebanon, the north-south mountain range west of the Beqa' Valley in Lebanon, were all noted for their fertility. If vegetation in these areas wilted and languished, the drought was indeed severe.

[5] The convulsions of the mountains and hills and the quaking of the earth are standard features of theophanies (Judg. 5:4; 2 Sam. 22:8 = Ps. 18:8 [7]; Isa. 13:13; 24:18; Jer. 4:24; 10:10; 51:29; Ezek. 38:19–20; Joel 4:16 [3:16]; Amos 9:5; Micah 1:4; Hab. 3:6, 10; Pss. 46:4; 68:9 [8]; 77:19 [18]). This imagery has often been associated with earthquakes, but the close association of these motifs with clouds, thunder, and lightning shows that another very important source for such imagery was the frightening phenomena of a strong thunderstorm in the mountains. Psalm 29, a psalm that probably goes back to a Canaanite original in honor of Baal, demonstrates this point quite clearly. (See H. L. Ginsberg, "A Phoenician Hymn in the Psalter," *XIX Congresso Internazionale degli Orientalisti* [Rome, 1935], 472–476; Cross, *CMHE,* 151–156; cf. Peter C. Craigie, *Psalms 1–50,* 241–246; J. L. Cunchillos, *Estudio del Salmo 29* [Valencia, 1976]; Oswald Loretz, *Psalm 29: Kanaanäische El- und Baaltradition in jüdischer Sicht* [UBL; Altenberg: CIS-Verlag, 1984]; and Carola Kloos, *Yhwh's Combat with the Sea: A Canaanite Tradition in the Religion of Ancient Israel* [Leiden: E. J. Brill, 1986] and the extensive literature cited there.)

[6] The function of all this theophanic imagery is to underscore the awesomeness of Yahweh in order to prepare the way for the prophet's announcement of judgment on the Assyrian enemy. In the light of this fearsome theophanic display of God's power, the questions in the first couplet of v. 6 can only be read as rhetorical. Obviously, no one can withstand Yahweh's indignation. No one can endure the heat of his anger. If seas and rivers dry up, the most fertile lands wilt, and mountains go into violent convulsions before his wrath, no human power, not even the Assyrian empire, will be able to stand against God's rage. As the second couplet states, when God's wrath is poured out like fire, even the rock cliffs are shattered by him, and if the rock of the primeval mountains cannot withstand his anger, how can the Assyrians?

[7] Nonetheless, this awesome God, whose violent temper cannot be resisted, is good to those who trust in him and seek their security in him. He will not disappoint them. He will acknowledge them and care for them in the day when judgment overtakes their world. The language of this verse and the first line of v. 8, which should really go with v. 7, is typical hymnic language, but it is perhaps worth noting that the imagery of the sweeping flood *(šeṭep ʿōbēr)* is used specifically in reference to the Assyrians in an earlier passage from Isaiah (*šāṭap wᵉʿābar,* "he will flood and sweep on"; Isa. 8:8). Yahweh will deliver those who trust in him from that sweeping flood.

[8] This sudden shift from the portrayal of God's violent rage to a celebration of his goodness may initially seem abrupt, but these two sides of God's character are in fact very closely connected. God's wrath is simply the reverse side of his goodness, because, as the continuation of v. 8 indicates, it is precisely Yahweh's violent judgment on his enemies that effects the salvation of his friends. He will save them by annihilating the enemy. To pursue one into darkness is equivalent to chasing him into the underworld, the realm of the dead (cf. Tromp, *Primitive Conceptions of Death,* 95–98).

[9] Verse 9 marks the transition point from the older acrostic to Nahum's application of it. In the light of the message of this cultic text, the prophet challenges his audience with an indicting question: "Why do you meditate against Yahweh?" It is difficult to decide precisely who is being addressed with this question. Similar language of "plotting against Yahweh" is also used in v. 11, where the author of such plots appears to be the Assyrian enemy. One might think, therefore, of the Assyrian enemy as the audience addressed, particularly since the Assyrian king seems to be addressed in v. 14. On the other hand, the plotter in v. 11 is clearly distinguished from the audience addressed in that verse, and the interchange between second- and third-person forms in vs. 9–13 suggests that the audience envisioned in v. 9 is a Judean audience. The second-person form used in v. 9 is a masculine plural in contrast to the feminine singular found in vs. 11–13, but the feminine singular can refer to Judah or Jerusalem as a collective, while the masculine plural could refer to the same audience as the citizens of that state or city. The second-person form in v. 14 is a

masculine singular, presumably referring to the king of Assyria, so it is not obvious that the different second-person forms in vs. 9 and 14 are referring to the same audience.

If the "you" of v. 9 is a Judean audience, the prophet is accusing them of harboring unworthy thoughts about Yahweh. Given the context, such thoughts must be doubts as to Yahweh's ability to deliver them from the Assyrian oppressor (Maier, *Nahum,* 187; Rudolph, 152). In response to this doubt, the prophet reasserts Yahweh's plan, in line with his character reflected in the older acrostic hymn, to wreak total annihilation on his enemies. The target of Yahweh's wrath will not rise up a second time to challenge him. This reference to a second time may suggest that Judah had recently experienced the hostility of Assyria, but if so, the precise background to this experience remains ambiguous. One might think of the brief exile of Manasseh, perhaps connected with the revolt of Babylon (650–648 B.C.), if the Chronicler's account of this exile can be believed (2 Chron. 33:10–13).

[10] No matter how invincible the Assyrians may appear, they will be utterly destroyed. Even if their troops are well-provisioned and arrayed in such numbers as to resemble an impenetrable, well-watered thicket of entangled thorns, they will be quickly burned up like very dry stubble.

[11] The feminine singular "you" in v. 11, taken by itself, could be interpreted as a reference either to Nineveh or to Judah or Jerusalem, but the similar references in vs. 12–13 can only be understood as referring to Judah or Jerusalem, so the reference in v. 11 should also be understood as addressing God's own people. Since the verses both before and after v. 11 appear to identify God's enemy with Judah's oppressors, the one who plotted evil against Yahweh should probably be identified with the Assyrian king or his representative. It follows, then, that the "going out" of this one from Judah or Jerusalem refers not to his point of origin, but to his departure from Judean territory. Taking the verb as a prophetic perfect, the sense of the verse is that the Assyrian will shortly depart from Judah. Yahweh will destroy Assyrian hegemony over Judah, and Judah will never again see this evil oppressor (cf. Isa. 33:18–19).

[12] Verse 12 continues this thought by alluding back to the metaphor in v. 10. The adjective *šᵉlēmîm,* "whole, complete," could refer either to the good health of the enemy soldiers or to the complete muster of the troops. Even if the Assyrian army is healthy, at full strength, and just as numerous as the thicket of thorns mentioned in v. 10, like the thicket in that metaphor, they will still be cut down and pass away. Yahweh had once used the Assyrians to afflict Judah (cf. Isa. 1:5–9; 10:5–19), but Yahweh will not afflict Judah again. The era of Assyrian oppression is over.

[13] Now Yahweh is about to break the Assyrian yoke and release Judah from the Assyrian bondage. In proclaiming this deliverance of Judah, Nahum is picking up both the language and the theme of older prophecies of Isaiah (Isa. 10:27a; 14:24–27).

[14] The second masculine singular form in this verse cannot represent a continuation of the direct address to Judah, for which the second feminine singular was used, but the switch to direct address of the Assyrian ruler appears quite abrupt. This has led a number of scholars to correct *'ālеykā,* "concerning you," to *'ālāyw,* "concerning him" (Rudolph, 159). Despite the fact that MT is supported by all the versions, this emendation may be correct. The corruption of the third-person suffix to the second person could have resulted from the following quotation, which does quite properly address the Assyrian in the second person. On the other hand, it is just possible that the abrupt address to the Assyrian ruler is due to the prophet himself, who anticipated the following quotation.

In any case, the judgment Yahweh announces against the Assyrian ruler is the extermination of his family, his gods, and his own life. Assyria is to be permanently destroyed, cut off without any future. Assuming the text is in order, the implication of Yahweh preparing the grave would appear to underscore the lack of anyone else to perform this task. There is no family left, and the dead ruler is too despised for anyone else to bother with his burial. It is left up to God to dispose of the body; the Assyrian will not receive proper burial. One should note how thoroughly this judgment was carried out in the collapse of the Assyrian empire, when Nineveh was permanently destroyed, the gods of Assyria desecrated, and the Assyrian monarchy brought to an end.

[2:1 (1:15)] The announcement of the arrival of the herald bearing good news could be seen as the introduction of a new oracle, but it does not seem to function that way here. The proclamation of the herald resumes the address to Judah in the second-person feminine singular, an address that had been briefly interrupted by 1:14, and in the prophetic vision it confirms the word of judgment the prophet had already spoken against Assyria. Just as the prophet had proclaimed, so the Judean messenger, presumably coming from Assyria, is about to confirm: The Assyrian scoundrel is totally cut off; he will never again pass through Judah. Because of this good news, Judah is to celebrate her festivals in honor of Yahweh and fulfill the vows she made to him. The implication seems to be that Judah could not celebrate her festivals appropriately as long as she was under the thumb of Assyrian oppression. It is no accident that one of the more important acts of Josiah's political and religious reform after Assyria's loss of control in the west was the public celebration of the passover festival (2 Kings 23:21–25). The vows are probably to be understood as vows made to Yahweh during the long period of Assyrian oppression, vows whose fulfillment was contingent on

Yahweh's deliverance of Judah from that oppression. In the light of that deliverance, those vows must now be paid.

3. THE FALL OF NINEVEH: 2:2–14 [2:1–13E]

2:2[1] A scatterer[1] has gone up against you.[2]
Man[3] the guard post,[4]
Watch the road;
Strengthen your loins,
Brace yourself with all your strength!
3[2] [For Yahweh is restoring the pride of Jacob,
Just as the pride of Israel;
Because plunderers have plundered them,
And have destroyed their branches.]
4[3] The shields of his warriors are dyed red,
His soldiers are clothed in scarlet;
The chariot attachments[5] are like fire[6]
In the day of his preparation,
And the spears[7] quiver.[8]
5[4] Through the streets[9] the chariots rush madly,
They race against one another[10] through the squares.
Their appearance is like torches,
Like lightning they dart.
6[5] He assigns[11] his commanders,[12]
They stumble[13] on their course,
They hurry to the wall,
And the siege shelters[14] are set in place.
7[6] The floodgates[15] are opened,
And the palace melts away.[16]
8[7] The princess is made to stand among the captives,[17]
Her maidservants are led away,[18]
Moaning[19] like the sound of doves,
Beating[20] upon their breasts.[21]
9[8] And Nineveh is like a pool of water,
Whose waters[22] are[23] running away.[24]
"Stop! Stop!"
But no one turns back.
10[9] "Plunder silver! Plunder gold!"[25]
There is no end to the supply,
An abundance of every precious object.
11[10] Desolation, and Destruction, and Devastation![26]
Melting hearts and tottering of knees!
There is anguish in all the loins,
And all their faces grow pale.[27]

12[11] Where is the den of the lions,
The cave[28] for the young lions,
There where the lion went,[29]
The lion's cub, and there was none to frighten?
13[12] The lion tore sufficient prey for its cubs,
And strangled for his lionesses;
He filled his holes with prey,
And his dens with torn flesh.[30]
14[13] Behold, I am against you,[31]
Says Yahweh of Hosts,
And I will burn your abundance[32] in smoke;
The sword will devour your young lions,
I will cut off from the land your prey,
And the voice of your messengers[33] will no longer be heard.

Textual Notes

[1]In place of MT's *mpyṣ,* "scatterer," LXX presupposes the reading *mpyḥ,* "blower," a participle from either *npḥ* (Ezek. 37:9) or *pwḥ* (Ezek. 21:36 [31]), construed as governing the following preposition *'l.* The letters *ṣ* and *ḥ* are not easily confused, so the corruption probably resulted from the influence of the idiom *hpyḥ/npḥ 'l* on an early copyist. LXX apparently equated *hpyḥ/npḥ 'l* with *hpyḥ/npḥ b-* and then interpreted *mpyḥ 'l* positively on the analogy with *npḥ b* in Ezek. 37:9. MT's *mēpîṣ* is a hiphil participle from the root *pwṣ,* "to scatter." This root is used to describe the dispersal of a people or an army as the result of a military defeat (1 Sam. 11:11; 2 Kings 25:5), so the enemy who imposed such a defeat could well be characterized as a "scatterer." Though the prophet does not immediately identify this enemy, Nahum 2:14 [13] implies that it is Yahweh. Moreover, "scatterer" is a particularly appropriate epithet for Yahweh, given Nahum's glorification of the deity in the traditional language and imagery of the divine warrior (ch. 1). Two ancient texts referring to the march of Yahweh as the divine warrior use the qal stem of *pwṣ* to characterize Yahweh's effect on his enemy (Num. 10:35; Ps. 68:2), and in a later prophetic reversal of holy war language Yahweh scatters (hiphil stem) his own people before the enemy (Jer. 18:17). Thus there is no reason to correct the text in order to derive the form from the root *npṣ,* "to smash, shatter."

[2]Read the 2 m. sg. suffix *pāneykā.* MT has the 2 f. sg. *pānayik,* but that is very suspect, since the direct address is continued in the next two lines with imperative forms, none of which are feminine. It is true that *nāṣôr* is an infinitive absolute used as an imperative, and the following three piel forms could also be analyzed as infinite absolutes, but the only reason for so analyzing them is the assumption that the subject is femi-

nine and therefore would not agree with m. sg. imperatives. Nothing in the text identifies the addressee as Nineveh; this is just a conclusion drawn from MT's 2 f. sg. suffix. The suffix was probably mispointed as a feminine due to the influence of the 2 f. sg. forms in 2:1 [1:15], but as already indicated, these forms have a different referent. Note the similar corruption in 2:14 [13] (see notes 38ff.).

[3]Hebrew *nāṣôr* is the qal inf. abs. used as the imperative, "guard!" LXX's *exairoumenos,* "one who saves," presupposes the reading *mṣyl* (see Hos. 5:14; Micah 5:7 [8]; Isa. 42:22; 43:13), but it is an obvious corruption. LXX was apparently interpreting this verse in the light of Ezek. 37:9 as a promise that God would breathe new life into his people and deliver them from affliction.

[4]The consonantal text *mṣrh* is pointed by MT as *m^eṣūrāh,* "rampart, fortification," from the root *ṣûr,* "to besiege." Following that understanding, one could translate the text "guard the ramparts." Given the Hebrew stylistic penchant for using cognate accusatives, however, it is more likely that the noun should be repointed as *maṣṣārāh,* "guard, guard post," from the root *nṣr.* A cognate of this noun is well attested in Akkadian, and it is probably hidden behind faulty pointing in a number of Hebrew texts. This pointing would give the cognate accusative, "Guard the guard post," i.e., "set the guard," or "man the guard post." LXX's "from affliction" is based on the reading *miṣṣārāh,* which is a result of the previous corruption of *nṣwr* to *mṣyl.*

[5]Hebrew *p^elādôt* presents a major problem of interpretation. LXX and V understood it to refer to the reins of the chariot. S takes it as the equivalent of *lappîdîm,* "lamps, torches." Others connect it to the Persian word for "steel," attested in Syriac as *pûlād* or *palādā',* and interpret it as referring to the metal decorations on the chariot and the gear of the chariot horses. Questions have been raised whether one would expect a Persian loanword in Hebrew this early, but Rudolph rightly points to the easy transfer of the name for cultural products from one language to another (p. 167). Cathcart (*Nahum,* 87–88), Keller (p. 121), and Dietrich and Loretz (*BO* 25 [1968]: 100–101) connect the word to Ugaritic *pld* (*UT* 1108.7; 1111.8, 12; 1112.1, 7; 1113.4, 7, 8; *CTA* 140[98].4), which refers to some kind of garment or covering. It could refer to the caparison for the chariot horses or to the decorative covering for the chariot pole attachment. Rudolph objects that the comparison to fire would not fit such coverings (p. 167), but that objection will hardly hold, since they were ornately and colorfully decorated, and those decorations included metallic pieces (see the representations in A. Henry Layard, *The Monuments of Nineveh* [London, 1819], plates 13, 14, 27, 28).

[6]One should probably make the slight correction from *b^e'ēš,* "in fire,"

to *kᵉʾēš,* "like fire." In the Aramaic square script, *b* and *k* are easily confused.

[7]Hebrew *wᵉhabbᵉrōšîm* literally means "and the junipers," but the name of the tree, either referring to the real juniper or to another conifer (such transference is attested with the Akkadian cognate, *CAD* b, 328), apparently came to be used to designate the spear either because its shaft was made of the wood of such trees or because it resembled the trunk of such trees. Compare the similar semantic development in the case of Greek *doru,* "stem, tree, shaft of a spear, spear itself" (H. G. Liddell and R. Scott, *Greek-English Lexicon,* rev. ed. [Oxford, 1940], 445), and the Aramaic *môrnᵉyān,* "ashtrees, lances," or *môrānît,* "spear, lance" (Marcus Jastrow, *Hebrew-Aramaic-English Dictionary,* repr. 1971, 750). Another possibility suggested by my colleague Leong Seow is to take the word as a reference to the wooden framework of the chariots. An Old Babylonian Sumerian text speaks of a *gigir šim.li* = Akkadian *narkabti burāši,* "a chariot of juniper wood" (*CAD* b, 327). This would have the advantage of providing somewhat closer parallelism to the dominant chariot imagery in the passage:

> The chariot attachments are like fire
> In the day of his preparation,
> And the chariot frames quiver.

LXX's *hippeis,* "cavalry," V's *agitatores,* "drivers," and S's *prš',* "cavalry," all presuppose the reading *wᵉhappᵉrāšîm* or *wᵉhabbᵉrāšîm.* The interchange between *p* and *b* is well attested in Hebrew (see Cathcart, *Nahum,* 89).

[8]The image seems to be that of a rippling or quivering effect in the sea of spears held aloft by the advancing spearmen of the attacking army. Alternatively, it would refer to the shaking, swaying, or quivering of the wooden frames of the chariots as they rushed into battle. Such movement would cause a flashing effect from the reflection off the metal decorations of the frame. Those who take *whbršym* to refer to the cavalry or chariot horses must either understand the verb to indicate tumult or confusion among these units, or assume a meaning for the verb *rʿl,* "quiver, shake, reel," otherwise unattested in Hebrew. Rudolph's translation, "and the horses stand in row and rank," takes the latter approach, based on the tenth conjugation of the Arabic root *rʿl* (Rudolph, 165, 167).

[9]LXX takes *baḥûṣôt,* "in the streets," with the preceding line, but the parallelism with *bārᵉḥōbôt,* "in the squares," shows that it should go with this line.

[10]The hithpalpel of *šqq* occurs only here, so its precise meaning remains problematic. BDB gives "they rush to and fro" (p. 1055), but the infixed *t* form could be interpreted as reciprocal, "to race against one

another" (cf. Rudolph, 167). LXX's rendering *sygchythēsontai ta harmata kai symplakēsontai en tais plateiais,* "the chariots were poured together and became entangled in the squares," suggests the engagement of opposing chariot troops at very close range, but the description of the chariots in the following two lines resembles the description of the attacking army in v. 4 [3], and that makes any attempt to find a reference to the defending troops in this verse more than problematic.

[11]MT's *yizkōr* would normally mean "he remembers," but the meaning "to remember" does not fit the context, so one should probably assign the verb the meaning "to command, to assign, to appoint" (cf. Akkadian *zakāru* [von Soden, *AHW,* 1503–1504]). Note also T's *yᵉmannôn,* "(the commanders of their camp) were appointed." LXX, S, and T read the verb as a plural, and LXX, T, and V all translate it as a passive. Thus one cannot rule out the possibility that the original text was *yizzākᵉrû,* "(his commanders) were given orders." There is no indication in the text that the prophet has shifted from his description of the attacking army to a description of the frenzied activity of the defenders of Nineveh. Rudolph claims that v. 6 [5] cannot refer to the attacking army because the mustering of the troops comes too late after v. 5 [4] (p. 167), but if v. 5 describes the preliminary assault to reach the city walls, v. 6 could very well describe the giving of orders to the various commanders for the actual assault on the walls.

[12]LXX's additional clause, "and they will flee by day," is unexplained, but it is probably a secondary expansion.

[13]The verb *kāšal,* "to stumble," normally has a negative connotation in military contexts (see Isa. 5:27), but the parallelism with *mahēr,* "to hurry," suggests that here it simply refers to the troops moving forward in extreme haste, perhaps struggling with the burden of the siege weapons. At any rate, this rapid advance leads up to the statement that the siege-shelters were set in place.

[14]The noun *sōkēk,* "shelter," from the root *sākak,* "to overshadow, screen, cover," apparently designates the various roofed and mobile siege towers that were used by besieging armies to protect their sappers and their troops manning the battering rams. LXX takes the noun as referring to the defenses within the city, but this seems highly improbable.

[15]Hebrew *šaʿᵃrê hannᵉhārôt,* "gates of the river," is the lexical equivalent of Akkadian *bāb nāri,* "door of the river," which was used to designate the sluice gates on canals and dams controlling the flow of rivers (von Soden, *AHW,* 95). The *bāb nāri* is mentioned in the Bavian inscription that celebrates Sennacherib's construction of the aqueduct and Bavian-Khosr canal, which brought the water of the Khosr River into the northeast side of Nineveh (T. Jacobsen and S. Lloyd, *Sennacherib's Aqueduct at Jerwan* [OIP 24; Chicago: University of Chicago

Press, 1935], 31–43; cf. Cathcart, *Nahum,* 95–96). Rudolph's interpretation of the Hebrew expression as referring simply to the city gates facing the Tigris (p. 171) is not convincing.

[16]The niphal of the verb *mûg* is normally used metaphorically of people "melting away" in fear, but the root is used in the qal, polel, and hithpolel for actual melting or dissolving, and one cannot rule out the possibility that the verb was chosen because of the prophet's view that flooding would contribute to the downfall of Nineveh.

[17]This line presents a major crux. Given the difficulties in the line, the translation offered above is far from certain. It is based on the emendation of the line suggested by Rudolph: *w*^{e}*huṣṣ*^{e}*bāh baggālūt hā'*^{a}*tallāh* (p. 168). The proposed emendation requires only some slight changes in the consonantal text: *whṣb glt[h] h'lth* < *whṣb[h b]glt h'tlh.* The loss of *h* at the end of *wḥsbh* and of *b* at the beginning of *bglt* is easily explained by the movement of a scribe's eye from the first to the second *b.* The addition of *h* to *glt* is due to dittography of the following *h,* and the transposition of *tl* > *lt* that results in a form from the more common root *'lh* presents no major problems.

MT's *w*^{e}*huṣṣab* has given rise to a host of interpretations, but none of them is convincing. The interpretation of the form as the proper name of an Assyrian princess or queen is a relatively late proposal, and there is no historical or inscriptional basis for it. The various attempts to find a noun behind the form that would refer to a princess have yielded at best *w*^{e}*haṣṣ*^{e}*bī,* "the beauty" or "the gazelle," and *haṣṣāb,* "the lizard," neither of which seems very convincing. The reference to "her maidservants" in the next line requires that there be some reference to a princess in this line, however, and that makes the reading *haṣṣāb,* "the litter, the wagon" (cf. T) or *haṣṣōb,* "the column, train" (Driver, *JTS,* n.s. 15 [1964]: 296–298), of little help. The various attempts to read the form as a masculine verb, either with a following feminine subject, or with *w*^{e}*hahêkāl,* "and the palace," of the preceding line as its subject, break down for the lack of a convincing root. Saggs's *naṣābu* (*JTS* 20 [1969]: 221) means "to suck" or "to lick;" its usage in Akkadian does not justify the extension of meaning to "are dissolved" (ibid., 225). Keller's Arabic root *ṣb,* "to pour out" (p. 122), is very problematic as a cognate for an early Hebrew root.

The emended form *hā'*^{a}*tallāh* would be cognate with Akkadian *etelletu,* "princess"; a form of the word (not the root *eṭēlu,* "to be manly") is probably also evidenced in the name of the Judean queen Athaliah (*'*^{a}*talyāh(û);* cf. Jeaneane D. Fowler, *Theophoric Personal Names in Ancient Hebrew: A Comparative Study* [JSOTS 49; Sheffield: JSOT Press, 1988], 162).

[18]Reading the pual participle *m*^{e}*nuh*^{a}*gôt* from *nhg,* "to drive, con-

duct," in place of MT's piel, *m^{e}nah^{a}gôt.* The passive is supported by LXX, V, and T. One could read the active form with the MT, if one followed S in deriving the form from *nhg,* "to moan," instead of *nhg,* "to drive, conduct." However, this analysis would produce the very unbalanced line, "her maidservants are moaning like the sound of doves," and it would leave the preceding line without any parallel. One should compare Lam. 1:1–4. It describes Jerusalem as a princess *(rbty/śrty,* Lam. 1:1) in distress, whose priests groan, whose virgins are afflicted *(nûgôt),* and whose children are taken into captivity. If one corrects *nûgôt* to *n^{e}hûgôt,* "(her virgins) are led away," following LXX (Lam. 1:4), the parallel would be even more striking.

[19]Restoring the qal active participle *hōgôt* from *hgh,* "to moan" (Isa. 38:14; 59:11), which was lost by haplography after the preceding participle with the identical consonantal ending, *m^{e}nuh^{a}gôt.* Both V and T reflect a text with both verbs over against LXX and S, which reflect only one of the two forms.

[20]Hebrew *m^{e}tōp^{e}pôt* is a polel participle from *tpp,* a denominative verb from *tōp,* "timbrel," meaning "to sound the timbrel, to beat."

[21]Hebrew *'al lib^{e}bēhen* here means "upon their breasts." Striking one's own chest was a sign of mourning (cf. Luke 18:13; 23:48). T catches the sense of the idiom, but LXX, V, and S all miss it with their rendering, "they were moaning in their hearts."

[22]Despite the claims of Cathcart (*Nahum,* p. 101), the MT can hardly be correct as it stands; Cathcart's own translation departs from it. Correct *mîmê hî',* "from days of . . . it(?)," to *mêmeyhā('),* "its waters," and read as the subject of an unmarked relative clause. LXX and V, both of which have "its waters," support the correction, and S at least reads "waters." Only T with its "from days of old" preserves MT's vocalization.

[23]Delete the *w^{e}* on *w^{e}hēmmāh,* since *hēmmāh* is serving as the copulative in the nominal clause *mêmeyhā hēmmāh nāsîm,* "its waters (they) are running away." LXX, S, and T have the *w^{e},* but it probably represents an early expansion of the text by a scribe who misdivided it as follows: "Nineveh's waters are like a pool of waters. (And) They are running away" (cf. LXX). This division cannot be correct, because it would make the first line too long and unbalanced compared to the following line.

[24]For the use of the verb *nws,* "to flee, run away," with reference to water, see Pss. 104:7; 114:3, 5. This imagery is rooted in the mythological portrayal of Yahweh as the divine warrior before whose might even the unruly waters of chaos are put to flight. It was particularly popular in the Zion Tradition's motif of Yahweh's protection of Zion, where the imagery of mighty waters is often just a powerful metaphor to convey

the cosmic significance of the attack of enemy kings (Pss. 46:6–10; 48:4–8 [3–7]; Isa. 17:12–14). Isaiah exploited this imagery to portray Assyria's conquest of Israel (Isa. 8:7–8a), but he claimed its raging tide could not finally defeat God's plans (Isa. 8:8b–10; 17:12–14). Nahum picks up on this older imagery to suggest that the mighty waters of Assyria are no longer a threat to anyone. The tide has turned, Assyria's hosts have fled, and Nineveh is left high and dry.

[25]LXX reads the verbs as perfects: "They plundered the silver, they plundered the gold." V and T support MT, however, and the more dramatic imperatives represent the superior reading.

[26]The translation is an attempt to catch the play on the similarity of sound in the original *bûqāh ûmᵉbûqāh ûmᵉbullāqāh.*

[27]Literally, "and the faces of all of them gather a glow/redness" (*HALAT,* 860). That could either mean that their faces became flushed, or *qibbᵉṣû* could have the sense of "to gather in and so take away" (cf. *'āsap*), in which case the idiom would mean that their faces became pale. The parallel use of the expression in Joel 2:6 shows that it is the reaction of terrified individuals, so the sense "to become pale" fits the context better. The versions all understood the idiom as connected to the word *pārûr,* "cooking pot," and their renderings are all a variation on "all their faces were black like a cooking pot."

[28]The versions all reflect MT's *mir'eh,* "pasturage," but this word is normally used to refer to a place of grazing for sheep and cattle, and occasionally in the same sense for grass-eating wild game. If correctly used in connection with beasts of prey, it must presumably refer to the place where they feed. It is better to adopt Wellhausen's emendation to *mᵉ'ārāh,* "cave" (p. 162). This would require the further emendation of MT's masculine pronoun *hw'* to the feminine *hy',* but *yod* and *waw* are easily confused in several periods, so this emendation is easily justified. The parallelism in the following verse between *ḥōr,* "hole," and *mᵉ'ōnāh,* "den," supports the emendation to *mᵉ'ārāh* and more than answers Maier's objection that *mᵉ'ārāh* is never used in the OT in connection with lions (p. 279).

[29]Reading *lābô',* "to go," for MT's *lābî',* "lion," with LXX, V, and S (Wellhausen, 162). Literally, "which the lion went to go there." Another word for lion would be redundant in the passage, but the corruption is easy to understand, given all the words for lion already mentioned in the passage.

[30]Hebrew *ṭᵉrēpāh,* "torn flesh," is simply the feminine of the word for prey, *ṭerep,* used in the preceding line.

[31]MT's second-person feminine suffix would require that one understand the addressee as Nineveh, though the preceding verse spoke of the action of the lion, i.e., of the king of Nineveh. Moreover, the final *-h* on

rbkh and *ml'kkh* are best explained as the use of the *mater* to indicate the long *ā* of the second-person masculine singular suffix (Wellhausen, 162). All the suffixes, some of which are written defectively *(-kā)* and some with the *mater (-kāh),* should be read as second masculine singulars referring back to the lion, the king of Nineveh.

[32]Read *rubbᵉkāh* with LXX's *plēthos sou,* "your multitude, abundance." S has a similar reading, while T and some texts of V at least have the second-person suffix. MT's *rkbh,* "her chariotry," is objectionable both because of the third-person suffix and because of the noun "chariotry." It breaks the consistent metaphor of the lion, and the chariotry mentioned earlier in the text was not Assyria's but that of her enemies. The original *rbkh,* "your abundance," was misread as *rkbh,* probably because the use of the *mater* for the 2 m. sg. was not recognized, and the influence of the earlier use of *rkb* in the chapter offered an easy correction. "Abundance" like "prey" later in the verse presumably refers to the plundered wealth stored up by the king in Nineveh.

[33]Read *mal'āke(y)kāh,* "your messengers." LXX and S have "your works," but V and T as well as the construal with "voice" and "to hear" support the rendering as "your messengers." The garbled form in MT *mal'ākēkēh* resulted from the failure to recognize the use of *-h* as a *mater* to mark the second-person masculine singular suffix.

Commentary

A new unit begins in 2:2 [2:1E]. After announcing the good news to Judah that the Assyrian oppressor was cut off and would never again pass through Judah (2:1 [1:15]), the prophet could hardly continue in the very next verse of the same oracle to give the contradictory announcement that a destroyer was coming up against Judah (2:2 [1]). This announcement is the beginning of a separate oracle, and the addressee is not Judah but Assyria or the Assyrian ruler, who is called upon to prepare for a siege. The announcement is continued in vs. 4–11 [3–10] with a graphic description of the attack on the Assyrian capital Nineveh in v. 9 [8]. One could treat vs. 12–14 [11–13] as a separate oracle, but since it is so closely related to the preceding material, it is perhaps better to treat it simply as the concluding rhetorical movement in the larger oracular composition in 2:2–14 [2:1–13]. However, v. 3 [2] does not fit easily in this composition. It interrupts the connection between vs. 2 and 4 [1 and 3] with a strangely discordant note. It is probably a secondary addition to 2:2–14 [2:1–13], perhaps with the intention of creating a closer logical link between this material and the preceding material in 1:2–2:1 [1:2–15]. Whether it can be attributed to the prophet Nahum himself is dubious.

[2:2 (1)] The prophet addresses the king of Assyria with the announcement that a "scatterer" has gone up to make war against him. In view of this imminent threat, the Assyrian should begin immediately making defensive preparations for the coming attack on his capital. Nahum does not identify this scatterer, but the traditional use of this verb in descriptions of Yahweh's march as the divine warrior and the announcement of Yahweh's hostility toward Assyria in v. 14 [13] suggest that Yahweh is the scatterer. The implication is that the human army soon to attack Nineveh is in Yahweh's employ.

[**3 (2)**] This verse interrupts the announcement with a statement about God's treatment of his own people, who had been plundered and ravaged by their enemies. Neither the logical connection of this verse to the preceding one, nor the precise meaning of this verse, taken by itself, is entirely clear. In prophetic literature the expression *gᵉʾôn yaʿᵃqōb,* "the pride of Jacob," and its parallels normally have a negative connotation. One most often reads of "the pride of Jacob or Israel" rebelling against God (Hos. 5:5; 7:10) and of God punishing such pride (Jer. 13:9; Amos 6:8; 8:7; cf. Ezek. 32:12; Zech. 9:6; 10:11). Psalm 47:7 [6] is almost unique as a positive occurrence of this expression. One might be tempted, therefore, to follow the LXX in understanding *šāb* in this verse in a negative sense: "Yahweh has turned aside the pride of Jacob just as he had turned aside the pride of Israel." Then the following reference to their plunderers could be taken as the explanation of this statement. Such a reading suffers the difficulty, however, that there is no clear transitive use of the qal of the root *šûb* with this negative sense. Because of that, Maier corrects *šāb* to *šab,* which he derives from the root **šābab,* "to cut off," and translates: "Because Yahweh hath cut off the pride of Jacob" (Maier, 227, 233). If one follows this line of interpretation, the logical connection between vs. 2 and 3 [1 and 2] would appear to be the following: Assyria should prepare for an attack, for Yahweh has already removed the pride of Jacob, having sent plunderers against them to carry out this punishment, and now, having finished his work on Mount Zion, he is about to punish Assyria for its pride (see Isa. 10:12).

If one stays with the MT's pointing, however, one must probably translate the transitive *šāb* in a positive sense. The form should be taken either as a prophetic perfect or as a participle; the word order with the subject following the participle may be unusual, but it is well attested (GKC, par. 116q). If this line of interpretation is correct, the thought would be as follows: Yahweh is about to restore the pride of Jacob, which has been ravaged by plunderers, and therefore Assyria should take warning, because these plunderers came from Assyria, and the restoration of Jacob can only be effected through the destruction of Assyria.

Neither interpretation, however, can make a convincing case for the originality of this verse, which appears to disrupt the close connection between vs. 2 and 4 [1 and 3]. Moreover, the parallelism between "the pride of Jacob" and "the pride of Israel" is basically empty of content. In the older prophetic literature both expressions were used for the northern kingdom (Hos. 5:5; 7:10; Amos 6:8). Contra Maier (*Nahum,* pp. 227–228), there is no basis for assuming that Jacob refers to Judah, while Israel refers either to the northern kingdom or to the nation as a whole. The imagery of the plunderers who destroy "their branches" appears to be dependent on the earlier prophetic motif of Israel as Yahweh's choice vineyard but, like the repetition of the word "pride," seems a weak imitation of earlier prophetic language rather than a poetic metaphor that can stand on its own. In short, on either interpretation the verse is probably to be understood as a later gloss, constructed out of older prophetic motifs and expressions, and inserted here to create a closer link between 2:2, 4–14 [2:1, 3–13], and the preceding oracle in 1:2–14.

[4 (3)] This verse returns to the thought of v. 2 [1] by describing the troops and equipment of the army of "the scatterer" that is about to attack Assyria's capital. The reddened shields, scarlet uniforms, elaborate chariot decorations, and rippling sea of spears or swaying chariots all underscore how professional and well equipped this army is. No ragtag collection of involuntary conscripts, this is a formidable military machine whose preparation for attack has been thorough and complete. Since the battle has not yet been joined, the red color of the shields and uniforms is not from bloodstains (cf. Isa. 62:3) but is simply an indication of how well outfitted this army is.

[5 (4)] Then the attack is unleashed. Verse 5 [4] portrays the mad dash of the chariot corps through the outlying streets of the suburbs to reach the city walls. Because of the mention of the streets, one might be tempted to think of this verse as portraying the confusion of the Assyrian army within the city rather than as portraying the charge of the attacking army, but the last two lines of the verse undercut any such reading. The description of the movement of the chariots as like torches darting about like lightning picks up the imagery of the chariot attachments that resemble fire in v. 4 [3], and this imagery is clearly intended to emphasize the frightening speed of the enemy's attack.

[6 (5)] Verse 6 [5] seems to continue this portrayal of the attacking army with a description of their assault on the wall. The "scatterer" assigns his commanders their objectives for this next stage of the assault, the assaulting forces stumble forward in haste to bring their siege equipment up against the wall, and the siege instruments are brought into place. This whole description emphasizes the speed with which the assault on the wall is carried out.

[7 (6)] The mention of the floodgates is probably due to Nineveh's famous system of dams and sluice gates that controlled the flow of water into Nineveh, particularly from the Khosr River on the northeastern side of the city. While that concrete reality is probably the reason for the choice of this imagery, it need not rule out the purely metaphorical use of the imagery itself. That is, the image may imply no more than that the enemy has breached the wall and that his troops are pouring through like water from opened sluice gates. The impact of this development on the Assyrian palace is for the Assyrian officials to lose heart. The imagery actually functions on two levels. On a literal level, one can think of the floodwater washing the palace away; on the metaphorical level, the language refers to the collapse of the will to resist.

There is a classical tradition that attributes the fall of Nineveh to floodwater that washed away part of its defenses, but it is difficult to evaluate that tradition (see Diodorus Siculus, *History* 2.26–27, esp. 27.1–3; Xenophon, *Anabasis* 3.4.12). The *Babylonian Chronicle* makes no mention of such an occurrence (Grayson, TCS V, no. 3:38–45), and in view of the traditional Mesopotamian use of flood imagery to describe the attack of an enemy army, it is possible that the Greek tradition arose from a misunderstanding of the metaphorical language of a lost Babylonian source. Even if an actual flood contributed to the fall of Nineveh, it is unlikely that Nahum was referring to such a specific event, for his prophecy probably dates some years before the fall of Nineveh. His description of the attack on the city is in the nature of a prophetic vision composed well before the event it envisions; thus one should be very hesitant in drawing too close a correspondence between his vision and the actual course of the final siege of Nineveh.

[8 (7)] With the collapse of resistance from the palace, the imagery shifts from the assault to the aftermath of the assault. Nahum speaks of the humiliation of a former princess who must now stand among the captives. Far from referring to a particular Assyrian woman, the prophet is probably personifying the city Nineveh as a royal princess who has lost her status (cf. the treatment of Babylon in Isa. 47:1–5 and Jerusalem in Lam. 1:1–4). In this topos, the unfortunate city's ladies-in-waiting presumably refer to the female population of the city. Both the princess and her servants go into exile, and, as might be expected, they go mourning and lamenting.

[9 (8)] Then there is a portrayal of Nineveh's defenders, which again makes use of water imagery. The well-watered city, whose mighty streams once inundated Israel and Judah (Isa. 8:7–8; 28:15,17–19) like the unruly waters of chaos (Isa. 17:12–14), is here compared to a pool of water whose dam has broken, allowing its water to drain away. Just as the waters of chaos fled before Yahweh's rebuke (Pss. 93:3–5; 104:7; 114:3; Isa. 17:12–14), so Nineveh's defenders flee, and the flight cannot be stemmed. When their commanders order them to halt, no one pays any attention. The rout is complete.

[10 (9)] This verse shifts the focus to the activity of the victors. The conquering soldiers are confronted by a vast abundance of booty to be plundered, and the cry goes up to begin the looting.

[11 (10)] Then the focus shifts back to Nineveh and its hapless inhabitants. In the city, there is nothing but desolation, destruction, and devastation. Its citizens can only wait in helpless and terrified anguish to know what terrible fate awaits them.

[12 (11)] Verse 12 [11] begins a new movement with its taunt of Nineveh and its rulers, but this new movement is very closely tied to the preceding context. The portrayal in v. 11 [10] of Nineveh's citizens cowering in helpless fear provides the necessary background to the taunting question of v. 12 [11]. These are hardly the ferocious and courageous denizens for which Nineveh had long been famous. Nineveh used to be a den of lions that none could frighten. What has happened to the old Nineveh that it is no longer itself? Where are the lions that used to inhabit it?

The lion is a traditional symbol for kingship throughout the Near East, but Nahum may have chosen the lion imagery for this taunt precisely because the lion figures so prominently in Assyrian reliefs and because the Assyrian kings loved to compare themselves to lions (Rudolph, 173). As Rudolph has suggested (p. 173), the elaboration of this metaphor suggests that the lion represents the Assyrian king, the lionesses his queens and their court, the young lions the army and state officials, and the lion cubs the general population of Nineveh.

[13 (12)] This verse continues with a further portrayal of Nineveh as it used to be. Maintaining the metaphor of the lion as a creature who provides prey for his den, the text depicts the Assyrian king of those former days as a ferocious and rapacious ruler who provided his royal court and the citizens of Nineveh with abundant wealth and booty.

[14 (13)] But those days are past. Yahweh announces his declaration of war against the Assyrian king. The wealth the Assyrian ruler has brought into Nineveh (v. 13 [12]) will go up in smoke, and the sword will devour his troops and officials. Yahweh will bring an end to the Assyrian king's plundering of other nations; the voice of his messengers will no longer oppress and terrify the surrounding nations. Nineveh's glorious days as a den of lions are finished.

4. A *hôy*-ORACLE AGAINST NINEVEH: 3:1–17

3:1 Hey, city of blood,
Which[1] is all lies,
Full of plunder,
Never without prey![2]
2 The sound of whip
And rattle of wheel,

Galloping horse
And bouncing chariot!
3 Charging horseman,
Flash of sword,
And gleam of spear!
A multitude of slain
And a mass of corpses,
Dead bodies without end—
They stumble over their bodies.
4 Because of the countless harlotries of the harlot,
The attractive and winsome mistress of sorcery,
Who made nations drunk[3] by her harlotries,
And clans by her sorceries,
5 I am against you,
Says Yahweh of Hosts,
And I will lift your skirts over your face,
And I will show nations your nakedness,
And kingdoms your shame.
6 And I will throw filth upon you,
Treat you with contempt, and make you a spectacle.
7 And everyone who sees you
Will flee from you and say,
"Nineveh is devastated.
Who will grieve for her?"[4]
From where will I seek
Comforters for you?[5]
8 Are you better than No[6]-Amon,[7]
Which sat among the streams of the Nile,[8]
Surrounded by water,
Whose outer wall[9] was the sea,[10]
Water[11] her rampart?
9 Ethiopia was her[12] strength,
Also Egypt, without limit,
Put and the Libyans
Were her[13] allies.[14]
10 Yet even she was fated for exile,
She went into captivity,
Her infants, too, were dashed to pieces
At every street corner;
Over her honored men they cast lots,
And all her nobles were bound in chains.
11 You also will become drunk,[15]
You will become[16] unconscious;[17]
You also will seek refuge from the enemy.
12 All your fortresses are fig trees
With[18] early figs;

If they are shaken,
They fall into the mouth of the eater.
13 Indeed, your troops are women within you,
To your enemies are opened wide
The gates of your land;
Fire consumes your bars.
14 Water for the siege draw for yourself,
Strengthen your fortifications,
Go into the clay,
And tread the mortar;
Take hold of the brick mold.[19]
15 There fire will consume you,
A sword will cut you off;
It will consume you like the young locust.
Multiply[20] like the young locust,
Multiply like the locust;
16 Though you increase your traders
More than the stars of heaven,
The young locust sheds[21] and flies away.
17 Your officials[22] are like locusts,
Your scribes[23] like a swarm of locusts,
Which camp on the walls on a cold day;
When the sun rises, they fly away,[24]
And the place[24] where they go[25] is not known.

Textual Notes

[1]The following clauses are all unmarked relative clauses.

[2]Literally, "(from which) the prey does not depart." LXX mistakenly derives *yāmîš* from *mšš,* "to feel, grope," rather than from *mwš,* "to depart." V reflects the direct address in the text with its rendering, "plunder does not recede from you."

[3]MT reads *hammōkeret,* "who sold," and this reading is supported by LXX and V. T's "deliver over" probably presupposes MT as well. S's *dmrby',* "who made great," is less clear, but if its reading resulted from an internal corruption (so Haldar, *Studies,* 67), it may also reflect MT. Despite this, many scholars have felt that *mkr,* "to sell," does not fit the context. If the MT is correct, the sense is apparently that Nineveh was able to treat the nations as mere merchandise through her seductive policies, but one might have expected the metaphor to have "buy" rather than "sell" (ICC, 338). Some have suggested assigning the root the meaning "to cheat, deceive" based on an Arabic cognate (Smith et al., ICC, 338; D. W. Thomas, *JTS* 37 [1936]: 388–389; *JTS,* n.s. 3 [1952]: 214; Zorell, *ZLH* 435b), but the existence of this meaning for the root in Hebrew remains uncertain (cf. Maier, *Nahum,* 306). Rudolph sug-

gested the correction of *hammōkeret,* "who sold," to *hakkōmeret,* "who ensnared" (p. 175), but this verb is not attested in biblical Hebrew. Cathcart, following Dahood, argued for *hammukkeret,* "who was known (by the nations for her harlotries)" (*Nahum,* 129), but this would produce a very lame metaphor implying no more than that Nineveh had a bad reputation. The translation given above is based on the emendation to *hammᵉšakkeret,* "who made (the nations) drunk" (cf. Jer. 51:7; Rev. 17:2). 4QpNah's *hmmkrt* could easily be explained as a corruption of *hmškrt*—in the late paleo-Hebrew script *m* and *š* differ only slightly apart from the tail on *m*—and once *š* had been corrupted to *m,* the second *m* would soon be dropped as an obvious dittography, thus producing the present text of the MT.

[4]V and S read "over you" under the influence of the surrounding second-person suffixes, but this is still part of the quotation of an onlooker, so MT's third-person suffix is the preferable reading.

[5]LXX has "for her" under the influence of the preceding third-person suffix.

[6]LXX has a triple reading of *htyṭby mn'.* Its translator apparently misunderstood the interrogative *h* and corrected the text to get the feminine hiphil imperative *hṭyby,* which could be rendered "prepare" or "make pleasant." The choice depends on the meaning of the following word *mn'.* The translator did not recognize the preposition *min* in front of the place name; as a result, he misanalyzed the form as either *mānāh,* "portion," or **mēn,* "string, stringed instrument." Apparently the translator could not make up his mind which reading to follow, and the result was the curiously conflated reading: "Prepare the portions, make the chord/string pleasant, prepare the portions."

[7]The name No-Amon *(N'iwt-'Imn)* is Egyptian for "the city of (the god) Amon," i.e., Thebes. This full transcription of the city name of Thebes is unusual, since most foreign transcriptions of the name drop both the divine name and the final *-t* of the word for city (Assyrian *Ni-'* [VAB 7, 800; AOAT 6, 261]; Hebrew *Nō'* [Jer. 46:25; Ezek. 30:14]; Greek *Nau*[*kratis*] [see *HALAT,* 621]). V's *Alexandria populorum* and T's *'lksndry' rbt'* both identify the city as Alexandria, and both of them seem to interpret *'āmôn* as *hāmôn,* "crowd, multitude." S misunderstands the city name as *ywn,* "Greece."

[8]The plural *yᵉ'ōrîm,* "rivers, streams of the Nile," presumably refers to the Nile and the system of canals in and around Thebes fed by the Nile (Rudolph, 181).

[9]As Rudolph notes (p. 181), one should add the suffix to the noun, *ḥêlāh,* "its wall," with 4QpNah and the versions. LXX's *hēs hē archē,* "whose beginning," apparently connected *ḥylh* with the hiphil infinitive of *hll,* "to begin." V's *cuius divitiae,* "whose wealth," derived the He-

brew word from *ḥayil,* "strength, wealth," rather than from *ḥēl,* "wall, rampart," but the parallelism shows that V's understanding is mistaken.

[10]The word *yām,* "sea," here refers to the Nile, as in Isa. 19:5 (see BDB, 411).

[11]Reading *mayim,* "water," for MT's *miyyām,* "from the sea," with 4QpNah, LXX, V, and S. T has *my ym',* "water of the sea."

[12]MT lacks the mappiq, but the suffix is clearly to be read with LXX, S, T, and some texts of V.

[13]MT has the 2 f. sg. suffix, but the context demands the 3 f. sg. that LXX and S offer.

[14]The word *'ezrāh,* "help," is used here in the concrete sense of "helper" or "ally" (BDB, 741).

[15]LXX, V, and T all support this understanding of MT. Cathcart follows Driver, Dahood, and others in rendering "hire yourself out" (*Nahum,* 119, 137–138), but in the context that seems highly improbable.

[16]One should read *tihyî,* the regular qal impf. 2 f. sg., instead of MT's *t*^{e}*hî.* There is no reason for the jussive form.

[17]The meaning of *na'*^{e}*lāmāh* is disputed. It is normally taken as the niphal f. sg. ptc. of *'ālam* I, "to be concealed," with the semantic extension "to become unconscious" (cf. *HALAT,* 789). LXX's "be overlooked, disdained" and V's "despised" probably presuppose the same text as MT. Cathcart's "become young again" does not fit the context (*Nahum,* 119). Other treatments involving emendation of the form do not significantly improve the MT.

[18]MT is supported by LXX and V. S and T do not reflect the preposition, but neither do they give any support for the popular emendation to *'am,* "people."

[19]S's senseless *mwlkn',* "counsel, advice," is simply a scribal error for *mlbn',* "brick mold." T's "buildings" is interpretative. LXX and V presuppose MT.

[20]MT's *hitkabbēd* should be analyzed as an infinitive used in place of the imperative. If it were the imperative, one would expect the feminine form, since Nineveh is the understood subject.

[21]The reference is to the final shedding of skin in the development of the locust from its crawling stage to its flying stage (so S and T). LXX and V offer less precise and less accurate translations.

[22]Hebrew *mnzr* is probably a loanword from Assyrian *maṣṣāru,* "guard," or, perhaps more likely, *manzāzu, manzaz pāni,* "official, courtier" (*HALAT,* 568). The versions offer little help. LXX has a verbal form from *exallomai,* "to leap out of, leap forth," but this may not be intended as a translation of *mnzryk* (see next note). V has "guards," S has "Nazirites," and T has "glittering plate or foil."

[23]Hebrew *ṭpsr* is a loanword from Assyrian *ṭupšarru,* "scribe" (*HALAT,* 362). LXX has *symmiktos,* "promiscuous," but Rudolph takes this as LXX's translation of *mnzr* understood as *mamzēr,* "bastard" (p. 182). If he is correct, LXX simply omits *ṭpsr* in its translation. V's *parvuli tui,* "your children," apparently misunderstood the initial *ṭp* in the word as *ṭap,* "children." T transliterates, and S has "fighter."

[24]The singular verb form *nôdad* and the singular suffix on *mᵉqômô,* "its place," are both acceptable, since *gôb gōbāy,* "a swarm of locusts," is a collective.

[25]Hebrew *'ayyām,* "Where are they?" is used here in an indirect question: "and its place where they are (now) is not known." LXX's "woe to them" is a mistranslation. The use of the interrogative particle here prevents one from interpreting "its place" as a reference to the former place of the locust swarm; the particle is in no way redundant.

Commentary

A new oracle begins in 3:1 with the *hôy*-saying against Nineveh. Several new thoughts are introduced in the course of this oracle, but the direct address to Nineveh is maintained through v. 17, and there are no clear introductory formulae suggesting that any of these new thoughts represent the beginning of a separate, independent oracle. Even the section about Thebes in vs. 8–11 appears to be only a new rhetorical unit, not an independent oracle with a different *Sitz im Leben.* Verses 18–19, however, which are addressed to the king of Assyria rather than to Nineveh, probably were originally an independent oracle, though their literary placement following the oracle against Nineveh seems quite appropriate.

[3:1] Using the genre of the *hôy*-oracle (for further discussion of this genre see the commentary on Hab. 2:6ff. and Zeph. 3:1), Nahum calls for Nineveh's attention, characterizing her as a city of bloody oppression and deceit, always full of plunder and never without the prey torn from other peoples. The mention of prey connects this verse with the end of the preceding oracle in 2:14 [13], and this catchword may be responsible for the literary placement of 3:1–17 after that oracle.

[2] After getting Nineveh's attention with his opening exclamation and his uncomplimentary characterization of the city, Nahum switches to a series of quick word pictures that portray the attack on Nineveh and the city's fall (vs. 2–3). The imagery of v. 2 may be compared to that in 2:5 [4]. It captures the movement and noise of the chariots and horses in the battle for the city.

[3] The first half of v. 3 continues this imagery and may be compared to 2:4–5 [2:3–4]. This portrait of the joined battle quickly takes a more gruesome turn, however, when the prophet directs his attention away from the flashing sword and gleaming spear to the corpses of the slain. There are so many dead bodies that the attackers stumble over them in their advance, and it seems clear from the larger context that these dead are the defenders and inhabitants of Nineveh. The city of bloody oppression is getting its own treatment in full measure.

[4] In v. 4, the prophet switches to another characterization of Nineveh, this time as a harlot. Like an attractive, seductive prostitute and accomplished sorceress who intoxicates and seduces her clients with her illicit love and black magic (cf. Prov. 6:24–7:27), Nineveh has intoxicated and seduced the nations. Precisely what actual behavior the prophet may have been referring to by this metaphorical language is not entirely clear. It might refer to the role of Assyrian trade in her imperial expansion. Economics was a major factor in Assyria's expansion, and trading missions typically preceded the Assyrian army into foreign territories. It might also refer to Assyria's willingness to come to the aid of embattled rulers in return for their submission to Assyria as loyal vassals (so, for example, Menahem [2 Kings 15:19] and Ahaz [2 Kings 16:7–9]). At any rate, Assyria's treatment of other nations did not promote their well-being. Like intercourse with a harlot (Prov. 7:27), involvement with Assyria led eventually to death.

[5] Because of this reprehensible behavior of Nineveh, Yahweh announces that he is against the city. Note the parallel to 2:14 [13]. One should also note that God's announcement of judgment to Nineveh makes explicit the direct address to the city in the second person that was already implicit in the opening of the *hôy*-oracle. Since Nineveh had behaved like a harlot, Yahweh imposes on her the punishment of a harlot. Just as a prostitute or faithless wife was subject to public stripping or shameful exposure (Hos. 2:5 [3]; Jer. 13:22, 26; Ezek. 16:37–41), so Yahweh will undress Nineveh before the nations and allow them to look upon her nakedness. While the motif of public exposure maintains the harlot metaphor, this language of looking upon a city's nakedness was often used to describe the enemy's treatment of a conquered city (Isa. 47:1–3; Micah 4:11). Thus the reality expressed by this figure is the imminent capture of Nineveh and the subsequent humiliating treatment of its surviving inhabitants.

[6] Verse 6 continues the same image of the humiliating treatment imposed on the harlot. As Nineveh stands shamefully exposed before the nations, Yahweh will ensure that the seductiveness of her beauty is destroyed. He will throw filth upon her, treat her with contempt, and turn her into a disgusting spectacle.

[7] As a result, the nations will no longer be captivated by Nineveh's charm, but they will turn and flee from her in disgust and fear. Up to this point the prophet has maintained the metaphor of the harlot, but the comment of the peoples as they turn aside from Nineveh slips briefly from the figure to the reality portrayed by the figure. One would hardly speak of a real prostitute as devastated *(šoddᵉdāh),* though this is appropriate language for a conquered and plundered city. The continuation of the quotation, however, resumes the metaphor. None of the nations that had been intoxicated by Nineveh's charms will mourn for her, for Yahweh has exposed her disgusting reality, and that leads Yahweh to ask where then he will find mourners for the doomed city (cf. Lam. 1:8–9). There will be none. Nineveh will die bereft of friends or lovers to mourn her demise.

[8] Such a prophetic prediction of Nineveh's downfall might well strike Nahum's Judean audience as unbelievable in view of Assyria's still unbroken power and Nineveh's impressive fortifications. Without denying these facts, Nahum attempts to counter the skepticism they engender by rhetorical means. He addresses an extended rhetorical question to Nineveh, comparing her to the equally powerful and well-fortified Thebes. "Are you," the prophet asks, "any better than No-Amon?" No-Amon or Thebes, as the city was known by the Greeks, was a major Egyptian city lying on the east bank of the Nile about 440 miles south of Memphis and 140 miles north of the first cataract of the Nile (Smith et al., ICC, 342–343). Despite Thebes's powerful fortifications, which Nahum portrays as similar to Nineveh's in including great moats, this Egyptian city was captured by Ashurbanipal's Assyrian army in 663 B.C.

[9] At the time of the fall of Thebes, Egypt was under the rule of the Ethiopian twenty-fifth dynasty (712–663 B.C.), but the population of Thebes was still predominantly Egyptian, so Nahum can speak of both Ethiopia and Egypt as the strength of Thebes. It was also supported by the Libyans and Put, who were allies of the Ethiopian ruler. Though Put is closely associated with Ethiopia or Egypt in a number of passages (Gen. 10:6; Jer. 46:9; Ezek. 27:10; 30:5; 38:5; 1 Chron. 1:8), the precise identification of this country remains uncertain. The reason for listing Libya and Put along with Ethiopia and Egypt is certain, however; it is to underscore how seemingly invincible Thebes once was.

[10] Nevertheless, despite her apparent invincibility, Thebes was fated for exile, and her people went into captivity. Her infants were brutally killed, and her nobles were treated with the humiliation normally accorded prisoners of war in the ancient Near East.

[11] Nahum's extended rhetorical question obviously assumes a negative answer. The implication is that just as Thebes's apparent invincibility failed to save her, so Nineveh's apparent invincibility will fail to protect her against the threat of Yahweh's punishment. This is now made explicit in v. 11. Nineveh will also fall into a drunken stupor and have to seek refuge from the enemy. The metaphor of the drunken woman has created problems for interpreters, but it should probably be read as an indication that Nineveh's defenses have been breached and that she is naked and open to the abuse of her conquerors (see vs. 4–5 above; and cf. Lam. 4:21). That is why she must seek a place of refuge.

[12] Even now, Nineveh's fortresses are like fig trees loaded with early figs ready to fall in the first strong wind. They need only to be shaken, and the figs will fall into the mouth of the eater. In other words, Nineveh's fortifications are ripe for the taking; they will offer little resistance to the attacker.

[13] Nahum captures this lack of resistance with two other images in v. 13. The deprecation of Nineveh's troops as women makes use of a traditional Near Eastern topos to indicate the defenders' lack of courage and will to resist (Isa. 19:16; Jer. 50:37; 51:30). The admonition to courage in battle might include the command to "be men" (1 Sam. 4:9). The second image is that of a land unprepared for an attack because the gates of its cities lie wide open. Moreover, they cannot be securely closed, because the enemy has already penetrated them, and the bars that could latch the gates are already burning.

[14] Yahweh urges Nineveh to prepare for the coming siege. She should secure her supply of water and strengthen her fortifications. For that work of strengthening the walls of her fortifications, she needs to make more mud bricks, so Yahweh urges her to work the muddy clay into the right consistency and then to take up the brick mold. One should note that the imperatives in v. 14 are all feminine singulars, not the masculine forms found in 2:2, where the Assyrian king is given a similar admonition to prepare for an attack.

[15] Nonetheless, despite Nineveh's best efforts, the outcome of the battle is certain. In the very midst of these preparations, fire and the sword will consume Nineveh. The destruction of the city will be as thorough as the destruction of a countryside under a plague of young locusts. The point of the comparison to locusts in this simile is their destructive power, but the mention of locusts leads to a use of the same figure with a different point in the following lines. The term locust is also used figuratively in Hebrew to symbolize a great multitude (Judg. 7:12), and that is the point of comparison in the following similes. As Yahweh urged Nineveh to prepare for the siege in the preceding verse, now he urges her to make her people as numerous as locusts. The multitude of Assyria's troops, traders, and officials must have made it very difficult for Nahum's Judean audience to believe his proclamation of Nineveh's imminent fall, and this ironic command is probably intended to undercut that objection to his message.

[16] That multitude will not prevent Yahweh from imposing his punishment on Nineveh any more than Nineveh's preparation for siege will prevent her destruction. Even if Nineveh should make her traders as numerous as the stars, their end is in sight. They will disappear as totally as a locust grub when it matures into a full-grown locust, sheds its skin, and flies away.

[17] Yahweh compares Nineveh's numerous officials and scribes to a locust swarm huddled together on a wall early in the morning on a cold day. Just as such a swarm flies away and is no longer seen, once the rising sun has warmed the locusts, so the multitude of the Assyrian officials will soon disappear forever.

5. An Oracle Against the King of Assyria: 3:18–19

3:18 Your shepherds are slumbering,
O king of Assyria,
Your nobles are asleep;[1]
Your people are scattered[2] upon the mountains,
And there is no one to gather (them).
19 There is no alleviation[3] for your fracture,
Your wound is incurable;
All who hear the news about you
Clap their hands over you,
For over whom has not passed
Your unceasing evil?

Textual Notes

[1]Reading *yāšᵉnû* in place of MT's *yiškᵉnû,* "they will camp." The verb *yšn,* "to sleep," provides a better parallel to *nwm,* "to slumber." LXX misconstrued the vocative as the subject of this verb and rendered, "the king of Assyria put your nobles to sleep," but it apparently read the verb *yšn,* not *škn.* Contra Maier (*Nahum,* 360), *škn* is never used absolutely to refer to the slumber of death (Rudolph, 183).

[2]The obvious meaning of *nāpōšû* is hard to derive from *pwš,* "to leap about," so one must probably assume a by-form of *pwṣ,* "to scatter," or correct the text to *nāpōṣû.* Neither LXX's "removed (themselves)" nor V's "hid themselves" catches the meaning of the verb.

[3]Hebrew *kēhāh,* from the root *khh,* "to grow dim, faint," apparently means "a dimming, lessening, alleviation" of an injury, but one may wonder whether it is a phonetic variant of *gēhāh,* "healing, cure" (Prov. 17:22). LXX renders as *iasis,* "healing," and V has *obscura,* "dimmed." S and T have "there is no one who hurts because of your wound."

Commentary

The change of address from Nineveh to the Assyrian king marks vs. 18–19 as a separate oracle, even if its thought is quite compatible with the theme of the rest of chapter 3. The oracle's placement here is probably due to the fact that, like vs. 16–17, it makes prominent mention of the Assyrian officials. In its present placement, certainly, if not in its original oral setting, it serves as a final comment to the Assyrian king suggesting that there is no hope for Assyria's recovery from its disastrous collapse. If most of Nahum's message could be attributed to the time of the siege of Nineveh (ca. 612 B.C.), this oracle would fit well in the brief subsequent period when the Assyrian remnant, including a new king, tried to establish a new royal base in Harran, only to lose it to the Babylonians in 609 B.C. However, since most of Nahum's message appears to have been given some years prior to the actual assault on Nineveh, one should probably regard this oracle too as a prophetic vision, not as a description of the actual, current political situation.

[3:18] The Assyrian king seems curiously unaware of the real situation. Yahweh has to inform him that his officials and nobles are asleep, that is, dead (cf. Isa. 14:18; Jer. 51:39, 57; Pss. 13:3 [2]; 76:5–7 [4–6]). With his officers and officials all sleeping the sleep of death, it is no wonder that his people are scattered over the mountains; there is simply no one left to gather them together. For this image of a defeated people, compare 1 Kings 22:17.

[19] Given this situation, there is no hope that the Assyrian king can find a cure for the fatal wound inflicted upon Assyria. There is no possibility of recovery, and for this news all of Assyria's neighbors are rejoicing. Everyone who hears of the Assyrian king's disastrous predicament shouts and claps for joy, because all have suffered at the hands of the Assyrian king in the past. Now at last he is getting a fatal taste of his own medicine, and no one can feel sorry for him.

Habakkuk

Habakkuk

INTRODUCTION

Habakkuk is not a typical prophetic book. Like other prophetic books, it consists of oracles that were given on different occasions during the ministry of the prophet, but unlike the typical prophetic book, these oracles have been arranged in the book of Habakkuk to develop a coherent, sequentially developed argument that extends through the whole book and to which each individual oracle contributes its part.

The book begins, following a very brief heading (1:1), with a lament by the prophet over the injustice rampant in Judean society (1:2–4). Yahweh responds to this complaint with the surprising announcement that he is sending the Chaldeans as his agents to take care of this problem of Judean injustice (1:5–10). Habakkuk is astonished by this announcement, and he reacts to it by uttering another lament in which he attacks God's announced solution to injustice as being more unjust than the original problem (1:11–17). Then the prophet takes up his position to await God's response to his second lament, which the prophet himself characterizes as a reproof (2:1). God answers this reproof with the announcement of a vision that will testify to a set time in the future. The prophet is told to record that vision clearly so that whoever reads it will be able to read it easily and live by its testimony. It is a reliable vision, its testimony is trustworthy, and Habakkuk is to patiently wait for its fulfillment even if it seems a long time in its coming. The fainthearted will not live by the vision, but the righteous person will find life in the trustworthiness of the vision (2:2–4). Still, the content of the vision itself is not revealed; instead, one finds the description of a third kind of response to life, that of the grasping, arrogant man who trusts in his amassed wealth rather than in God's vision for life. His object of trust will prove far less reliable than the vision Habakkuk is to record. The nations will rise up to mock this greedy man, the embodiment of Chaldean imperial power, and ultimately all the earth will have to recognize that Yahweh is still in control of the world (2:5–20). It is not until chapter 3 that the vision is finally recorded. The chapter begins, after a liturgical superscription (3:1), with another prayer of Habakkuk (3:2), and then one finds a vision of the march of the divine warrior to rescue his people (3:3–15). This vision of Yahweh's coming intervention against the powers of chaos, embodied at the moment in the Babylonians, makes a tremendous impression on the prophet, and he confesses his willingness to wait patiently for God to resolve the problem of injustice that the prophet had struggled with so long (3:16).

He vows to trust in God's ultimate salvation even if things get worse (3:17–18), and he ends on a statement of confidence, which is followed by a final liturgical subscript (3:19). One may outline the book as follows:

Outline

- I. The problem of divine justice
  - A. Superscription (1:1)
  - B. Habakkuk's initial lament (1:2–4)
  - C. God's response (1:5–10)
  - D. Habakkuk's second lament
    - 1. God's answer unsatisfactory (1:11–17)
    - 2. Habakkuk awaits new answer (2:1)
- II. God's announcement of a resolving vision
  - A. Instructions about the vision
    - 1. Record it (2:2)
    - 2. Wait for it (2:3)
    - 3. Trusting in it means life (2:4)
  - B. Wealth is far more deceitful than the vision
    - 1. The greedy oppressor will not succeed (2:5)
    - 2. The nations will make fun of him (2:6–19)
    - 3. Yahweh is still in control (2:20)
- III. The resolution
  - A. Liturgical superscription (3:1)
  - B. Habakkuk's third prayer (3:2)
  - C. The vision of God's coming (3:3–15)
  - D. Habakkuk accepts the vision
    - 1. Will wait for Yahweh's intervention (3:16)
    - 2. Vow of trust (3:17–18)
    - 3. Statement of confidence (3:19a)
  - E. Final liturgical subscription (3:19b)

Date

Despite the coherence between the discrete oracles in the development of the overall argument of the book, and despite the initial impression made by the arrangement in the book that lament, divine response, new lament, new divine response, and so forth, followed upon one another in quick succession, there are clear indications that the individual oracles that make up this compositional whole were originally given at widely separated times in the prophet's ministry. The evidence for this is clearest in 1:5–10 and 1:11–17. God's announcement that he was about to surprise his Judean audience by raising up the Chaldeans as his agents for punishing injustice (1:5–6) could hardly date later than 605 B.C. Once the Chaldeans or Neo-

Babylonians under Nebuchadnezzar had destroyed the Egyptian army at Carchemish and its remnant at Hamat, the threat of Nebuchadnezzar's appearance in Palestine would not long remain unbelievable; after Nebuchadnezzar appeared on the Philistine coast in 604 B.C., Habakkuk could hardly announce his coming as a big surprise. Habakkuk's description of the Babylonian oppressor in 1:11–17 and the nations' characterization of him in 2:6–19, however, presuppose a much longer experience of Babylonian rule over Judah. These oracles probably date originally from the time after Nebuchadnezzar's first capture of Jerusalem in 597 B.C. Moreover, if Habakkuk's initial lament about injustice concerns internal Judean affairs, as seems probable, this lament probably dates to the reign of Jehoiakim, sometime between 609–605 B.C., prior to the rise of the Neo-Babylonian threat.

A number of scholars have identified the evil oppressor in Hab. 1:2–4 with the Assyrian power, and this has led them to date the book much earlier than 605 B.C. Thus Fohrer dates the book between 626 and 622 B.C. (Georg Fohrer, *Introduction to the Old Testament* [Nashville: Abingdon Press, 1988], 455), while Otto Eissfeldt (*The Old Testament: An Introduction* [Oxford: Oxford University Press, 1965], 422) and Artur Weiser (*The Old Testament: Its Formation and Development* [New York: Association Press, 1961], 263) date it between 625 and 612 B.C. It is difficult to square the description of the Chaldeans in 1:6–10 with such an early date, however. Until 616 B.C. they were basically fighting a defensive war in their own territory; they were hardly the terror of distant kings and princes. The situation changed somewhat after the fall of Ashur (615 B.C.) and Nineveh (612 B.C.), but it was not until after Babylon's decisive defeat of Egypt in 605 B.C. that Babylon's imperial expansion was assured and her armies acquired the aura of invincibility reflected in Hab. 1:7–10. Moreover, as A. Bentzen noted (*Introduction to the Old Testament* [6th ed., Copenhagen, 1961], II, 152), nothing suggests that the people described in 1:12–17 are different from those described in 1:5–10, and, as already noted, 1:11–17 and 2:6–19 clearly suggest that Judah has already experienced a period of oppression at the hands of the Babylonians.

A date between 605 and 597 B.C. is suggested by most recent commentators (Keller, 140: 605–601 B.C.; Rudolph, 194: 605–597 B.C.; Van der Woude, 9–10: 605–598 B.C.), but, if my argument is sound, some of the oracles date from before 605 B.C. and others from after 597 B.C. In other words, the prophet or a very creative editor has taken oracles originally given by Habakkuk over a period of years and has put them together in a connected meditation over the problem of divine justice. The book is composed sometime after 597 B.C., and it addresses the problem from that historical perspective, but it incorporates oracles from an earlier period to illustrate solutions to the problem that cannot be the final word. The treatment of these earlier oracles can be seen as a critique, not only of Yahweh's earlier responses to Habakkuk, but of the similar proclamations to be found in the contemporary oracles of Jeremiah as well. Running through the book is the underlying conviction that judgment cannot be God's final word to his people.

Since the prophet has shaped his earlier oracles into an organic whole, reflecting his post–597 B.C. perspective, it is possible that some of the oracles in the book have been significantly reworked to serve this purpose. Some of the *hôy*-oracles in 2:6–20, for instance, may have originally been formulated against a Judean oppressor like Jehoiakim, as a number of scholars have suggested (so Otto Eckart, "Die Stellung der Wehe-Worte in der Verkündigung des Propheten Habakuk," *ZAW* 89/1 [1977]: 73–107, and Jörg Jeremias, *Kultprophetie und Gerichtsverkündigung in der späten Königszeit Israels* [WMANT 35; Neukirchen: Neukirchener Verlag, 1970], 57–89). But in their present form they clearly envision the Babylonian oppressor. The vision in 3:3–15 also appears to involve the reworking of an older text, in this case an archaic hymn that has been reworked by the prophet as an expression of his visionary experience.

Text

There are relatively few secondary insertions in this carefully edited book. Apart from the glosses in 2:13a and 14, the transposition or gloss in 2:18, and the insertion of the liturgical notations in 3:1, 3, 9, 13, 19, the work can be regarded as a unified composition of the prophet or a very good editor. The text of chapters 1 and 2 is in relatively good condition, though there are a number of difficult cruxes, but the textual difficulties in chapter 3, where one must deal with the reworking of an archaic hymn, are quite formidable. One may doubt whether the prophet fully understood all the lines in this archaic hymn, and at many points the modern commentator's understanding of Habakkuk's new construal of the text can be little more than educated guesswork. All but the first colon of 3:14 is extremely problematic, most of a line appears to be omitted by haplography in 3:11, and there are a few other places where modesty might have dictated foregoing a translation in favor of simply indicating the difficulty. Nevertheless, the general sense of the text is clear enough to follow the prophet's line of argument.

The Prophet and His Message

One can say very little about the person of the prophet. He was obviously very familiar with the cultic and liturgical traditions of his people, but whether he had employment in the service of the cultic establishment remains a disputed question. Moreover, it is not clear that a firm answer to that question, whether negative or positive, would contribute significantly to a better understanding of the prophet's message. A theological evaluation of the message can only be based on its content, not on the prophet's position inside or outside the establishment.

The prophet is deeply concerned about the injustice he sees in Judean life, and he is dissatisfied with prophetic theologies of history that resolve that injustice through the use of foreign agents as God's chastening rod. To Habakkuk, such a solution simply appears to compound the problem. Such a response could at best be only a partial answer. There must be something beyond punishment for the people of God. Habakkuk finds his answer in the powerful testimony of the ancient communal hymns of his people. One such hymn provides the catalyst for the prophet's own powerful vision of the coming intervention of Yahweh on behalf of his people. Habakkuk's vision of God as the mighty conqueror of chaos endows him with hope for the future and instills within him the triumphant courage to endure a dismal present in the joyous confidence that this vision of God will prove reliable.

Habakkuk's stance in the interim between Yahweh's ancient victories and his coming intervention, between vision and fulfillment, is strikingly similar to that of the Christian. The Christian lives after God's victory over evil in Jesus' death and resurrection but prior to his final victory at Jesus' second coming and the general resurrection. Thus it is no accident that Hab. 2:4 has become a key text in describing the Christian's eschatological lifestyle. Nor have the intervening centuries robbed the book of its ability to give new courage to the modern believer in his or her struggle to live in the present. Its vision of the awesome divine warrior whose will is to save his people can and does still serve to refocus the modern believer's perceptions, enabling the believer to see through appearances and to fix his or her gaze on ultimate reality.

COMMENTARY

1. The Title: 1:1

1:1 The oracle which Habakkuk the prophet saw.

Commentary

[1:1] This opening superscription to the book of Habakkuk identifies the content of the book, or at least the content of the first two chapters—the final chapter has its own superscription—as a prophetic oracle *(maśśā')* of Habakkuk the prophet *(nābî').* This meager information, which amounts to little more than the prophet's name, is all that is known about the prophet apart from what can be gleaned indirectly from the prophecy itself. The prophet is mentioned in the deuterocanonical book, Bel and the Dragon (vs. 33–39), and the Old Greek version of this work (v. 1) identifies Habakkuk as a Levite with a father named Jesus. However, these deuterocanonical traditions are of little or no historical value, since they are probably the creation of late midrashic speculation.

Moreover, the prophet's name provides no clue to the personality of the prophet or to the interpretation of the book. Habakkuk appears to derive from Akkadian *ḫabbaququ,* the name of a garden plant. The Greek form *Ambakoum* is the result of simple dissimilation; it does not suggest a different derivation of the name. Thus the name Habakkuk belongs to a common Israelite name type in which plant names are used. Other examples of this name type include Tamar, Elon, Keziah, and Hadassah. The presence of such an Akkadian loanword in seventh-century Judah is not surprising, given Assyria's domination of Palestine since the late eighth century.

Finally, the designation of the prophet as a *nābîʾ* and of his message as a *maśśāʾ* does not add much to our understanding of the book. Some scholars have taken the use of these terms as a clear indication that Habakkuk was a cult prophet employed by the temple, but it is more than doubtful whether either term will bear the weight this interpretation places upon it. The designation *nābîʾ,* presumably an old passive participle from a root cognate to Akkadian *nabû,* "to call," hence meaning "one who is called (by God)," is a general term for prophet; it is not restricted to just those figures who were clearly employed by the crown or the temple. Neither Isaiah nor Jeremiah is generally considered a professional cult prophet, but each is occasionally designated as a *nābîʾ* (Isa. 38:1; 39:3; Jer. 1:5; 20:2; passim). Nor is the term *maśśāʾ* used only for the oracles of cultic prophets. The term is probably a technical term for "oracle," derived from the idiom *nāśāʾ* + a word designating either voice or a spoken message. (Cf. *nāśāʾ dābār/qînāh,* "to lift up a word/lamentation" [Amos 5:1]; *nāśāʾ māšāl,* "to lift up a saying" [Hab. 2:6; Num. 23:7, 18; 24:3, 15]; *nāśāʾ qôl,* "to lift up the voice" [Cathcart, *Nahum,* 36].) Hence this use is distinct in meaning from the more general use of *maśśāʾ* in the sense of "burden." Nevertheless, the fact that the same word was used for both these meanings easily led to the conception that Yahweh had placed the "burden" of the message on the prophet. Because it was a favorite term used by his opponents, Jeremiah came to object to the prophetic use of the term *maśśāʾ* (Jer. 23:33–39), particularly since he did not think God had anything to do with the message which "burdened" his opponents. The word, however, is used unblushingly as a designation for some of Isaiah's oracles (note esp. Isa. 17:1; 19:1; 22:1; 30:6).

The content of the book shows that the prophet Habakkuk was familiar with Israel's liturgical forms. There is no reason to doubt that the temple was the locus of at least some of his prophetic activity, but the evidence does not allow one to say more. Even if Habakkuk were a professional prophet employed in the temple, that offers no basis for a theological evaluation of his message and certainly not for a denigration of it. Opposition to the establishment is not necessarily an indication of theological truth, and a position within the establishment is not necessarily an indication of the rejection of theological truth. There is actually little justification for the sharp dichotomy drawn by much contemporary scholarship between the professional cult prophets—the "false prophets"—and the non-professional, independent, classical prophets—the "true" prophets. This sharp distinction is based on a problematic reading of Amos 7:14 and a few other highly polemical passages, and it fails to take into account how little we know of the sources of income of any of the prophets—true or false. The classical prophets as a group may have been just as professional as the false prophets as a group. To judge from the account of the encounter between Jeremiah and Hananaiah (Jer. 28:1–17), the contemporaries of the prophets had no such easy yardstick for deciding who was a true prophet.

2. Habakkuk's Initial Lament: 1:2–4

1:2 How long, O Yahweh, shall I cry out
And you not listen,
Shall I shout to you, "Violence!"
And you not save?
3 Why do you make me see iniquity and trouble?[1]
[Why] do you idly watch,[2] while plunder and violence are before me?
While there is strife and contention arises?[3]
4 That is why the law is ineffective,
And justice never comes forth.
For the wicked person hedges in the just—
That is why justice comes forth perverted.

Textual Notes

[1]The correct division of the poetic lines is problematic, as the ancient versions indicate. The traditional division suggested by the accents of the MT is rejected, partially following the ancient versions, on the basis that *'āwen wᵉʿāmāl* and *šōd wᵉḥāmās* are parallel pairs, each dependent on a single verb. Since the second verb is intransitive, in order to keep it in the second person to match the first verb, it was necessary to introduce the second parallel pair with *wᵉ* as a circumstantial nominal clause.

[2]If one takes "trouble" *(ʿāmāl)* as the object of "you watch" *(tabbîṭ),* following the traditional division of the text, the resulting paral-

lelism between a causative and simple transitive verb is awkward. There is no clear evidence that the hiphil of the root *nbṭ* ever has a causative sense, however. Because the versions misunderstood the circumstantial nominal clause *wᵉšōd wᵉḥāmās lᵉnegdî,* "while plunder and violence are before me," they felt this awkwardness and tried to correct it. LXX and V finessed the problem by translating the verb *tabbîṭ* with an infinitive, and S and T corrected the verb to a first person, but neither correction appears to be based on a different Hebrew text. The similar use of *habbîṭ* in v. 13 appears to confirm both the text and the translation given above.

[3]Either one must assume an unusual intransitive sense for the qal of *nāśā'* (cf. the textually uncertain Hos. 13:1; Nahum 1:5; Ps. 89:10 [9]) or one must correct *yiśśā'* to *niśśā'*. One might also consider *'eśśā',* "while there is strife and *I endure* contention?"

Commentary

Habakkuk 1:2–4 gives voice to the prophet's questions about God's justice in the form of an individual lament. In traditional fashion, Habakkuk complains that God does not intervene to save the just and punish the wicked. The conditions that provoked this lament, if one may judge from the vocabulary used and from the fact that the Babylonians are offered as God's solution to the problem (vs. 5ff.), appear to be problems internal to Judean society. Jeremiah also used the lament form and similar language to express his conflicts with Judean society (Jer. 12:1–4; 15:10; 20:7–8).

[1:2] "How long" *('ad-'ānāh)* is a typical way of introducing a question that implicitly complains about the other person's behavior. God uses it to complain about his people's disobedience (Ex. 16:28; Num. 14:11), humans use it to complain about the behavior of other humans (Ps. 62:4 [3]; Job 18:2; 19:2), and a human worshiper may use it to complain about God's behavior (Ps. 13:2 [1]). The expression is normally followed by the imperfect, but the perfect is found here and in Ex. 16:28. Both the verb "to cry out" *(šiwwā')* and its derived noun "outcry" *(šaw'āh)* refer to a cry for help, and the complaint implicit in the question is clear when one notes that Israelite religious tradition confidently asserted that Yahweh would listen to the cry of his faithful (Ps. 34:16 [15]; 145:19). In the light of that tradition Habakkuk wants to know "When?"

The interrogative particle is not repeated in the second half of the verse, but it is understood, and the second half presents a parallel question. "Violence!" *(ḥāmās)* appears to be what the prophet cries out (cf. Jer. 20:8; Job 19:7). It was a desperate cry for help like our cry "Thief!" or "Fire!" When, then, is God going to respond to save his servant? The very nature of the cry suggests that time is of the essence.

[3] "Why" *(lāmmāh)* is another interrogative particle that typically introduces the accusatory questions so typical of individual laments (Pss. 10:1; 22:2 [1]; 42:10 [9]; 43:2; 44:24–25 [23–24]; 74:1, 17; 79:10; 80:13 [12]; 88:15 [14]; Jer. 15:18). "To make one see" here carries the sense of "cause one to experience." "Iniquity" *('āwen)* and "trouble" *('āmāl)* refer to the wrongs done to the prophet or other righteous individuals in his society and the resulting hardships that he and they had to endure.

As in v. 2, the second line in v. 3 presupposes the interrogative particle though it does not repeat it. The syntax of the two verses is similar. In both verses the interrogative particle, expanded by the vocative "Yahweh" in v. 2, is followed immediately by the verb in the first line, but the parallel line omits the interrogative particle and any vocative expansion and simply begins with the verb:

> How long, O Yahweh, shall I cry out . . .
> shall I shout to you . . . (v. 2)
> Why do you make me see . . .
> do you idly watch . . . (v. 3).

The verb translated "idly watch" *(tabbîṭ)* implies that Yahweh is watching while the prophet or other righteous individuals in his society are oppressed; though he sees the wrongdoing, God does not do anything about it. The prophet cannot understand why, because Israelite religious tradition affirmed that Yahweh's eyes were too pure for him to idly watch while evil was done (v. 13). "Plunder" *(šōd)* and "violence" *(ḥāmās)* would appear to refer to property being taken from the prophet or his neighbors by force, though the possibility of metaphorical usage makes it impossible to identify precisely the nature of the acts to which Habakkuk is referring. The word pair can be used for the oppression, perhaps even in some sense legal, of a populace by the officials of its own government (Amos 3:10; Ezek. 45:9). Jehoiakim and his officials were certainly guilty of such oppression, involving among other things the use of forced labor (Jer. 22:13). That oppression also involved actual physical violence, however, since both Jeremiah (Jer. 22:17) and the Deuteronomistic Historian speak of Jehoiakim as shedding the blood of the innocent during his reign (2 Kings 24:4). He tried to kill Jeremiah, and he succeeded in executing another prophet, Shemaiah from Kiriath-jearim (Jer. 26:20–24). Habakkuk may have been a member of the reform party open to Jeremiah's message. At any rate, he was clearly opposed to the abuses of justice that characterized Jehoiakim's reign. How can God idly watch, the prophet wants to know, while these things are done before Habakkuk's very eyes?

"Strife" *(rîb)* and "contention" *(mādôn)* are both terms derived from the legal sphere; while they could refer to actual litigation, they could also refer more generally to conflict that had not reached the level of the courts.

Jeremiah used the same terms to describe the conflicts in which he was embroiled, conflicts that sometimes led to his imprisonment and public humiliation but at other times simply resulted in the public's profound hatred for the prophet (Jer. 15:10). It would appear that Habakkuk, like Jeremiah, experienced the pressure of official disapproval and perhaps some measure of persecution. This situation existed, according to Habakkuk, because God had not intervened to make clear whose side he was on.

[**4**] The conjunction *'al-kēn,* used twice in this verse, points back to the preceding verses as the explanation for why the situation expressed in the following clause exists. One may take the term translated "the law" *(tôrāh)* as a more general reference to priestly instruction, a prophetic oracle, or perhaps even the decision of a law court. But since Habakkuk's ministry falls after the deuteronomic reform of Josiah, it is likely that the reference is to the famous *tôrāh* scroll found in the temple, to the corpus of deuteronomic law that fueled Josiah's reform and was in turn promoted by that reform. The verb *pûg,* translated above as "is ineffective," means "to be numb from cold," "to be powerless, ineffective." Habakkuk's thought is that Yahweh's failure to act and to punish wrongdoing has crippled the Deuteronomic law's effectiveness as a tool for justice in Judean society. Since that law used the promise of reward for obedience and the threat of punishment for disobedience as a fundamental motivation for observing the law, and since it is clear that after Josiah's death in 609 B.C., his successors, particularly Jehoiakim, paid little attention to the demands of the deuteronomic law, Habakkuk's complaint is easy to understand. Because God did not uphold the sanctions, the credibility of the law's demands had been undermined, and thus justice never emerged.

To say it differently, because God allows the wicked person *(rāšā')* to "hedge in" *(maktîr)* the just or righteous person *(haṣṣaddîq),* the only justice that emerges is a perverted, crooked justice. Habakkuk is probably using both the terms "wicked" and "righteous" in their generic senses well attested in psalmic and wisdom literature. It is doubtful whether he has in mind a particular individual for either figure, though he clearly sees himself as a righteous person. The use of the verb *haktîr,* "to surround, encircle, hedge in," suggests the imposition of severe limitations on the freedom of action of the encircled party, the frustration of the righteous man's plans and expectations. Habakkuk may be thinking of his own experiences of frustration at the hand of powerful enemies, but it is hard to read his words without thinking of the experiences of Jeremiah, his contemporary. Jeremiah, whose enemies dogged his heels (Jer. 12:6; 18:20, 22–23; 20:7–10), certainly felt hemmed in, and he, like Habakkuk, blamed his situation on God's slowness in executing divine judgment on his evil oppressors (Jer. 15:15–18).

3. God's Response: 1:5–11

1:5 "Look among the nations[1] and watch,
Stare in astonishment, be astounded;[2]
For a work is about to be done[3] in your days
That you would not believe even if it were told.
6 For lo, I am about to raise up the Chaldeans,[4]
That fierce and impetuous nation
That crosses the wide expanses of the earth
To seize habitations not belonging to him.[5]
7 He is terrifying and dreadful;[6]
His law and his majesty[7] proceeds from himself.
8 His horses are swifter than leopards,
Fleeter than wolves of the steppe.[8]
His steeds[9] gallop and fly,[10]
From afar they come flying.
Like a vulture rushing toward food,[11]
9 Each one of them comes, bent on violence.
All their faces[12] forward,
And he amasses[13] captives like sand.
10 He scoffs at kings,
And princes are a joke to him.
He laughs at every fortress;
He piles up[14] earth and captures[14] it."[15]
11 Then the spirit passed on,
It departed, and I was astonished:[16]
"This one (takes) his might as his god!"

Textual Notes

[1]LXX and S have misread *bgwym,* "among the nations," as *bwgdym,* "you treacherous ones," possibly under the influence of 1:13 and 2:5.

[2]One might delete the *waw* before *hittamm*ᵉ*hû* or add a *waw* before the following *t*ᵉ*māhû* or both (cf. Isa. 29:9), but there is no justification for emending either of the two imperatives in this line; they balance the two imperatives in the preceding line. LXX's *thaumasia* has been taken as an indication that the second form was originally an infinitive absolute *tāmôah,* but the additional word in the LXX may simply be an attempt to give a fuller rendering to the longer hithpalel form.

[3]The MT has the active participle here, but that is difficult, since with the active participle one expects a pronominal form to indicate the subject, as one has in v. 6. LXX and S read the active participle, translating it with the first person, probably under the influence of v. 6, but one should probably correct *pō'ēl* to the passive participle *pā'ūl* (cf. the passive rendering in T and V).

[4]Some Greek manuscripts, including A, Q, and W, add *tous machētas,* "the warriors," after "the Chaldeans," and the Göttingen edition of the Septuagint accepts this as the original reading, bracketing *tous Chaldaious,* "the Chaldeans," as a secondary gloss. This can hardly be correct. Other Greek manuscripts, including B, S, V, and a group of Lucianic texts, lack *tous machētas,* and the reading is not attested in the other versions V, S, or T. As Rudolph has convincingly argued (pp. 203–204), it is far more likely that the less well-attested *tous machētas* (= Heb. *gibbôrîm*) is the secondary gloss. It was presumably introduced in the exegetical tradition when, in later historical situations, readers felt compelled to apply this old description of the Babylonian enemy to a more contemporary enemy power. One can see the hints of this development in the Habakkuk pesher from Qumran, where the reference to the Chaldeans in this verse is interpreted as referring to "the Kittaim (= Romans) . . . who are swift and mighty warriors *(gbwrym)* in battle" (col. ii).

[5]The third masculine singular suffix here refers back to the noun "nation," so normal English usage would require "it" rather than "him," but the lack of the neuter in Hebrew makes possible a certain fluidity between the nation, personified as a male, and the nation's king, as the embodiment of the character of the nation. It is to preserve that ambiguity in the Hebrew that I have translated both this suffix and the following series of third masculine forms, all of which have "nation" as their grammatical antecedent, with the masculine singular pronoun. The general tendency of the standard translations to render these forms with plural pronouns obscures this feature of the original text.

[6]The LXX mistakenly derives *nôrāʾ* from *rāʾāh,* "to see," rather than from *yārēʾ,* "to fear."

[7]LXX, S, and V all appear to be reading *maśśāʾ,* "oracle, burden," instead of *śᵉʾēt,* "dignity, majesty," (see v. 1), but the reading is no improvement on the MT.

[8]The word *ʿereb,* "evening," should be emended here and in Zeph. 3:3 to *ʿᵃrābāh,* "steppe," as suggested by the parallel *zᵉʾēb ʿᵃrābôt,* "a wolf of the steppes" (Jer. 5:6), or one must assume a masculine form of the noun synonymous to *ʿᵃrābāh.* LXX's "wolves of Arabia" presupposes the MT, but it indicates that translator's dissatisfaction with "wolves of the evening" as an appropriate translation for the expression.

[9]The Hebrew *pārāšāyw* could be translated either as "its steeds" or as "its cavalrymen."

[10]The text here is a very difficult crux. MT divides after *ûpāšû pārāšāyw,* taking the second *ûpārāšāyw* with the following line. That could suggest a reading, "And its steeds gallop, and its cavalrymen come from afar. . . ." One would expect the second *pārāšāyw* to have a different

meaning than the first, because the same word is seldom repeated in poetic parallelism of this type. The main difficulty with this division of the text is that such a two-word line would be anomalous in this section, where most of the lines contain three or sometimes four words. The Habakkuk pesher has *pšw wpršw pršw,* which suggests it was reading the second form as a verb. Since the Qumran texts make no orthographic distinction between *š* and *ś,* one could read *pāšû wᵉpārᵉśû pārāšāyw.* My translation presupposes either this text or a slight variant with the last two words transposed and understands the verb as a pregnant expression for *pārᵉśû (kanpēyhem),* literally, "they spread (their wings)" = "they flew" (See Jer. 48:40; 49:22; Job 39:26; and for the omission of "wing" see 1 Chron. 28:18). Many other suggestions have been proposed, most of which require more radical emendation, but one should note the suggestion of Duhm (*Habakuk,* 24–25), followed by Rudolph (p. 204), to read *ûpāšû paršê pārāšāyw,* "and the steeds of his cavalrymen galloped."

[11]The last three words of v. 8 are to be construed with v. 9.

[12]The expression *mᵉgammat pᵉnēyhem* is a crux. My translation presupposes a derivation from a root *gmm,* "to be abundant," and a nominal form *mᵉgammāh,* meaning "totality." Another possible derivation would be from a middle weak root *gāma,* "to seek, desire," which would yield a nominal form *mᵉgûmāh* or *mᵉgōmāh,* perhaps meaning "thrust" or "impulse." If one opts for the second derivation as Rudolph (p. 204) and JPSV do, one could take *pānîm* in the military sense of "van" (Joel 2:20) and translate the expression with JPSV as "the thrust of their van." Either explanation suggests much the same meaning for the thought as a whole, but the first derivation has the advantage of emphasizing the parallelism between *kol,* "all, each," and *mᵉgammāh,* "totality."

[13]The verb should be repointed as an imperfect with simple *waw: wᵉyeʾᵉsōp.*

[14]Both these verbs should be repointed as imperfects with simple *waw.*

[15]The feminine suffix on this verb is suspect, since its antecedent *mibṣār,* "fortress," is masculine. Either the antecedent is elliptical for the feminine phrase *ʿîr mibṣār,* "fortified city" (1 Sam. 6:18; 2 Kings 3:19; 10:2; 17:9; 18:8; Jer. 1:18; Ps. 108:11 [10]), or read the suffix as *-ēhû* with the Habakkuk pesher.

[16]Reading *wāʾeššōm,* the qal imperfect consecutive, first-person singular from *šāmēm.* The verse is a very difficult crux, and extensive discussion of the text and translation will be found in the exegetical discussion.

Commentary

Taken in isolation, Hab. 1:5–11 could be read as a simple oracle of judgment addressed to Habakkuk's contemporaries, but its literary placement between two laments of the prophet (1:2–4; 1:12–2:1) forces one to read it as God's response to Habakkuk's first lament. One could argue that this arrangement represented a secondary, compositional unity, though that would be hard to prove, and if the prophet himself were responsible for such compositional unity, the fact that it may have been historically secondary would be largely irrelevant to the interpretive task.

In Israelite religious practice a petitioner, whether an individual or a community, who approached Yahweh with a lament hoped for a response from the deity in the form of a favorable oracle mediated either through a priest or a prophet. When the petitioner was himself a prophet, that response could come as a revelation direct to the petitioner (see Amos 7:1–8; Jer. 12:5–6; 14:13–14; 15:19–21). That is what one has in Hab. 1:5–10. Even though v. 5 lacks any transitional formula to indicate the shift in speaker, the same could also be said of God's response (Jer. 12:5–6) to one of Jeremiah's laments, and it is clear from the continuation in Hab. 1:6 both that there is a new speaker and that this speaker is Yahweh. In contrast to the Jeremiah parallel, however, Yahweh's response to Habakkuk's lament is not addressed to Habakkuk as an individual. Formally, Hab. 1:5–10 is an oracle of judgment addressed to the whole Judean community. This is a surprising, unexpected response to Habakkuk's individual lament, but the content of the response suggests that the surprise is intentional. Both form and content underscore that Yahweh's solution to Habakkuk's complaint will be shocking, what Isaiah would call a "strange work" (Isa. 28:21). Verse 6a identifies that solution as Yahweh's use of the Chaldeans as his agent for correcting the injustice in Judean society, and vs. 6b–10 give a frightening portrayal of this foreign power's military prowess.

Verse 11 is a crux, but the first part of the verse is probably to be understood as marking the end of Yahweh's oracular response to Habakkuk, and the last part of the verse records the prophet's shocked response to Yahweh's word.

[1:5] Although Habakkuk's lament was expressed as the lament of an individual, Yahweh's response to him, framed in a series of plural imperatives, is clearly intended to address a larger audience. That audience is called upon to observe international developments with both care and astonishment. Something was about to happen among the nations in their days that they would not believe even when they were told. A similar motif of an unbelievable report about international developments as well as very similar vocabulary is found in the later exilic oracle in Isa. 52:15–53:1, but there the nations are the audience astounded by the revelation of Israel's significance, and it is a joyful significance that points to salvation. In Habakkuk, it is a Judean audience that will be astounded by the sudden intervention of Babylon in the west, and it is hardly a joyful astonishment. It is rather the astonishment of dismay as in Isa. 29:9–12 and Jer. 4:9, because this is in fact a word of judgment. In short, God's answer to Habakkuk's complaint is to give him a word of judgment to announce to his people.

"In your days" is a general indication of a date during the lifetime of the prophet and his contemporary audience, but the tenor of the oracle suggests that one would not have to wait years for its fulfillment; the rise of Babylon was imminent. That suggests a date for the oracle sometime around 605 B.C., possibly after Babylon's defeat of Egypt at Carchemish, but prior to the appearance of the Babylonian army in the Philistine plain in 604 B.C. After that event, the prophetic announcement could hardly be presented as astonishing.

[6] Even though Hab. 1:6 does not explicitly state that the purpose for God's raising up the Chaldean nation is to punish Judah, the numerous parallels to the motif make that obvious. The closest literary parallel to God's announcement, "For lo, I am about to raise up the Chaldeans . . ." is in Amos 6:14, where God says, "For lo, I am about to raise up against you, O house of Israel, says Yahweh God of Hosts, a nation, and they will oppress you from Lebo Hamat to the wadi of the Arabah." Amos clearly had in mind the Assyrians, whom God would use to punish Israel for its transgressions. Isaiah, though he used different language, made use of a similar motif (Isa. 5:26–30; 9:9–10 [10–11]; 10:5–6), and the concept of enemy nations as agents that Yahweh could raise up to punish his own people was incorporated into the Deuteronomistic History (e.g., 1 Kings 11:14, 23), the first edition of which dated to the time of Josiah, prior to Habakkuk's prophecy. Jeremiah, a contemporary of Habakkuk, spoke of God's "calling" or "bringing" a people from the north to punish Judah (Jer. 1:15; 4:6–9; 6:1, 22–24; 10:22), and, whatever the background of this prophecy, by the time of the battle of Carchemish in 605 B.C. Jeremiah had identified these northerners with the Babylonians under King Nebuchadnezzar II (Jer. 25:1, 9; 46:24). Thus both Jeremiah and Habakkuk were giving very similar messages during the reign of Jehoiakim around 605 B.C.

The Chaldeans were an Aramaic tribal group that first appeared in the area of lower Mesopotamia around the beginning of the first millennium B.C. and that became one of the dominant elements in the Neo-Babylonian kingdom founded by Nabopolassar (626?–605 B.C.) and turned into an empire by his son Nebuchadnezzar II (605–562 B.C.). However accurate it might be, the following description of this nation's character and prowess in war continues a well-known tradition in prophetic oracles of judgment of describing any enemy army used as Yahweh's agents of judgment in as frightening a manner as possible (see Isa. 5:26–30; 13:17–18; Jer. 4:7, 13;

6:22–23). In other words, the description probably owes more to literary conventions than it does to any firsthand knowledge Habakkuk may or may not have had concerning the Babylonian army.

The Babylonian army's reputation for being "fierce" (*mar,* lit. "bitter") probably developed from reports reaching Judah during the long and bitter seesaw war between Assyria and Babylon in the years 626–609 B.C., but the characterization as "impetuous" *(nimhār)* suggests more recent events. Apart from S, the versions treat this verbal adjective as though it simply meant "swift," a positive attribute for an army, but in most occurrences the term actually has a negative connotation implying a careless, frantically hurried behavior (Isa. 32:4; 35:4; Job 5:13). Up until 605 B.C., the Babylonian accounts of the campaigns against Assyria and its Egyptian ally do not impress one with Babylonian "impetuousness" or "daring," but when Nebuchadnezzar defeated the Egyptian army at Carchemish, he immediately pursued them to Hamat, a distance of slightly more than 150 miles, in order to follow up the first victory with another crushing defeat; then, learning of Nabopolasar's death, Nebuchadnezzar, with only a small bodyguard, quickly returned to Babylon to secure his succession. Those actions were both impetuous and daring. They also provide a good background for the following statement that the Babylonians crossed wide expanses of the earth to seize the habitations of others. Nebuchadnezzar's impetuous pursuit of the defeated Egyptian army in 605 B.C. gave the Babylonians control of Egypt's former vassals in the vast area of north and central Syria, and Nebuchadnezzar soon expanded that control farther south.

One should note the tone of disapproval in the statement, "to seize habitations not belonging to him." The Babylonians may be God's punishment on Judah for injustice, but Habakkuk presents the Babylonians as no paragons of justice. Whatever God's purpose with them, they are in it for their own satisfaction, just as the Assyrians were in Isaiah's time (Isa. 10:7–14).

[7] Verse 7 continues this negative portrayal of the Babylonian nation by characterizing it as one that makes its own rules. That is, it is terrifying and dreadful because it does not abide by traditional norms of conduct. It does what it pleases and expresses its majesty as it chooses. In short, its might makes right whatever it wants, and that leaves the other nations in sheer terror. Again the prophet accomplishes two purposes with this description. On the one hand, it heightens the threat of judgment on sinful Judah, but, on the other hand, it heightens the reader's sense that such a judgment, using such an unjust agent, can provide no real resolution to Habakkuk's original cry for justice.

[**8**] The various comparisons of the Babylonian horses to leopards, wolves, and a vulture rushing toward food all convey the idea of the speed

with which the Babylonian cavalry reaches its objective, but the choice of these animals of prey as the terms of comparison already intimates the nature of that objective. As v. 9a makes explicit, each cavalryman comes "to do violence" *(lᵉḥāmās).*

[9] Despite the difficult crux *mᵉgammat pᵉnēyhem,* discussed in the textual notes, the first two parallel lines of v. 9 convey the thought that every horse and rider in the Babylonian cavalry is pressing forward for the kill. There is no laggard, or coward, or squeamish individual in the lot. The parallel lines simply offer different imagery for basically the same motif found in Isa. 5:27. The last line of v. 9 adds the further thought that the Babylonian army takes prisoners in massive numbers. This may again reflect the outcome of Nebuchadnezzar's very successful campaign against the Egyptians and their allies in north Syria.

[10] Babylon's success leads it to make light of enemy kings and princes. Having destroyed the imperial Egyptian army, what possible respect could it have for the petty kings and princes of Egypt's vassals in Syria, Phoenicia, and Palestine? The thought here is very similar to that in Isa. 10:8–9, 13–14. Fortified cities presented no serious obstacle to the Babylonian march of conquest; the Babylonians simply put them under siege and quickly captured them. "Piles up earth" refers to the very ancient siege practice of piling up dirt to construct earthen siege walls around a besieged city or to construct earthen ramps leading up to the wall of the besieged city. These ramps could be used for bringing up siege machines to make a breach in the wall as well as providing an easy approach for infantry to attack the wall or exploit any breach made in it. The Babylonians, like the Assyrians before them, were masters at siege warfare. They were not always so successful as this picture suggests, however, as Nebuchadnezzar's later fourteen-year siege of Tyre demonstrated.

[11] This verse is a very difficult crux, but the difficulty is largely exegetical rather than textual, though almost all exegetes regard the form *wᵉʼāšēm* as corrupt. Most translations and exegeses assume that v. 11 continues the description of the Chaldean nation, but that assumption encounters difficulties with the word *rûaḥ,* "wind" or "spirit." It forms the obvious subject of the verb *ḥālap,* "to change" or "pass by," and, if *rûaḥ* is the subject, how does that relate to the Chaldean nation? The ancient versions apparently all take *rûaḥ* as the spirit of the Chaldean king, but they differ radically in their treatment of the rest of the verse. LXX is not entirely clear, but it seems to imply that the Chaldean king will repent and make propitiation for his sins. V implies that the spirit of the Chaldean king will be changed, pass from him, and he will fall. Both these renderings may be dependent on the story of Nebuchadnezzar's madness in Daniel 4. S and T also seem dependent on Daniel, but their emphasis is on the guilt the king will incur by his pride and, in the case of T, by the honor he ascribes to his idols. None of these renderings appears very convincing, though a few modern exegetes follow LXX in assuming that *ḥālap rûaḥ* means "(his) mind changes."

Most recent commentators either emend *rûaḥ* to *kārûaḥ,* "like the wind" (see *BHS*), or they take *rûaḥ* to be an adverbial accusative of comparison with the same meaning as the form with the preposition *kᵉ* (see Rudolph, 205). This results in a translation like "Then he sweeps by like a wind, passes on, and . . . ." In addition to the difficulty with *rûaḥ,* another difficulty with this interpretation is the problem of tenses. The verb forms used to describe the Chaldean nation in vs. 6–10 are generally imperfects or converted perfects, i.e., present or future forms of the verb. There are three exceptions in vs. 9–10, all converted imperfects and all generally corrected to the expected simple imperfects by the slight change of *wayye/i-* > *wᵉye/i-* (see *BHS* and Rudolph, 205). Verse 11, however, is introduced by a temporal adverb that suggests a change in the sequence, and it is followed by a perfect and a converted imperfect, both past tense forms. Given the break in the sequence introduced by the temporal adverb, the emendation of the perfect *ḥālap* to the imperfect *yaḥᵃlōp* is quite improbable (contra *BHS*), and Rudolph's more cautious explanation of it as a prophetic perfect (p. 205) is not very convincing either.

The closest parallel to the first half of Hab. 1:11 is found in Job 4:15, and it suggests the quite different solution to the crux found above in our translation. Job 4:15 and Hab. 1:11 both juxtapose the noun *rûaḥ* and the verb *ḥālap* in clauses that would suggest that *rûaḥ* is the subject of the verb; if that is the case, the noun *rûaḥ* is treated as masculine, contrary to normal usage, in both examples. (The subject of the feminine verb *tᵉsammēr* in Job 4:15b is not *rûaḥ,* but *śaʿᵃrat,* an archaic form of *śᵉʿārāh,* a feminine synonym of *rûaḥ.* See the commentaries.) The Job passage occurs in a context, extending from 4:12–16, in which Eliphaz is describing the onset of a revelatory experience:

> Now a word came to me stealthily,
>   and my ear caught just a whisper of it.
> Amid disquieting thoughts from night
>   visions,
>   when deep sleep falls upon men,
> Terror confronted me and trembling,
>   and it made all my bones shudder.
> A spirit *(rûaḥ)* passed by *(ḥālap)* my face;
>   a gust made my skin bristle.
> It stood still,
>   but I could not recognize its appearance.
> A form was before my eyes;
>   silence, then I heard a voice: . . .

The objection has been raised that *rûaḥ* in the Job passage really means "wind," not "spirit," but that is in many ways a modern and largely irrelevant objection, because the ancient Hebrew did not make that sharp distinction; to the ancient the "wind" could be the sign of the presence of the "spirit" (cf. Acts 2:1–4). However one translates the term *rûaḥ* in Job 4:15, it is clear that its "passing by" *(ḥālap)* is the indication of the presence of a spiritual reality through which the revelation is given to Eliphaz. Moreover, the identification of the *rûaḥ* as the source of prophetic inspiration is common to the Deuteronomistic History (1 Sam. 10:6, 10; 19:20, 23; 2 Sam. 23:2; 1 Kings 22:21–24) and to classical prophecy (Micah 3:8; Ezek. 2:2; 3:12, 14, 24; 8:3; 10:11; 11:5, 24; 37:1; 43:5). One should note that the second verb used with *rûaḥ* in Hab. 1:11, *'ābar,* also occurs with *rûah* as its masculine subject in Zedekiah's question to Micaiah ben Imlah in 1 Kings 22:24, where it expresses the idea of the departure of the inspiring spirit, and thus the end of the revelation: "Which way did the spirit *(rûaḥ)* of Yahweh pass *('ābar)* from me to speak with you?"

In view of these parallels, it is best to take v. 11a not as a continuation of the description of the Babylonians but as a notice by the prophet that the revelation which brought him Yahweh's response to his lament ended at this point. The spirit departed, and Habakkuk was left to ponder the inspired message. If one adopts this interpretation, one does not have to emend the tenses of the first two verbs, assume an unusual prophetic perfect, or explain *rûaḥ* as the equivalent of *kārûaḥ.*

Everyone, however, has to emend *wᵉ'āšēm,* "and he will become guilty." Even if the meaning of the verb were defensible, the tense clearly does not fit with the two preceding verbs. Moreover, the Qumran pesher has *wyšm,* not *w'šm,* which shows that even the ancients had trouble with the text. On the basis of the Qumran reading, scholars who understand v. 11 as a continuation of the description of the Babylonians have suggested two interpretations of the verb form involved. Rudolph reads *wayyaššēm,* a hiphil from *šāmēm,* and translates "and devastates." The sense of the verse, then, would be, "Then he sweeps by like a wind, passes on, and (continues) to devastate (new territories)." Apart from the difficulties already mentioned, Rudolph has difficulty explaining the following line introduced by the demonstrative or relative pronoun *zû,* to which he assigns a rather ad hoc meaning. Other scholars have read *wayyāśem,* from the root *śym,* and, by taking the following demonstrative as the subject, ended up with a translation such as "and this one makes/made his strength into his god." In addition to the problems already noted, this rendering must assume a very unusual syntactical use for *zû.* Neither *zû* nor *zeh,* the more common form of this pronoun, normally occurs as the subject of a verbal clause following the verb. I could find only one other occurrence, and it is not really parallel because it uses the distributive idiom *zeh . . . wᵉzeh* (2 Kings

22:20). A third alternative, which adopts this last reading, either deletes *zû* altogether or emends it and the following word *kḥw,* "his strength," to *mizbēaḥ,* thus arriving at one of the two following translations: "and he makes his strength into his god" or "and he sets up an altar for his god."

In contrast to these explanations, I keep the consonantal text of the MT and simply repoint it as the first-person converted imperfect of *šāmēm,* "to be astonished." It continues the past tense sequence of the preceding two verbs and expresses the reaction of the prophet to the revelation that he has just received: "And I was astonished." One should note that the prophet's reaction is precisely what the opening words of the revelation (v. 5) said that the reaction of its recipients would be, though different vocabulary is used. The end of v. 11 is a simple nominal clause introduced by a demonstrative that gives expression to the prophet's exclamation of resentful astonishment. As such it marks the end of this unit and provides the transitional link for the prophet's next lament. How can God use this nation to solve the problem of injustice in Judah, when the Chaldean makes his own might into his god?

4. Habakkuk's Second Lament: 1:12–17

1:12 Are you not from of old, O Yahweh?
My holy God,[1] you[2] will not die, will you?[3]
Yahweh, did you place him for judgment?[3]
O Rock,[4] did you establish him to reprove?[3]
13 You who are too pure of eye to look upon evil,
Who are not able to gaze upon trouble,
Why do you idly watch the treacherous?
Keep silent when the wicked swallows one
more righteous than he?
14 You have treated humans like the fish of the sea,
Like the creeping things that have no ruler.
15 Every one he brings up[5] with a fishhook,
He drags him into his net,
And he gathers him into his seine.
That is why he rejoices and exults,
16 That is why he sacrifices to his net,
And burns incense to his seine.
For by them his portion is fat,
And his food is rich.[6]
17 Shall[7] he then keep[8] drawing his sword[9]
To slay nations without sparing?

Textual Notes

[1]Reading *'ᵉlōhê qodšî* as suggested by the LXX. MT would have to be translated "my God, my Holy One." Neither reading is attested elsewhere in scripture.

[2]Reading *tāmût.* The MT has *nāmût,* "we do not die," but this is one of the eighteen so-called "corrections of the scribes," made for dogmatic reasons (see Christian D. Ginsburg, *Introduction to the Massoretico-Critical Edition of the Hebrew Bible* [London: Trinitarian Bible Society, 1897], 348–363). One could not bear the thought of speaking of God dying, even if the thought was negated, so the pious scribe altered the text.

[3]There is no morphological indication of a question, but the context suggests that this clause continues the initial question in the verse. One should note that the following verse also contains two questions, only the first of which is marked by an interrogative morpheme.

[4]Rock *(ṣûr)* is a very common epithet for God, used especially in the Psalms to characterize God as a source of refuge and safety (Pss. 18:3 [2], 47 [46]; 19:15 [14]; 28:1; 62:3 [2]; 73:26; 78:35; 89:27 [26]; 92:16 [15]; 94:22; 95:1; 144:1). It normally occurs either with a suffix or in construct with a noun with a suffix, but it does occasionally occur without the suffix (Deut. 32:18, 37; 1 Sam. 2:2; 23:3; Isa. 26:4; 30:29; 44:8; Pss. 18:32 [31]; 31:3 [2]; 71:3). The ancient versions all misunderstood the epithet here. LXX and S took it as the verb *ṣûr,* "to fashion," which led to the further misconstrual of *ysdtw,* "you founded him"; S omits this word, and LXX reads it as *yswrw,* "his discipline." V and T both take the epithet as an adjective, "strong," modifying the enemy God established to discipline Judah.

[5]Reading *ya'ᵃleh* with 1QpHab.

[6]One should read the masculine *bārī'* in place of MT's feminine form. Cf. 1QpHab's *bry.*

[7]The interrogative particle is omitted by 1QpHab and all the ancient versions except T. If it is deleted, the verse would be an indicative statement parallel to those in vs. 15–16, "That is why. . . . "

[8]Omit the *waw* before *tāmîd,* and construe it with the first line of the verse following the Qumran pesher. Cf. S.

[9]Reading *ḥarbô* with 1QpHab. The fishing metaphor is not continued in v. 17, and the verb *rîq* is well attested with the object *ḥereb* (Ex. 15:9; Lev. 26:33; Ezek. 5:2, 12; 12:14; 28:7; 30:11).

Commentary

Yahweh's response to Habakkuk's first lament shocked the prophet. In astonishment he exclaimed, "This one takes his might as his god!" (1:11). How could God use such an obviously evil nation to discipline his own people? This is the question the prophet elaborates in his second lament (1:12–17). The second lament may have actually been formulated some time after the initial lament. It seems to presuppose a significant experience of Babylonian oppression, so it could date several years later than the original lament, perhaps as late as the Babylonian destruction of the temple in 597 B.C., which would have raised serious questions about the Babylonians as God's agents. The present compositional arrangement of the oracles places no emphasis on such a passage of time, however.

[1:12] The logic of Habakkuk's opening question is not immediately apparent, and that has created some debate about the predicate in this nominal clause. Rudolph (p. 208) and Van der Woude (p. 28) have argued that "Yahweh" is the predicate, not a vocative, which results in a translation such as the following: "Are you not Yahweh from of old, my God, my Holy One, who does not die?" The alternative, they claim, is to take the following epithet as the predicate: "Are you not from of old, O Yahweh, my holy God who does not die?" If either "Yahweh" or "my holy God" is the predicate, the logic would be that God's action in using the Babylonians as his tool is inconsistent with his character revealed in the name Yahweh or in his being as holy God. This understanding of the text is very problematic, however. It destroys the poetic parallelism in the verse. If one adopts the syntactical analysis of Rudolph and Van der Woude, the parallelism between the expressions "Yahweh" and "my holy God" and between "from of old" and "you will not die" is undermined.

The predicate is actually the temporal expression "from of old" in the first clause and the verbal clause "you will not die" in the second line. In other words, God's eternal existence is the basis for the prophet's argument. This motif is found several times in the Psalms, including Ps. 90:2, where *'ēl,* if it is original at all, is not the predicate, contrary to Van der Woude (p. 28), but a vocative (cf. Pss. 93:2; 102:13 [12]). There is probably an allusion here to the dying god of the Mot-Baal myth, as the imagery in the following verse indicates. Yahweh is not supposed to be a dying god like Baal, but if he is a living god, why does he not see what is going on and do something about it? How could a living God propose the Babylonians as a solution for Judean injustice? That hardly provides a long-term solution to the problem of injustice; it simply replaces one source of injustice with a greater one. A living God who is really in control of the world ought not resort to such stopgap measures.

Thus Habakkuk addresses a series of reproving questions to Yahweh:

Yahweh, did you really set him up to render judgment upon the wicked in Judah? O Rock, did you really establish him in order to reprove the disobedient among your people? Rock *(ṣûr)* is an epithet that conveys Yahweh's role as a source of security to his people, so its use here underscores the incongruity of Yahweh's action: Has Judah's source of security brought the Babylonians upon us? God's response to Habakkuk was congruent with the message of Habakkuk's contemporary Jeremiah and with the earlier prophetic message of Isaiah. Both of these prophets interpreted the major foreign enemy of Judah in their time as a tool God was using to punish Judah. Habakkuk's questioning of his oracle suggests that he had some difficulty accepting this theological interpretation of history. This understanding may have prophetic tradition behind it, but how can this be just?

[13] According to the tradition, Yahweh was too pure and holy to look upon evil. Evil would provoke his intervention in human affairs to vindicate the innocent and punish the wicked. How then could Yahweh idly watch while the Babylonians, who were far worse than the wicked in Judah, swallowed up God's own people? The imagery of the wicked swallowing up the righteous recalls the imagery of the Mot-Baal myth, where Mot, the god of death, swallows Baal (*CTA* 5, i 5–8; ii 2–4). That Habakkuk was conscious of this mythological background to his imagery seems apparent from his language in Hab. 2:5 where, in a similar description of the voracious appetite of the wicked Babylonian, the prophet explicitly compares the Babylonian to Sheol and to death *(Māwet)*. One should also compare Psalm 73, a similar lament over God's apparent inattention to the wicked's oppression of the righteous (vs. 3–12), where the psalmist describes the wicked as insatiable, again in imagery strikingly reminiscent of the Mot-Baal myth (v. 9):

> They place their mouth in the heavens,
> And their tongue goes to the earth.

Note the Mot-Baal myth's similar description of Mot's voraciousness (Herder, *CTA* 5, ii. 2–3):

> [A lip t]o the earth, a lip to the heavens,
> [. . . , the t]ongue to the stars!

Another motif that may be attributed to this dying god myth is found in several other Israelite laments, where the psalmist appeals to Yahweh to "wake up" and "intervene" (Pss. 35:23; 44:24 [23]; 59:5–6 [4–5]). In the Baal myth, Baal eventually returns to life, and, because he lives, his people are saved. The prophet seems to suggest to Yahweh by analogy, "If you live, should you not also save your people?"

In contrast to Hab. 1:4, where *rāšāʿ*, "the wicked (man)," referred to a native Judean wrongdoer, here in Hab. 1:13 the term refers to the Babylonian enemy, and "the one more righteous than he" refers to Judah. There might be a problem of injustice in Judah, but it was nothing compared to the injustice that the Babylonians wreaked on the world.

[14] If God was using the Babylonian as his agent for punishing Judah, then God was treating mankind as having no more value than the fish of the sea or the creeping things that have no ruler. "That have no ruler" is a disparaging comment to suggest a very rudimentary level of social development (Prov. 6:7; 30:27); it simply underscores the lack of value human existence has to a God who would use the Babylonian as his agent. One might also take this expression as another allusion to the myth of the dying god. When Baal is found dead, El exclaims, "What will become of the people of Dagan's son? What will become of his multitudes?" (*CTA* 5, vi. 23–24). Similarly, the treatment meted out to Judah suggests that they are without a ruler, that Yahweh their real king who delivered them from their enemies (Judg. 8:23; 1 Sam. 8:7; Pss. 47:3–10 [2–9]; 89:19 [18]) has either died or deserted his people.

[15] Verse 15 develops the fish metaphor by describing how the Babylonian king treats people. He drags in the various nations on his fishhook, or he snares them in his net or seine. Other nations were to the Babylonian no more than fish to be caught for his own pleasure and use. The net was a very ancient Mesopotamian symbol associated with military power; it occurs in Mesopotamian art and literature as a weapon in which the gods ensnare the naked enemies of their favorites. In the cosmogonic myth, it is one of the major weapons Marduk uses to conquer Tiamat. Habakkuk may have known of this symbolism, and, if so, it may have influenced his choice of the fishing metaphor.

[16] The fishing metaphor is continued in v. 16. Because his net and seine bring in such an abundance of rich food, the Babylonian worships the tools by which he obtains this abundance as though they were divine. Habakkuk's point is that Babylon worshiped its military power because its military power brought such a high standard of living to Babylon. Habakkuk's comment is hardly a fair appraisal of the religious situation in Babylon, but there is a certain truth to his statement in terms of the ultimate significance Nebuchadnezzar placed upon his military. It raises the broader contemporary question whether we in our own way deify the means to our high standard of living. To do so is to ignore the true God and almost inevitably to disparage other humans as mere creatures significant only for our convenience and pleasure.

[17] Habakkuk concludes his lament by asking whether the Babylonian would ever cease slaying other nations. Or, if one follows the Qumran pesher and the versions in reading the verse as a statement, Habakkuk attributes the Babylonians' slaughter of other nations to their deification of their military might. In either case, the prophet has dropped the fish imagery to speak clearly of Babylon's military activity. And in either case God is held responsible for the activity of the Babylonians. How can God permit the Babylonians to go on killing nation after nation? How can that bring about justice?

5. Yahweh's Second Response: 2:1–4

2:1 Upon my watch let me stand,
And let me station myself upon my post,[1]
That I might watch to see what he will say to me,
And what he[2] will reply to my reproof.
2 Then Yahweh answered me and said:
Write the vision clearly[3] upon the tablets
So that the one who reads in it might run.[4]
3 For the vision is a witness[5] to the appointed time;
It is a testifier[6] to the end, and it does not lie.
If it seems slow, wait for it.
For it will surely come; it will not delay.
4 Now the fainthearted,[7] his soul[8] will not walk[9] in it,
But the righteous person will live by its[10] faithfulness.

Textual Notes

[1]Since the parallelism suggests that *māṣôr* is a synonym of *mišmeret,* it is probably to be pointed as *maṣṣôr,* derived from *nāṣar,* "to guard," and treated as cognate with Akkadian *maṣṣartu,* "guard, guardpost." The normal meaning of *māṣôr,* "wall, fortress," does not fit here. LXX and S apparently connected the word with *ṣûr,* "rock, cliff." 1QpHab adds a suffix to the word, *mṣwry,* but since its preceding parallel term, *mišmartî,* already has a suffix, it need not be repeated with *maṣṣôr.*

[2]Reading *yāšib* with S. It is clear from the context that the prophet is awaiting Yahweh's response to Habakkuk's reproof. Rudolph keeps MT on the assumption that one can translate *'āšîb* as "(what) I will bring back (as an answer to my reproof)" (p. 212), but this seems quite dubious. It is likely that the text was altered to avoid the idea that the prophet could reprove God. Note that the Vulgate has "what I will respond to the one reproving me." The T's passive is just an attempt to keep the sense of the context without altering the text.

[3]"Write the vision and make it plain" is a hendiadys for "write the vision clearly." There is no need to follow Rudolph in treating *ûbā'ēr,* "and make plain," as an adverbial use of the infinitive absolute (p. 212).

[4]The translation of this line is problematic and will be discussed extensively in the notes.

[5]Repoint *'ôd,* "yet," to *'ēd,* "witness," because of the parallelism with *yāpēaḥ,* "testifier." The error crept into the text after the tradition forgot the noun *yāpēaḥ* and misanalyzed this form as a verb.

[6]The word *yāpēaḥ* (also spelled *yāpîaḥ* and *yāpīaḥ*) often occurs in parallelism with *'ēd,* and both terms are further specified by identical syntactical constructions in which they are placed in construct with a following noun. The context makes clear that both terms are nouns meaning "witness," further specified by the construct chain as either "witness of lies/false witness" or "witness of truth/truthful witness" (Ps. 27:12; Prov. 6:19; 12:17; 14:5, 25; 19:5, 9; see Loewenstamm, *Leš* 26 [1962–63]: 205–208). Proverbs 12:17 is particularly clear:

> *yāpîaḥ 'ᵉmûnāh yaggîd ṣedeq*
> *wᵉ'ēd šᵉqārîm mirmāh*
> A truthful testifier declares what is right,
> But a lying witness deceit.

The word *ypḥ* is also clearly attested in Ugaritic as a noun meaning "witness" (*UT,* 413). It apparently dropped out of common Hebrew usage sometime after the exile, because none of the ancient versions recognized the word as a noun. Once *yāpēaḥ* was misconstrued as a verb, the corruption of its synonym *'ēd* into *'ôd* was just a matter of time.

[7]MT contains a pual perfect 3 f. sg. verb form *'ūppᵉlāh,* "she/it was puffed up(?)," but this does not fit the context. The parallelism with *ṣaddîq,* "the righteous man," in the next line leads one to expect a noun or a nominalized adjective here; and the masculine suffix on *napšô,* "his soul," shows that the form should be masculine like *ṣaddîq.* LXX reads the form as a 3 m. sg. verb, "if he shrinks back," but it is unclear how it arrived at that meaning for the verbal root, and its construal of the rest of the line is improbable. S reads the form as an abstract noun, "wickedness," which leaves the parallelism in the verse ambiguous, dependent on whether one takes the antecedent of "his" to be God or the righteous man: "And in wickedness his soul does not delight, but the righteous man shall live by faithfulness." T paraphrases the term as "wicked men," but, apart from the recognition that one should expect a noun to contrast with "righteous man," neither S nor T offers much help for correcting the text. V renders the form as *qui incredulus est,* "the one who is unbelieving," which would be an appropriate contrast to *ṣaddîq,* but it is not clear how V came up with this rendering. Scholars have proposed several emendations of the form to arrive at an appropriate nominal term for the context. Among those suggestions are *'appāl,* "the arrogant" or "the heedless(?)," *hā'awwāl,* "the wicked," *'āṣēl,* "the sluggard," and *hanneʿᵉlāp,* "the fainthearted." Given the preceding verse that urges one to wait patiently for the fulfillment of the vision, I would expect a negative term that

suggested the failure to wait. The original root behind the corrupt form *'ūpp^elāh* is likely to be *'lp, y'p,* or *'yp,* all of which imply exhaustion, weariness, or fainting away. Based on the idiom in Jer. 4:31, one could read the qal masculine singular participle of *'yp* and obtain an appropriate sense without changing the consonantal text: *hinnēh 'āp lōh,* "Now the one who faints before it . . . ." This is the emendation presupposed by my translation, but the text remains a difficult crux, and other emendations remain possible.

There is a whole series of emendations that see behind the form *'ūpp^elāh,* not the parallel or contrast to *ṣaddîq,* but a verbal form or clause standing in contrast to the clause "shall live by faithfulness." Then, in order to provide the contrasting poetic member for *ṣaddîq,* this requires that one take *lō' yāš^erāh napšô bô* as an unmarked relative clause meaning "whose soul is not upright in him." Such a rendering of this clause is problematic, however (see below, note 10), and that renders the underlying analysis of *'ūpp^elāh* problematic as well.

[8]LXX reads a first-person suffix, "my soul," understanding the antecedent to be God, but it misconstrues the verbal idiom, and it is more natural to follow MT, with its third-person suffix referring back to the "fainthearted."

[9]As J. Gerald Janzen has shown (*HTR* 73 [1980]: 63), the customary rendering of this verbal clause as "his soul is not upright in him" is quite unnatural Hebrew. As he says, "it is so unlikely as to be an impossible or at least an outlandish rendering." The normal construction of verb + *nepeš* + *b-,* illustrated by such passages as Gen. 49:6; Num. 21:4; Isa. 46:2; 66:3, suggests a common general usage of the idiom "to characterize the relation of the soul or self, by way of its attitude, feeling or desire, or action (often locomotive) toward something other than itself" (p. 66), and the use of the verbal construction *yāšar b^e-* in 1 Sam. 6:12 suggests that the expression here means "to walk straight in it."

[10]LXX has a first-person suffix, referring to God, but while this catches the general sense of the passage, it hardly represents the original text. MT is original, but the antecedent of its third masculine singular suffix on "faithfulness" is the "vision" and its testimony about the end.

Commentary

[2:1] Following Habakkuk's second lament, the prophet takes up his position to await Yahweh's oracular response to his complaint. The verse makes clear that Habakkuk, like Jeremiah (Jer. 28:1–12; 42:7), had to wait for a word of Yahweh. No true prophet could produce one on demand, and the true prophet was quite capable of distinguishing between such a divine word and his or her own thoughts on a subject.

The designation of the place where the prophet waits for a new word from Yahweh as a "watch post" or "guard post" has a very close parallel in the thought and wording of the oracle in Isa. 21:8:

And the seer (*hārō'eh,* following 1QIsaa) cried:
Upon the watch post *(miṣpeh),* O Lord, I continue standing day after day,
And upon my guard post *(mišmartî)* I remained stationed every night.

This language probably derives from a widespread self-understanding of the prophet as a spiritual watchman for the people. Ezekiel spells out this concept of the prophet as watchman *(ṣōpeh)* in detail (Ezek. 3:17; 33:7), but the concept is neither unique to nor original with Ezekiel (see Jer. 6:17; Micah 7:7; cf. Ps. 5:4 [3]). It is unclear, however, whether one is to understand the language in Habakkuk as referring to a specific place where the prophet went to await an oracle or whether one should take the language as merely metaphoric for prophetic waiting for an oracle. There is some slight evidence that prophets followed a set pattern when awaiting an oracular response. Balaam went aside from the place of sacrifice "to meet" the omens (Num. 23:3, 15; 24:1), and one of the Mari letters seems to refer to waiting on a prophetic oracle as "guarding the tent sanctuary" *(maškanam naṣārum;* A1121 + A2731, lines 32–33, 42–43; *RA* 78 [1984]: 7–18). By analogy, Habakkuk may also have had a particular place where he went to await an oracular response from Yahweh, and that place could have been in the temple complex, but the evidence is insufficient to demonstrate either point.

Despite the visual language of "seeing" and "watchpost," the prophet also uses aural language of "speaking" and "answering" to refer to God's response. It is unlikely that further investigation of either set of metaphorical language could tell us whether visual or auditory phenomena were primary in Habakkuk's experience of revelation. One may wonder, in fact, whether the sharp contrast between the two is really appropriate to the biblical phenomena, since the biblical text often mixes these metaphors unashamedly. One thinks especially of the "word" *(dābār)* that certain prophets "saw" (*ḥāzāh;* Isa. 2:1; Amos 1:1; Micah 1:1).

The use of the term "my reproof" *(tôkaḥtî)* shows that the prophet characterized his second lament as a reproof or rebuke of Yahweh. He was unwilling to accept God's first response as appropriate, and certainly not as the final response to the problem he had originally raised, so Habakkuk talked back to God just as other great men of faith in the Old Testament had done or were to do. One thinks especially of Abraham, Moses, Amos, Jeremiah, and Job, to mention only the most prominent.

[2] The text does not specify how long Habakkuk had to wait before Yahweh responded to the prophet's reproof, but eventually God did answer

with another oracle. In it God commands the prophet to write down his vision clearly on the tablets. Precisely what these tablets were is unclear, though it is possible that prophetic oracles were sometimes inscribed on stone or wooden tablets and displayed somewhere in the temple complex in order to reach a wider audience. A similar command for writing down an oracle on a tablet as a witness for the future is found in Isa. 30:8, and the language suggests a tablet of wood or stone.

The command to make the writing clear may harbor a double meaning. Inscriptions on stone, if they are not cut carefully and deeply enough, can be very difficult to read, and the obvious sense of the command is simply to write the inscription clearly enough so that it will be easy to read. It is possible, however, that the command carries a second level of meaning, that is, make the import of the vision plain. This possibility for a double meaning is enhanced by the ambiguity in the following line on the proper construal of the suffixed preposition *bô,* "in/from it." The verb *qārā',* "to read," is often construed with the preposition b^{e}- + the source from which one reads (Deut. 17:19; Jer. 36:8, 10, 13; Neh. 8:3, 18; 13:1; 2 Chron. 34:18). One should note that ancient readers read aloud, hence in all these examples one should render the idiom as "to read from," not "to read in." If one construes Hab. 2:2c following this pattern, one could translate the line as "so that the one who reads from it might run." In this case the verb "to run" should be assigned the metaphorical sense "to read quickly." The text certainly does not mean that someone running down the street need not stop in order to read the inscription.

The construal of the suffixed preposition discussed above is probably the one that would occur to a reader first, but there is a slight grammatical problem with it. In all the examples cited, it is the document *(sēper),* not the contents *(tôrāh)* of the document, from which one reads. If the construction in Habakkuk followed that pattern, one would expect the masculine plural suffix on the preposition, since the document is designated as "tablets" *(lūḥôt),* a masculine plural noun. The only masculine singular antecedent for the suffix to refer to is the vision *(ḥāzôn),* the contents written on the tablets. This difficulty, as slight as it may be, suggests that one try construing *bô,* not with the participle *qôrē',* but with the verb *rûṣ,* "to run." Proverbs 18:10, which contains this construction, is quite suggestive:

> The name of Yahweh is a strong tower;
> The righteous man will run into it *(bô-yārûṣ)* and find
> security *(niśgāb).*

Following the hint provided by that parallel, one might render the line from Habakkuk as "so that the one who reads might run into it (for refuge)." In this case the antecedent of the pronominal suffix is clearly the vision, in which the reader may find refuge while awaiting its fulfillment.

I am inclined to think the prophet intentionally played with such a double meaning. Behind the surface meaning, "Write the vision legibly on the tablets so that the one reading from it can read quickly," lies the deeper meaning, "Write the vision on the tablets and make its import plain so that the one reading can take refuge in it."

One should note that up to this point the content of the vision has not been revealed. The prophet has been told to write it down, but the attentive reader is still waiting to hear the vision.

[**3**] Verse 3 does not end that waiting; it does not contain the vision but, rather, gives the reason for writing it down and the assurance that the vision can be relied on. The vision is a witness to what God is going to do at a set time in the future. Because God's intervention is to take place in the future, the testimony about it is to be written down and preserved as a witness until the events of that day confirm it. A similar motif is found twice in Isaiah. Once in connection with the oracular promises associated with the child Maher-shalal-hash-baz (Isa. 8:1–4), Isaiah gives the command, "Bind up the testimony *(t*[e]*'ûdāh),* seal the teaching among my instructed ones," and in the meantime, says Isaiah, "I shall wait for Yahweh who is hiding his face from the house of Jacob, and I shall trust in him" (Isa. 8:16–17). The other occurrence is in Isa. 30:8:

> Now go, write it on a tablet *(lûaḥ)* with them,
> And on a document *(sēper)* inscribe it,
> That it might be for a future day,
> As a witness [reading *'ēd*] for ever.

A comparison of those two parallels shows that the practice of writing down the prophetic message as a witness or testimony had two purposes. On the one hand, it was done because of the disbelief of the people who did not want to hear the message (Isa. 30:8–11). When the word was fulfilled, its testimony would leave the unprepared without excuse. On the other hand, the written word would serve in the meantime as a source of reassurance and guidance for those who believed (Isa. 8:16–17). It is this latter function which is highlighted in Habakkuk's use of the motif.

Habakkuk is assured that the vision is a safe guide for the present, because its testimony about the future was true. The vision was not a lying witness; its fulfillment would come at the appropriate time. The parallel terms "appointed time" *(mô'ēd)* and "end" *(qēṣ)* suggest a fixed point for the fulfillment of the vision whose term can neither be rushed nor delayed. The word *mô'ēd* is used for the end of term of a woman's pregnancy (Gen. 18:14), and, just as the nine-month term for a pregnancy is fixed, though it may often seem to the pregnant woman that her condition will never change, so the vision will be fulfilled at its appointed time. If it seems slow in coming, wait for it, for like the birth of a child, it cannot be delayed.

[4] After this admonition to patiently await the fulfillment of the vision, the vision itself is still not related; there follows instead a portrayal of two contrasting responses to the vision. The textual difficulties in the verse makes it difficult to characterize the first response with any degree of certainty. Any interpretation of this response will be clouded by a certain amount of hypothetical guesswork. If my structural analysis in the text-critical notes is correct, the first response is that of one who faints or loses heart in the presence of the vision. In other words, it is the response of one who gives up and no longer expects the vision to be fulfilled. Such a one will not continue to walk unwaveringly in the light of the vision. The verb *yāšar,* when followed by the expression *bᵉʿênê,* "in the eyes of," means "to be right in the eyes of," "to be pleasing to." This is the most common use of the verb, and it has tended to distract interpreters of Hab. 2:4, even though that idiom is not found here. Habakkuk 2:4 has the simple verbal construction *yāšar bᵉ-,* a construction that is used to express consistent, unwavering movement along a certain path, as in 1 Sam. 6:12, where the two young cows pulling the wagon to return the ark of the covenant walked straight in the road that led to Beth-shemesh and did not turn aside either to the right or the left. Habakkuk's meaning is that the fainthearted individual will turn aside from a manner of life consistent with the message of the vision; he or she will not continue to walk straight and unwaveringly in its light. One should note that this rendering underscores the prophet's continuing use of verbs of motion in his metaphorical language describing human response to the vision. Compare the use of *rûṣ bᵉ-,* "run into," in v. 2.

In contrast to the fainthearted, the righteous individual will find in the reliability or trustworthiness of the vision the strength to go on living. The noun *ʾᵉmûnāh* means "firmness, steadfastness, fidelity, reliability, trustworthiness," not faith, and it refers to the reliability of the vision, and ultimately of God who gives the vision, not the reliability or the fidelity of the righteous person. The thought is a continuation of the claim in v. 3 that the vision is not a lying witness, that it can be trusted, and that one should wait for its fulfillment, even if subjectively it seems to be a long time in coming. Nonetheless, the appropriate human response to the trustworthiness of the vision is to believe it and live in a way that reflects that faith. Thus the New Testament appropriation of this passage (Rom. 1:17; Gal. 3:11; Heb. 10:38) is justified, even if its translation of the passage involves a slight shift of meaning. Hebrews 10:38, in particular, remains very close to the original intent of the Habakkuk passage when the author of Hebrews cites Habakkuk in order to encourage despairing Christians, to reassure them that God's promised intervention will surely come at its appropriate time. Paul's use of the passage is more abstract and general, less tied to the specific context of the oppressed waiting for vindication, but it may be more profound. Life is to be found by trusting in God's promises rather than by earning it through one's own meritorious deeds. It is a gift rather than an achievement.

In the context of Habakkuk's oracle, however, the verb "will live" refers to life in the interim before the time fixed for the fulfillment of the vision. It expresses the ability of the righteous person to endure and to engage the necessities of the present with the eschatological patience and joy that only the certainty of the coming end could give. Because the righteous person trusts in the reliability of God's promise contained in the vision, he or she is free to live in the present, no matter how unjust or oppressive it may be.

6. The *hôy*-Oracles: 2:5–20

2:5 How much more shall wealth deceive[1] the arrogant man,
And he shall not succeed[2] who has made his maw as wide as Sheol,
Who is like Death, which is insatiable,
Who has gathered in for himself all the nations,
And has collected for himself all the peoples.
6 Will not all these[3] take up a parable against him,
A satire,[4] epigrams about him?
One will say:[5]
Hey,[6] you[7] who amass what is not yours[7]—
How much longer?—
And make ever heavier your[7] load of debt!
7 Will not your creditors suddenly arise,
And those that terrify[8] you awake,
And you will become their object of plunder?
8 Because you plundered many nations,
All the remaining peoples will plunder you—
For shedding human blood[9] and the violence against the land,[10]
Against the city[10] and all its[10] inhabitants.
9 Hey, you[11] who acquire unjust gains
To the ruin[12] of your[11] own house[13]
In order to set your[11] nest in the height
To escape the reach of misfortune!
10 You have plotted shame for your own house
By cutting off[14] many peoples,
So sinning[15] against your own life.
11 For a stone from the wall will cry out,
And a beam[16] from the woodwork will answer it.
12 Hey, you[17] who build a city by bloodshed,
And establish[18] a town by iniquity,
13 [Are not these[19] from Yahweh of Hosts?][20]
So that the peoples exhaust themselves only for the fire,
And the nations grow weary for nothing!

14 [For the earth will be filled so that it knows
the glory of Yahweh as the waters cover the sea.][21]
15 Hey, you[22] who give your[22] neighbor to drink from the goblet[23] of your[24] wrath,
Even[25] making them drunk that you[22] may look upon their[26] nakedness![27]
16 You have sated yourself with shame instead of glory.
Drink, you too, and expose yourself![28]
The cup in the right hand of Yahweh will come around to you,
And there will be shame in place of your glory.
17 For the violence done to Lebanon will cover you,
And the destruction of the animals will shatter you,[29]
For shedding human blood[9] and the violence against the land,[10]
Against the city[10] and all its[10] inhabitants.
18 What has the carved image availed
That its fashioner has carved it?
The molten image and false oracle,
That the one who fashioned his product has trusted in it,
Making dumb idols?
19 Hey, you[30] who say "Wake up!" to wood,
"Awaken!" to inert[31] stone!
Can it give an oracle?
Though it is encased in gold and silver,
There is no breath inside it.
20 But Yahweh is in his holy temple;
Keep silent before him, all the earth!

Textual Notes

[1]Reading *w'p ky hwn ybgwd,* following 1QpHab. One can do nothing with MT's "wine is treacherous"; the many other emendations that have been suggested lack textual support and involve more radical correction of the text.

[2]The verb *yinweh* is derived from a root *nwh,* cognate with Arabic *nawāy,* and it means "to reach a goal, accomplish a purpose, succeed."

[3]The demonstrative pronoun is lacking in 1QpHab.

[4]The asyndetic construction which juxtaposes the singular *mᵉlîṣāh,* "satire," with the plural *ḥîdôt,* "epigrams, riddles," and makes them both dependent on the verb in the first clause is difficult but not impossible. The singular *mᵉlîṣāh* and plural *ḥîdôt* also occur together in Prov. 1:6. Contra Rudolph (p. 219), the Qumran reading *mlyṣy ḥwdwt* does not offer a better reading. It is unclear how Rudolph can move from a construct participial construction, "the scoffing makers of riddles," to his verbal translation "whereby they fashion riddles about him." One is still missing a verb. If one could also delete the initial *waw* on *wywmrw,* one

could translate "and the scoffing makers of riddles will say to him," but such an emendation has no support in the textual tradition. MT remains the preferable text.

[5]Qumran, LXX, and S have the plural, but this is just a stylistic improvement in the translation of MT's impersonal use of the singular.

[6]The particle *hôy* is a simple exclamation or vocative particle normally followed by direct address. Like the colloquial English "Hey," its function is to get the attention of the hearer, and any overtones it may acquire derive from the context, not from the inherent meaning of the word.

[7]The saying introduced by *hôy* is direct address, as the second-person forms in v. 7 clearly indicate. Verse 6 contains two third-person suffixes, but this use of the third person in direct address following a participle is a syntactical feature of Hebrew and other Semitic languages. A translation into English, which makes use of similar syntax only sparingly in prayers or hymns, cannot render these suffixes as third person without obscuring the fact that one is rendering direct address. Note that T also introduces second-person forms to more clearly indicate the direct address in v. 6.

[8]The pilpel participle from the root *zw'* literally means "those who cause you to shake."

[9]The expression *midd*ᵉ*mê 'ādām,* "on account of the blood of man," refers to human blood shed in abundance by violent acts—murder, war, and so forth.

[10]The singular here does not refer to a particular city or land; it stands for the class, for all the lands and cities against which Babylon committed crimes of violence.

[11]See note 7 above.

[12]The noun *beṣa'* carries the negative connotation of "profits obtained illegally or unjustly," thus it is difficult to take *rā',* "evil," as an adjective modifying *beṣa'*. That would be redundant. It is more likely a noun designating the disastrous impact of this action on the greedy man's house. It thus anticipates the similar thought in v. 10a.

[13]S has *lnpšh,* "to himself," because of the influence of v. 10.

[14]The versions translate *qṣwt* as a finite verb, so some scholars assume they were reading *qaṣṣôtā,* qal 2 m. sg. perfect from the root *qṣṣ,* "to cut off." MT's *q*ᵉ*ṣôt,* the qal inf. const. from the root *qṣh,* "to cut off," is an equally good reading, however, and one may wonder if the finite verbs in the versions are not simply for the ease of translation.

[15]Reading the inf. abs. *ḥāṭô'*. The present reading may have been influenced by Prov. 20:2, where the same expression occurs, but in a syntactical context where the participle is appropriate. LXX and V make *napšekā,* "your life," the subject of the verb, which they appear to read

as a perfect *ḥāṭā'*, but that is abrupt in the context, and one would have expected a feminine form to agree with the gender of the noun.

[16]The noun *kāpîs,* "beam, plank," is a rare word that gave the ancient translators problems. LXX, editio sexta and editio septima, misunderstood it as some kind of insect or larvae in the woodwork. Aquila, Symmachus, and Theodotion took it to be a mass, knot, or bond in the woodwork.

[17]See note 7 above.

[18]The MT has the polel infinitive absolute *wkwnn,* 1QpHab has the polel imperfect *wykwnn.* Either reading would fit in the context; the meaning would be the same in either case.

[19]Reading *hēnnāh* with LXX, V, and S, since *hinnēh* is unlikely following the interrogative *hᵃlō'.*

[20]This whole line is a marginal gloss. See the commentary.

[21]This slightly variant quotation of Isa. 11:9b is another marginal gloss. See the commentary.

[22]See note 7 above.

[23]Reading *missap ḥᵃmātᵉkā* by analogy with the clear expression *kôs ḥᵃmātô/î,* "the cup of his/my wrath" (Isa. 51:17, 22; cf. Jer. 25:15–17, 28; 49:12; 51:7; Ezek. 23:30–34). Simple dittography of the initial *ḥ* on *ḥᵃmātᵉkā* resulted in the corruption of *msp* to *msph̩* and the subsequent vocalization of the form as a participle from a root *sph̩,* "to pour out." LXX's *anatropēi tholerai,* "with a filthy outpouring," S's "dregs of your wrath," V's *mittens fel suum,* "pouring out his own gall," and T's "and he poured (it) out in wrath," all presuppose MT, but a second participle in the opening line of the *hôy*-saying is awkward and improbable.

[24]Contra Rudolph (p. 220), the second-person suffix here is not impossible. Once one recognizes that *hôy*-sayings involve direct address, the occasional replacement of the syntactically conditioned third-person form by the semantically correct second-person form is only to be expected. Note the second-person forms in the following verse.

[25]The expression *wᵉ'ap,* "and also," assuming it is original here, is only slightly stronger than a simple "and," which is all the ancient versions use to render it. As the introduction to the second line, it makes an already overly long line even longer, and that makes it suspect. One could also understand *wᵉ'ap* as "and anger" and take it as a secondary gloss on *ḥᵉmātᵉkā* at the end of the preceding line, "your wrath and anger."

[26]The plural suffix here indicates that the singular "neighbor" is to be understood as a collective.

[27]1QpHab has *mw'dyhm,* "their festivals," but that is the result of the easy confusion of *d* and *r.* LXX's "their caves" is due to their confusing

the word with the noun *m*ᵉ*ʿārāh.* Neither is possible in the context. For the sense, see Gen. 9:21–22.

[28]The niphal imperative *hēʿārēl* must be derived from the root *ʿrl,* having to do with the foreskin, so its literal meaning is probably "show the foreskin," that is, "expose your uncircumcised member." The same thought, though using the hithpael of the root *ʿrh,* is found in Lam. 4:21. T supports the MT, but LXX, V, and S presuppose the reading *hērāʿēl,* from the root *rʿl,* "to stagger," and this reading has turned up in 1QpHab. It appears that the scribe from Qumran knew the other reading as well, however, for in his interpretation he plays on the concept of uncircumcision, explaining that the wicked priest had not circumcised the foreskin *(ʿwrlt)* of his heart. In the context of Habakkuk, the MT reading seems preferable; as in Lam. 4:21, it involves the poetic justice of the oppressor suffering the same shameful exposure to which he had subjected others.

[29]Reading *y*ᵉ*ḥittekā* with LXX, S, and T. MT has the 3 f. pl. suffix and would require the translation "the destruction of the animals which he shattered," but that would destroy the parallelism between the first two lines in the verse.

[30]See note 7 above.

[31]LXX construes both imperatives in the verse with "wood," then misreads *dwmm* as *rwmh* or *rwmy* and takes it as a third imperative, "rise up," addressed to the stone.

Commentary

[2:5] Despite the detailed instructions on what to do with the vision in Hab. 2:1–4, the actual content of the vision has not been revealed, and Hab. 2:5–20 still does not supply the missing vision. Very serious textual problems make the interpretation of Hab. 2:5a hazardous, but if v. 4 portrays the outcome of two possible responses to the vision, v. 5 seems to portray the outcome of a life not directed by God at all. The opening expression *w*ᵉ*ʾap kî* normally follows a clause introduced by *hinnēh* in a construction with the sense "behold, . . . is so, then how much more will . . . be so." Thus v. 5 appears to jump over the positive example in v. 4b and link up with the negative example in v. 4a. That may suggest that vs. 5–20 were not an original part of the same divine response to the prophet as vs. 2–4, but that they are a compositional expansion put together from other, perhaps earlier, oracles.

Assuming the correctness of the Qumran reading discussed in the textual notes, the connection in thought between v. 5 and v. 4a seems to be the following: If the fainthearted person does not trust the vision, if he considers it unreliable and thus refuses to walk in it, how much more will wealth prove deceitful to the one who seeks life by pursuing it? The arrogant man who reaches for wealth and power with insatiable, unbridled lust will not reach his goal. Thus the reliability of the vision is set over against the deceitfulness of wealth and power.

The identification of this arrogant man is initially left open; the first couple of lines could apply equally well to a greedy, arrogant Judean ruler like Jehoiakim (Jer. 22:13–17) as it could to a Babylonian king like Nebuchadnezzar. The final two lines of the verse, however, make clear that the Babylonian ruler, whose actions have already been portrayed in Hab. 1:6–10 and 1:15–17, is the model for the arrogant man. The image of him opening his maw as wide as Sheol is a mythological metaphor for a prodigious appetite. Sheol is a poetic term for the mythological place where all the living go at death (Prov. 1:12), hence the insatiability of Sheol, like that of Death, was proverbial (Prov. 27:20; 30:16). The metaphor is not simply dependent on the human experience of the universality of death, however. The image of the insatiable maw, opened wide to swallow another victim, recalls Habakkuk's earlier complaint that the wicked one was swallowing up one more righteous than himself (1:13), as well as the psalmist's similar lament (Ps. 73:9), and underscores the mythological background of this imagery in all three passages. The imagery shows clear cultural, if not literary, dependence on the specific Canaanite myth of Mot, the god of death, swallowing up Baal, the god of life and fertility.

One must read the "gathering in" of the nations and peoples in the light of that mythological background. This is no benign gathering in of the scattered and oppressed as imperialistic propaganda might wish to portray it; rather, it is a devouring of the nations that would destroy their identities as they are absorbed into the body of the Babylonian empire. The parallel to Isaiah's portrayal of Assyria's gathering together of the wealth of the nations is striking (Isa. 10:14).

[6] The nations plundered by the Babylonians, however, will have their turn to gloat. As in Isaiah's famous taunt song *(māšāl)* against the king of Babylon (Isa. 14:4–23), these nations will rise up to taunt the Babylonian king. The three terms used to designate the form of these taunts are synonyms and sometimes difficult to clearly distinguish. The term *māšāl* is derived from a root which means "to be like, to be similar," and the basic meaning of the noun seems to be "a clever, insightful comparison." It is used to designate both very short, individual proverbs and much longer poetic comparisons. Very often the comparison involved in such texts is quite disparaging; the various expressions for someone "becoming" or "being made" into a *māšāl* are uniformly negative (Deut. 28:37; 1 Sam. 10:12; 1 Kings 9:7; Jer. 24:9; Ezek. 14:8; Ps. 69:12 [11]; 2 Chron. 7:20). Such a person is belittled as a negative model to warn others away from similar behavior. Because of these negative, disparaging overtones, one can sometimes translate *māšāl* as "taunt song." The term *m^e^lîṣāh* is from the root *lîṣ,* which in the hiphil means "to mock, to deride" (Ps. 119:51), but the hiphil participle from the same root means "interpreter" or "mediator," so the noun may have a broader meaning than "satire" or "mocking poem" (BDB). In this context, however, the negative rendering is appropriate. The term *ḥîdāh* designates a riddle or an enigmatic saying.

As in Isaiah's taunt song (Isa. 14:8–20), the taunters address their oppressor with direct address. As indicated in the notes to the translation, the particle *hôy,* which introduces the so-called "woe-oracles," does not mean "woe"; it is a simple exclamation or vocative particle whose function is to get the attention of the hearer, and as such it is normally followed by direct address. It is used in laments over the dead (1 Kings 13:10; Jer. 22:18), because in such laments the dead person was often addressed directly by the mourner (2 Sam. 1:25–26; 19:1 [18:33]), but it is also used in other contexts of direct address where there is no trace of funerary gloom, as in Isa. 55:1:

> Hey *(hôy),* all you who thirst! Come to the water!
> And whoever has no money! Come, buy grain and eat!
> Come and buy grain without money!
> And without price wine and milk!

There is not the slightest justification for distinguishing the use and meaning of the particle in this passage from its use and meaning in its other occurrences. Thus any overtones one may ascribe to a *hôy*-saying must derive from the larger context and cannot be attributed to the inherent meaning of the simple particle *hôy.*

The particle is normally followed by a noun or participial phrase that characterizes the one addressed, and here the nations characterize their oppressor as one who amassed property that did not belong to him and made even heavier his burden of debt. Between those two parallel characterizations, however, the nations insert a parenthetical question characteristic of laments, "How much longer?" The question anticipates the rhetorical question in v. 7 and the positive statement of judgment in v. 8, and its parenthetical nature is expressive of the agitation of the nations, impatient to see Babylon's coming reversal of fortune. The impunity with which Babylon continues its brutal treatment of its neighbors cannot long continue.

There is a certain ambiguity in the imagery used to characterize Babylon's actions, and that ambiguity continues into v. 7. The term translated "load of debt" *('abṭîṭ)* occurs only here in the Bible, and there is a dispute whether it means "a heavy debt of loans borrowed from others" or "a weight of pledges taken to secure loans made to others." It is clearly related to the noun *'^a^bôṭ,* "an article or person pledged as security for a debt," and to the verb *'ābaṭ,* "to give or receive a pledge as security for a debt." Since the Babylonian king is characterized as amassing property that did not belong to him, one may be tempted to understand the parallel line with *'abṭîṭ* as referring to the mass of hostages that Babylon took to secure the loyalty of its vassals. On the other hand, v. 7 seems to portray Babylon as the debtor, not the creditor. The possessions it has obtained by conquest are thus seen, not as Babylon's own, but as simply on loan, as a burden of debt too heavy to pay back or to secure with pledges. The ambiguity may be an intentional device of the prophet to show the sudden fall of Babylon from creditor to debtor, from conqueror to conquered.

[7] The commentators and dictionaries are divided on whether the qal participle *nōšᵉkêkā* means "those who pay you interest = your debtors" or "those who take interest from you = your creditors." The verb is a denominative from the noun *nešek,* "interest," or perhaps more precisely, "interest deducted from a loan prior to issuing it." In such a loan, the borrower would have to sign a contract to repay the full amount of the loan, but he or she would only receive what remained of that amount after the interest had been deducted off the top. The deducted interest, normally at least 20 percent in the ancient Near East, would be a major bite out of the capital provided by the loan, and the noun *nešek* appears to reflect this observation. It probably derives from *nāšak* I, "to bite," and literally means "a bite." If this understanding of the semantic development is correct, the active participle probably means "your creditors," not "your debtors." The variation between the use of the qal and the hiphil of this verb in Deut. 23:20 [19] provides no clear evidence that the qal means "to pay interest" in contrast to the hiphil "to charge interest." Most standard English translations find no such distinction. Note the recent JPSV rendering:

> You shall not deduct *(taššîk)* interest from loans to your countrymen, whether in money or food or anything else that can be deducted *(yiššak)* as interest.

The understanding of *nōšᵉkêkā* as "your creditors" also fits the context better, since the threat of creditors arising to collect what was owed them was a constant fear of debtors, and many debtors found themselves an object of plunder to their creditors. One should probably also see in the use of the participle from the root *nāšak* II an intentional double entendre playing on the primary meaning of the root *nāšak* I. Dropping the metaphor of creditor and debtor, one could read the participle with the versions as "those who devour you."

[8] Verse 7 was introduced as a rhetorical question expecting a positive answer, but v. 8 is framed simply as a statement of fact. Together these two verses provide the explicit judgment that concludes the first *hôy*-saying. The judgment against Babylon is grounded in Babylon's own behavior. It will

receive what it dished out to others. There is poetic justice here, but whether that is inherent in the nature of reality as created by God, or whether it is the result of a particular judicial decision of God is not clearly indicated in this passage.

Rudolph argues that the expression *kol-yeter 'ammîm,* "all the remaining peoples," must mean all the nations other than Babylon, not the remaining peoples who had survived or escaped subjugation by the Babylonians, because v. 5b makes clear that no nation or people had escaped his net (p. 220). One may doubt whether the prophet was such a literalist. The language of v. 5 is clearly hyperbolic, for, in fact, neither the Medes nor the Persians who eventually destroyed Babylon were ever subjected to the Neo-Babylonian kingdom, not to speak of the many other peoples, like the Greeks, who were on the periphery of the prophet's world. It is more natural to take the expression in its context in v. 8 as a simple contrast to the "many nations" plundered by the Babylonians. The remaining peoples, those who have survived or escaped the plundering meted out by the Babylonians, will in turn plunder Babylon.

The reason for this judgment on the Babylonians is then elaborated by a kind of addendum to the verse, which spells out what was involved in Babylon's plundering of the nations. The same lines are also found in v. 17, but there is no justification for deleting the addendum in v. 8 as a late gloss. Babylon's sin included the shedding of human blood in the killing that goes with war and conquest, but the reference to the "violence against the land, the city, and all its inhabitants" suggests a more profound understanding of the evil of wars of conquest. Such conflicts do violence to the ecology of the countryside, the culture of the city, and the well-being of even those inhabitants of the conquered territory who survive the bloodshed. The curse of war is far more pervasive than death, and in some ways the survivors feel its violence more profoundly than the dead.

[9] The second *hôy*-saying characterizes the oppressor as one who acquires gain unjustly in a vain attempt to construct a secure abode for himself. Embedded already in the characterization is an intimation of the judgment to come. The pursuit of unjust gain, far from bringing the security it was intended to buy, will result in the opposite, in the ruin of the oppressor's house. In isolation, v. 9 could be seen as a characterization of a Judean ruler like Jehoiakim, but, taken with v. 10 and the larger context, it clearly refers to the Babylonian oppressor. Unjust gain, then, must refer to the tribute and plunder that the Babylonians took from the conquered nations, and the prophet accurately portrays the motivation for that imperialistic oppression as an attempt to gain security for oneself. The reference to setting his nest in the height as well as the later references to building a city may allude to Nebuchadnezzar's impressive building activity in Babylon, his capital city.

[10] Verse 10 develops further the thought briefly anticipated in v. 9. Though the Babylonian ruler thought he was planning for the security of his house or dynasty, his plans would actually bring shame upon it. His destruction of other peoples, far from enhancing his own security, was a sin against himself. Between the lines one may read the thought of v. 8: as Babylon had done to others, so others would do to it. In contrast to v. 8, however, that implicit fate cannot be understood here as a simple act-consequence sequence inherent in the structure of reality, since the logical connection to v. 11 with its reference to witnesses implies an impending judicial decision of God.

[11] The Babylonian will not find security in the building he constructed by oppression, for even the inert material used in that construction will cry out in witness against him. The verb *zāʻaq,* "to cry out," is normally used for a cry for help that the oppressed direct either to a human authority (2 Sam. 19:29 [28]; Prov. 21:13) or to God (Ex. 2:23; Judg. 3:9; Jer. 11:11; Hab. 1:2; Pss. 22:5 [4]; 107:13; passim). When the cry of the oppressed was stilled only by death, particularly by violent death, there was the conception in Israel that nature itself might take up the cry. Though it uses the synonym *ṣāʻaq* rather than *zāʻaq,* God's response to Cain after he had murdered Abel expresses well this conception: "What have you done? Listen! The blood of your brother is crying to me from the ground!" (Gen. 4:10). Job expresses the same idea, using a noun derived from our verb *zāʻaq,* when he prays that his unjust suffering not be hidden from the eyes of heaven (Job 16:18–19):

> May the earth not cover up my blood,
> May there be no place for my cry *(zaʻᵃqātî).*
> Even now in the heavens is my witness,
> The one who testifies for me is in the heights.

Job also gives expression to this conception in his oath of innocence (Job 31:38–40):

> If my land cries out *(tizʻāq)* against me,
> And its furrows weep together,
> If I have eaten its produce without payment,
> And the life of its owners I have made to expire,
> Then instead of wheat, may thorns come forth,
> And instead of barley, darnel.

The verb *ʻānāh,* "to answer," is often used to express Yahweh's positive intervention in response to a cry for help (see Micah 3:4), but that cannot be the meaning of the verb in Hab. 2:11. The "response" of the beam is simply a parallel action to the "cry" of the stone, just as the "weeping" of the furrows parallels the "crying out" of the land in Job 31:38. If the parallelism in Hab. 2:11 conveys anything more than the normal seconding characteristic of Hebrew poetry, it may suggest that the beam "confirms" the testimony of the rock. Two witnesses continue to cry out against the oppression of the Babylonian, even after he has cut off many peoples. The city built on oppression will not be secure, for even if the accusing voice of the oppressed peoples is suppressed, the very stones and beams of which the city is constructed will take up their cry, and the implication is that God will not ignore indefinitely such a continuous cry (cf. Gen. 18:20–21).

[**12**] Since v. 11 threatens that stones and beams will cry out against the oppressor but does not give the content of their cry, it is tempting to read this third *hôy*-saying as a direct quotation of these inert objects. In any case, this *hôy*-saying continues the characterization of the oppressor as one who builds a city through injustice, but it is an incomplete or elliptical saying in that it is not concluded with an explicit threat or a word of judgment. Such elliptical *hôy*-sayings are not uncommon, particularly in a series of *hôy*-sayings, where the larger context would remove any possible doubt that a threat is implicit in the very characterization of the addressee's behavior (cf. Isa. 5:18–24). The formulation of the characterization is very similar to and probably dependent on Micah's attack on Judean officials, whom he accused of "building Zion by bloodshed and Jerusalem by iniquity" (Micah 3:10), but Habakkuk has clearly adapted the formulation with the Babylonian oppressor in mind.

[**13–14**] The meaning of the initial question in v. 13a is not immediately transparent. Two possibilities suggest themselves. "Are not these things from Yahweh of Hosts?" could be understood to mean that Babylon's oppression of the other nations was the work of Yahweh, since Babylon was his agent for punishing the nations for their sins (cf. Isa. 10:5–6; Hab. 1:5ff.). Or one could understand it as conveying a thought similar to Ps. 127:1–2:

> If Yahweh does not build the house,
> Its builders labor in vain on it.
> If Yahweh does not guard a city,
> The guard watches in vain.

In other words, Hab. 2:13a would mean that the building of a city and its protection depends on Yahweh of Hosts.

If one adopted the first interpretation, Hab. 2:13b would mean that the nations oppressed by the Babylonians did not enjoy the fruit of their labors, because God was punishing them. If one adopted the second interpretation, Hab. 2:13b would mean that all the efforts the oppressed nations had spent on building Babylon would come to nought, because God was not protecting that city built on blood. Either thought is appropriate enough in itself, but neither fits the context of the prophet's portrayal of the Babylonian tyrant as a wicked oppressor of other peoples. In that context it would make little sense to suggest that the peoples were just getting what they deserved. The second interpretation would be easier, but it does not fit well either, because the oppressed nations would hardly be sad at the failure of their labor, if it meant the fall of Babylon. In the context of the prophet's characterization of wicked Babylon, the meaning of Hab. 2:13b can only be that Babylon's oppression of the other nations has prevented these nations from enjoying the fruits of their own labors. It is an indictment of the selfish cruelty of the Babylonians. If this third reading of Hab. 2:13b is the only one that fits the context, then Hab. 2:13a must be considered a late gloss, added after the book of Habakkuk had already been put together as a compositionally unified work.

One may hazard a guess as to the reason for the gloss. Habakkuk 2:13b, in a slightly variant form, is either quoted in the later oracle in Jer. 51:58 or tacked on to it as a gloss, and the new context in Jeremiah forces a new meaning on the bicolon. The destruction of Babylon predicted in the same verse implies that the labors of the nations on behalf of Babylon will come to nought, but there is no hint in the Jeremiah context that such labor was forced on the nations by Babylonian oppression. On the contrary, the context in Jeremiah suggests that the nations had a vested interest in the stability of Babylon. They are portrayed as gazing on Bel of Babylon with joy (Jer. 51:44), but their joy in Bel and their investment of labor for the security of Babylon will be brought to nought by the fall of Babylon and its gods. Apparently a reader influenced by this use of the bicolon in Jer. 51:58 wanted to impose the same interpretation on the couplet in Hab. 2:13b; to do so, he glossed it with the introductory question in Hab. 2:13a, thus changing an indictment of Babylon for its treatment of the nations into a comment on the futility of the nations' attempt to build the city of Babylon.

The same glossator is probably also responsible for inserting Hab. 2:14, which is just a partial and somewhat garbled quotation of Isa. 11:9. In the light of the glossator's obvious attempt to read Hab. 2:13b in the manner of Jer. 51:58, Hab. 2:14 should be understood almost as an expression of praise to Yahweh over the coming fall of Babylon. Yahweh's destruction of Babylon will make God's glory transparent to the whole world.

If my analysis is correct, both these glosses miss the point of the original *hôy*-saying in Hab. 2:12 + 13b and of the larger compositional unit in which it is placed. Such an observation makes very problematic the recent claim of some canonical critics that the final form of the Masoretic text, including glosses and pre-Jamnia textual corruptions, should control biblical interpretation. One can interpret what the glosses in Hab. 2:13a, 14 mean, but one cannot interpret the whole context of Hab. 2:5–20 in the light of these glosses, because the glossator, who was concerned with a single bicolon that he knew from another prophetic book, did not interpret, much less understand, the whole text. If one wants to interpret Hab. 2:5–20 as a unified composition, one must bracket out such secondary glosses that confuse the argument.

With these glosses bracketed out, the third *hôy*-saying simply addresses the Babylonian tyrant as one who builds his city by oppressing others and so deprives them of the expected fruits of their own labor. No judgment is explicitly threatened, but the nature of the characterization and the larger context makes evident enough that such behavior will not go unpunished.

[15] The fourth *hôy*-saying addresses the Babylonian oppressor as one who has made his neighbors drunk so that he can look upon their nakedness. This characterization of the oppressor is clearly to be understood metaphorically, however, since the intoxicating agent that the oppressor gives his neighbors to drink is identified as the oppressor's anger. The prophet is not concerned here with the evils of alcohol abuse, but merely uses imagery drawn from a particularly shocking abuse of it to illustrate the evils of imperial power, which is Habakkuk's real concern. His metaphor exposes the disgusting brutality of imperialistic conquest, which, after rendering the conquered peoples helpless, systematically strips away their dignity and honor for the conqueror's own selfish, shameful, and insatiable gratification. Though the particular word Habakkuk uses for nakedness *(mā'ôr)* occurs only here, synonyms from related roots are often used metaphorically elsewhere either to describe the weak points in a country's defenses (Gen. 42:9, 12) or to describe the shameful treatment of conquered lands or cities (Isa. 47:1–3; Nahum 3:5). The metaphor was rooted in the actual practice of leading away prisoners of war naked (Isa. 20:4; 2 Chron. 28:15; see *ANEP,* nos. 358–359), not to mention the widespread sexual abuse of women captives characteristic of ancient imperial conquests.

The oracle against Babylon in Jeremiah 51 picks up this metaphor, but just as it did with the bicolon in Hab. 2:13b, it gives the metaphor a new twist (Jer. 51:7):

> Babylon was a golden cup in the hand of Yahweh,
> It made all the earth drunk.
> From its wine the nations drunk,
> That is why the nations behave as if mad.

Though both Habakkuk and Jeremiah promise that Babylon's turn for punishment will come, the two prophets give different emphases to their treatments of Babylon's imperial conquests. Jeremiah stresses Babylon's role as the agent for God's punishment of the nations, while Habakkuk lays more stress on Babylon's abuse of its power.

[16] The first line of v. 16 is similar to vs. 9b and 10a in that it describes the actions of the Babylonians as accomplishing precisely the opposite of what they were intended to accomplish. Babylon's imperial conquests were for the glory of Babylon, its gods, and its king, but the prophet claims that those actions have sated Babylon with shame, not brought it the glory it desired. There are possibly two ideas in this statement. On the one hand, there is an implicit redefinition of the term glory. The imperial understanding of glory based on self-elevation at the expense of others is rejected in favor of an understanding rooted in the concept of justice. Babylon has sated itself with shame, because its treatment of other nations, far from being glorious, is inherently shameful. The thought is similar to Jeremiah's definition of what constitutes true kingship (Jer. 22:15–16). On the other hand, there is the threat that Babylon's actions will bring the same fate upon itself that it has meted out to others. Babylon has sated itself with shame, because God, in retaliation for its actions, is about to make Babylon drink from the same cup it had administered to other nations.

The command in v. 10b is a graphic resumption of the metaphor in v. 15. It is Babylon's turn to become drunk and expose its nakedness. The cup of God's anger will come round to it, and it will then experience shame instead of the bogus glory to which it has become accustomed. This metaphor of the wine cup to designate the punishment God is about to pour down the throat of those who have angered him became a very popular image at the beginning of the Babylonian exile, and it is difficult to be sure who first coined it (Isa. 51:17–22; Jer. 25:15–28; 49:12; 51:7; Ezek. 23:30–34; Lam. 4:21).

[17] Verse 17a ties this threatened judgment to Babylon's violent treatment of the Lebanon. As Rudolph has shown (p. 228), this probably refers to Nebuchadnezzar's exploitation of the forests of the Lebanon for his building activities. Such exploitation was seen in Judah as a mark of hubris (Isa. 14:8; 37:24), because those forests were thought of as Yahweh's own (Ps. 104:16). One can see traces here of the ancient conception of the cedar forest of the gods attested, among other places, in the Huwawa/Humbaba incident of the Gilgamesh Epic (Tablet V, *ANET* 82–83, 504–505). Because Nebuchadnezzar had cut down these forests, Babylon would be covered, not by the shade of the cedars (Ps. 80:11 [10]) in their fine buildings, but by the same violence that had desecrated the sanctity of God's forests. The destruction of the animals could refer either to the abuse of work animals in transporting the lumber from the Lebanon to Babylon or to the destruction of wildlife in the forest regions decimated by Nebuchadnezzar's lumbering activity. In either case, the verse points to humanity's abuse of its authority over the rest of creation (Gen. 1:28; Ps. 8:6–9 [5–8]). It is one thing to rule over creation, respecting it as God's creation entrusted to one for the moment (cf. Deut. 22:6–7; 25:4; Prov. 12:10; 27:23); it is quite another thing to exploit it unmercifully as though it belonged to one absolutely, as though one were not accountable for it to its creator. What the Babylonian has meted out to these animals, he will receive in turn.

The last half of v. 17 is also found in v. 8, so some critics consider it a secondary gloss here, inserted to provide a stronger basis for judgment than the abuse of forests and animals mentioned in v. 17a. That is possible, but the bicolon supplements rather than clashes with v. 17a, so the repetition in v. 17b may go back to the prophet or editor responsible for the compositional unity of the book. It need not be taken as a secondary gloss.

[18] The placement of v. 18 is very peculiar. It is not a part of the preceding *hôy*-saying, but it comes before the introductory *hôy* of the following saying (2:19), with which it shares the same theme of the folly of idolatry. Many scholars transpose v. 18 after v. 19, therefore, assuming that it has been accidentally displaced in the course of textual transmission. Others, noting its more prosaic character, treat it as a later, but inappropriately inserted, gloss. Still others treat all of vs. 18–20 as a secondary insertion. Rudolph argues for the authenticity of both the verse and its present placement (p. 229). According to him, it was Habakkuk's response to those members of the pro-Babylonian party in Judah who defended Nebuchadnezzar as the agent of Yahweh or who pointed to Nebuchadnezzar's support of the Babylonian cult as a sign of Nebuchadnezzar's piety. Against any such justification of the Babylonian ruler, Habakkuk underlines the fact that Nebuchadnezzar worshiped dead idols, not Yahweh, the living God. Rudolph's explanation may have some merit in providing the reason for the inclusion of the final *hôy*-saying against idolatry in this series of *hôy*-sayings, but it fails as a convincing explanation for the placement of v. 18 before v. 19. Verse 18 needs an introduction; it can hardly stand alone to mark the transition to a new line of thought. As such it would be both awkward and unparalleled. It must either be regarded as a misplaced gloss or transposed after v. 19, where it would fit well.

The initial question in the verse is a rhetorical question that calls for a negative answer. The carved image has not helped the one who carved it. Scholars have debated the meaning of the expression *môreh šāqer,* translated here as "false oracle," literally "teacher of a lie." The same expression is used in Isa. 9:14 [15] to characterize a prophet who gives false oracles, but, since Habakkuk links it with molten image as a parallel expression, it probably alludes here to the use of idols in obtaining oracles (see Hos. 4:12; Isa. 46:7). In addition to the use of the term *môreh* in proper names for places where oracles were customarily given (*'ēlôn môreh* [Gen. 12:6] or *'ēlônê mōreh* [Deut. 11:30], "the terebinth(s) of the oracle giver," and *gib'at hammôreh* [Judg. 7:1], "the hill of the oracle giver"), note the use of the hiphil impf. *yôreh* in the sense of "give an oracle" in v. 19. The point of Habakkuk's characterization of the image with this expression is to underscore the folly of seeking an oracle from such an idol. It was a giver of false oracles not only because the oracles were untrue but also because such an idol was dumb, unable to speak; the real source of the oracle was not the idol at all, but the humans who made the idol and manipulated it. Thus it was folly to put one's trust in such a product of one's own imagination (cf. Jer. 10:3–15; Isa. 44:9–20; 46:5–7).

[19] The fifth and final *hôy*-saying in the series begins at v. 19. It characterizes the Babylonian conqueror as one who foolishly tries to waken inert stone and wood in order to obtain an oracle from his image. Habakkuk asks whether such an image can give an oracle, and he answers his own question by asserting that elaborate gold and silver plating on the outside of the image cannot make up for the lack of breath and life inside it. Verse 18 would make an appropriate continuation of this thought, and unless it is a later gloss, its original position must have been here rather than before v. 19.

Even if v. 18 is deleted as a secondary gloss, however, there is no convincing reason to treat vs. 19–20 as secondary. The fifth *hôy*-saying, with or without the transposed v. 18, lacks an explicit threat of judgment, but the same is also true of the third saying (2:12–13); as noted there, such incomplete or elliptical *hôy*-sayings are not at all uncommon. Other scholars have argued that such a saying against idolatry would not be appropriate in the mouths of the nations conquered by Babylon to whom these sayings are attributed (Hab. 2:6), but v. 19 is so distant from v. 6 that one may doubt whether the prophet was still aware of his fictive spokesmen. However, it should be noted that Judah was among the nations and peoples conquered by Babylon, and if "all of them" (2:6) took up a taunt song against Babylon, it should not be surprising to find in it words appropriate to the conquered Judeans. Contra Van der Woude (p. 50), the saying hardly contains a humble confession of the Gentile nations who renounce their idolatry in favor of Yahweh. Finally, contrary to many scholars, the saying's treatment of idolatry does fit in the context of Habakkuk's argument; the theme is not at all isolated or unprepared for in the book. Earlier in the book, Habakkuk had characterized the Babylonian conqueror as one who made his own strength into his god (Hab. 1:11), as one who sacrificed and burned incense to his tools of conquest (2:16). The new characterization of the conqueror as one who depends on divine images, which are no more than the work of the craftsman's hands, paid for by the crown, does not differ radically from these earlier characterizations. In each characterization the Babylonian has deified what is not divine, and in the long run, trust in any such false god will prove deceitful.

That suggests the reason for putting this particular attack on idolatry as the last in the series of *hôy*-sayings. Given Babylon's conquest of the other nations, including Judah, Habakkuk's Judean audience might be inclined to accept the mistaken belief that the gods of Babylon had proved themselves superior to Yahweh and that there was therefore little reason to hope that Yahweh would actually ever bring Babylon to justice. Against such a resigned acceptance of imperial injustice, Habakkuk employs humor polemically, making fun of the gods of Babylon as mere lifeless objects, the work of human hands. Such dumb idols cannot give reliable oracles to direct the policies of the Babylonian court, much less, the prophet implies, save Babylon from the coming judgment.

[20] In contrast, the true God, Yahweh, remains enthroned in his holy temple. The implication is that he can and will act decisively, therefore the whole world had best keep a respectful silence before him. It is unclear whether Habakkuk has in mind God's heavenly abode in distinction from the temple in Jerusalem that Nebuchadnezzar desecrated in 597 B.C.; but if this composition dates prior to 587/6, when the Jerusalem temple was completely destroyed, one may well doubt whether the prophet made such a distinction between the earthly temple and its heavenly prototype. The verse serves as a transition to the vision in chapter 3, a vision that may be understood as arising in the context of continued communal worship in the temple, and that suggests that Habakkuk included the earthly temple in Jerusalem in his conception of Yahweh's holy temple. The point is that Yahweh had not deserted his people. Despite his apparent silence, he still remains with them; he has not lost control of their destiny. One should wait upon him in the awed silence that is often the most appropriate expression of true worship.

7. The Vision: 3:1–19

3:1 The prayer of Habakkuk the prophet. In the mode of Shigionoth.[1]

2 Yahweh, I have heard the report[2] about you,
I am awed,[3] Yahweh, by your work.
When the years[4] draw near,[5] revive[6] it,[7]
When the years[4] draw near,[5] make it[8] known,[9]
In agitation[10] remember to show mercy.[11]
3 God[12] is coming from Teman,[13]
And the Holy One from Mount Paran.[14] [Selah.][15]
His majesty covered the[16] heavens,
And his glory[17] filled[18] the[16] earth.
4 Brightness[19] like lightning[20] appears,[21]
A double-pronged bolt projects from his hand,[22]
He places[23] the covering[24] for his might.
5 Before him marches Plague,[25]
And Fever[26] goes forth at his heels.[27]
6 He stood and shook[28] the earth,
He looked and startled[29] the nations.

The ancient[30] mountains were shattered,
The primeval hills sank down,[31]
His are the primeval routes.[32]
7 Instead of the iniquity that I saw,[33]
The tents of Cushan quiver,
The curtains of the land of Midian.
8 Is it against River[34] that burns,[35] O Yahweh,[36]
Against[37] River,[34] your anger,
Against Sea, your rage,
That you mount[38] your horses,[39]
Your chariot[40] of victory?[41]
9 Indeed[42] you bare[43] your bow,
You sate[44] the shafts[45] of the bowstring.[46] [Selah.]
You split open[47] the earth with rivers.[48]
10 Having seen you, mountains[49] writhed,
The clouds[50] poured down[51] waters.
The Deep gave its thunder,
It lifted[52] its hands[53] on high.[54]
11 ⟨The brightness of the light⟩ of the Sun ⟨ceased⟩,[55]
The moon stayed in its lordly abode.[56]
For light[57] your arrows dart about,[58]
For brightness[57] the lightning of your spear.[59]
12 In indignation you tread[60] the earth,
In anger you trample the nations.
13 You went forth for the salvation[61] of your people,
For the deliverance[62] of your anointed one.[63]
You struck the back[64] of the wicked one,
You laid him bare,[65] from bottom[66] to neck.[67] [Selah.]
14 You pierced[68] his[69] head with your[70] shafts.[71]
[72][His followers[73] you blew away,[74]
Scattering them[75] in a secret place[76]
As food[77] for the sharks of the sea.[78]][72]
15 You trod upon Sea with your horses,[79]
On the surge[80] of many waters.
16 I heard,[81] and my bowels churned,
At the sound my lips quivered,[82]
Rottenness[83] entered into my bones,
And beneath me my steps[84] wavered.[85]
I will wait quietly[86] for the day[87] of affliction
To come upon the people who attack us.[88]
17 Though[89] the fig does not bud,[90]
And there be no produce on the vines,
The olive yield fails,
And the fields[91] produce no food,
Though one cut off[92] the sheep from the fold,[93]

And there be no cattle in the stalls,
18 Yet I will exult in Yahweh,
I will rejoice in the god of my salvation.
19 Yahweh my lord is[94] my strength,
He makes my feet like the hinds',[95]
On my high places[96] he lets me tread.

For the leader.[97] With instrumental music.[98]

Textual Notes

[1]The term *šigyōnôt* is one of those words often found in the superscriptions of Psalms whose exact meanings are not known. It is presumably the plural of *šiggāyôn,* which occurs in Ps. 7:1, apparently as the name of a genre of sung prayer or lament. It has been associated with the Akkadian *šēgu,* a type of lament prayer, but the contents of Habakkuk 3 bear only faint resemblance to either Psalm 1 or the Akkadian *šēgu.* LXX may have read *nᵉgînôt* as in v. 19, since it translates with ǭdē, "song," in both places. Apart from Barb, which follows the LXX, the other Greek versions, V, S, and T all connect the word with the root *šgh* or *šgg,* "to commit a sin of ignorance or inadvertence."

[2]S mistakenly reads *šmk,* "your name," instead of *šm'k,* "your report."

[3]LXX and Barb contain a secondary double reading, due apparently to the easy confusion between the form *yārē'tî,* "I feared," and the form *wᵉrā'îtî,* "and I saw:"

> Lord, I heard your report and I feared;
> [Lord,] I saw your works and I was astounded.

The need to redress the poetic imbalance created by the double reading of *yr'ty* led in turn to the introduction of the final verb, "to be astounded." V, S, and T reflect only the verb *yārē'tî,* "I feared." The verb is introduced by the *waw*-conjunctive in V and S, but that is probably secondary, influenced by the interpretation derived from the double reading in LXX. Rudolph and others emend the MT to *rā'îtî,* "I saw," following the second reading of LXX, on the basis that it provides a better parallel to "I heard" (p. 233), but the argument is quite problematic. In public laments, one may refer to having "heard" of Yahweh's former work recited in the cult (Ps. 44:2 [1]), or one may remember and reflect on Yahweh's former work (Pss. 77:13 [12]; 143:5), but that is not parallel to "seeing" it. To "see" Yahweh's work implies one's own experience of his action (Pss. 90:16; 95:9). The contrast is expressed very well in Ps. 48:9 [8]: "As we have heard *(šāma'nû),* thus we have seen *(rā'înû).*" The psalmist, speaking for his cultic community, claims that they have now seen in their own experience the kind of divine deliverance of Jerusalem that they had long heard about in the cult. Habakkuk is reflecting on Yahweh's former work that he has heard about in the cult; he has not yet "seen" it in his own experience, or he would not ask in the following verse for God to revive it and make it known. "To fear" or "to be in awe," on the other hand, fits quite well in the context. When one hears Yahweh's mighty work recited in the cult, the appropriate response is fear or awe and a desire to see those ancient marvels repeated in the present. The MT clearly offers the better text.

[4]LXX and Barb have a double reading for *šānîm* in the first line, which they render twice. In the first rendering, they treat the Hebrew word as though it were *šᵉnayim,* "two." In the second rendering of the first line and in the second line, they read it as "years" or "season, set time."

[5]LXX and Barb also have a double reading for *bᵉqereb* in the first line. The first reading is simply *en mesǭ,* "in the midst of," but the second reading and the reading for the second line apparently vocalize as *biqrōb,* the qal inf. const. of the root *qrb,* "to draw near": *en tǭ eggizein ta etē,* "when the years draw near;" *en tǭ pareinai ton kairon,* "when the set time arrives." If the MT vocalization were correct, the expression "in the midst of the years" might be taken by analogy with the expression *baḥᵃṣî yāmāw/y,* "in the middle of his/my days," as a request to shorten the appointed time for Yahweh's intervention (Mowinckel, *TZ* 9 [1953]: 10). This is preferable to Hiebert's translation, "through the years," which is based on the mistaken notion that the expression occurs in a description of past events rather than in a prayer for Yahweh's future intervention (HSM 38:13). It is better, however, to revocalize as the infinitive *biqrōb* with the LXX. So also Humbert (p. 59) and Albright, who has pointed to parallels to this construction in other poetic passages ("Psalm," 13).

[6]MT has the piel imperative of the verb *ḥyh,* "to bring to life, revive, preserve life." LXX and Barb have a double reading. The first rendering of the first line, *en mesǭ dyo zǭōn gnōsthēsę̄,* "in the midst of two living creatures you will reveal yourself," apparently reads *ḥywt ḥwh/ḥwwt/ḥwyt* instead of MT's *ḥyyhw.* The "living creatures" *(ḥayyôt)* were probably understood as the two cherubim that stood on either side of the ark of the covenant in the inner sanctum of the temple, where God was thought to reveal himself (Ex. 25:22). The variant *dyo zōōn,* "two lifetimes," simply exploits another possible meaning of *ḥayyôt,* and this may also be behind the reading in S, "in the midst of the years of life." The verb *gnōsthēsę̄* in LXX and Barb's first rendering of the first line and the verb *epignōsthēsę̄* in the second rendering of the first line both presuppose a piel imperative *(ḥawwēh),* a piel infinitive absolute used as an imperative *(ḥawwôt),* or, far less likely because of the tense, a piel perfect 2 m. s. *(ḥawwîtā)* from the root *ḥwh,* "to declare, make known."

The parallelism with the hiphil of *yd‘,* "to make known," might suggest the emendation to *ḥawwêhû,* "declare it," but the MT reading offers the more striking imagery and probably should be retained. An emendation to the perfect *ḥawwîtā,* "you declared," would not work, because one needs an object with the verb, and the context of the prayer calls for an imperative or future tense. Hiebert's emendation to *ḥiyyîtā,* "(through the years) you sustained life" (HSM 38:13) does not work because of this contextual requirement, and one may also question whether it provides an adequate parallel to "you revealed yourself."

[7]Humbert's argument for deleting the following line as a mere doublet of this line (pp. 58–59) ignores the widespread presence of this abc/abd style of poetic repetition elsewhere in Hebrew poetry as well as its popularity in the Ugaritic poetry of the second millennium (Albright, "Psalm," 3–8). Both lines are original.

[8]The suffix on *ḥayyêhû* need not be repeated with the following verb that stands in parallel to it.

[9]LXX, Barb, and S read the niphal imperfect *tiwwādēa‘,* "you will reveal yourself," but that is probably a misreading caused by the absence of the suffix on the second of two parallel verbs. MT offers the better text.

[10]LXX and Barb have a double reading that appears to have arisen out of the ambiguity of the unsuffixed Hebrew form *bᵉrōgez.* In addition to *en orgę̄,* "in wrath," they have the reading *en tǭ tarachthēnai tēn psychēn mou,* "in my soul being troubled." Rudolph explains the latter reading as based on a corruption of the Hebrew text from *brgz rḥm* to *brgz rḥy,* which was read as *birgōz rūḥî* (p. 233). There is no evidence that *eleous (=rḥm)* was missing in any Greek text, however, and if the Hebrew text *brgz rḥy rḥm* ever existed, it probably originated because the unsuffixed form *brgz* left open the possibility of interpreting *rgz* as either the "agitation" of Yahweh or as the "agitation" of the prophet or his community. S has "in anger let your mercy be remembered," and T has "in the midst of your anger remember mercy." (See the commentary for the possibility that Habakkuk was exploiting the ambiguity of the form to express a double entendre.)

[11]The versions all translate *rḥm* as a nominal form, but MT's *rahēm* is the piel infinitive absolute.

[12]The word for God here is the singular form *'ᵉlôah,* not the normal word *'ᵉlōhîm.*

[13]Barb, Theodotion, V, and T interpret the construction with the proper name as meaning "from the south." This is probably due to the widespread use of the term in the Bible as a simple directional designation (Ex. 26:35; 27:9; Josh. 12:3; passim), but this is a secondary use of the original proper name. Teman came to mean "south" because Teman lay far to the south of Palestine. Cf. the texts from Kuntillet ‘Ajrud,

which speak of "Yahweh of Teman" *(yhwh tmn)* and of the theophany of "God when he shines forth" *(wbzrḥ . . . 'l;* see M. Weinfeld, "Kuntillet 'Ajrud Inscriptions and Their Significance," in *Studi epigrafici e linguistici* [1984], 121–130).

[14]LXX interprets the proper name as "(from) the shaded, thickly wooded *(daseos)* mountain." Rudolph attributes this rather strange rendering to the equation of Mount Paran and Seir (Deut. 33:2), and the interpretation of Seir based on the LXX rendering of *śē'ār,* "hair" (Gen. 25:25; 2 Kings 1:8) and *śā'īr,* "hairy" (Gen. 27:11, 23) with the Greek word *dasys,* "shaggy, hairy, thickly wooded" (p. 233). Others assume the translator associated the name with the Hebrew noun *pō'rāh,* "bough," but the noun is never translated in the LXX with either *kataskios* or *dasys.*

[15]"Selah" is a technical Hebrew term found elsewhere only in the Psalms. Its exact meaning is unknown, though it seems to have something to do with the musical recitation of the Psalms. It is clearly a technical rubric of some kind and not a part of the actual text of the prayer. It is omitted by S and one manuscript of Barb.

[16]"Heavens" does not have the article in Hebrew, and the article before "earth" is probably secondary, introduced by dittography of the final *h* on *ml'h.* The article is rare in old poetry and often secondary.

[17]The word *tᵉhillāh* normally means "praise," and that is its traditional rendering in this passage. "Praise" seems a weak parallel to "majesty," however, and a number of scholars have suggested that the word used here is not the normal word for praise, but a homonym meaning "splendor," derived from the hiphil of the root *hll* I, "to shine" (Rudolph, 234; Eaton, "Origin," 148; Van der Woude, 60). "Glory" or "splendor" is the appropriate translation in this passage, but one may question whether that requires the assumption of a separate noun from a different root. The same term could be used to designate the glorious deeds or qualities for which one praises God as well as to designate the act of ascribing praise to God (BDB, 240).

[18]"Earth" could also be taken as the subject of the verb *ml'h:* "the earth was filled with his praise" (LXX, Barb, V, S, and T), but taking "praise" as the subject provides a better parallel to the preceding line.

[19]LXX, V, S, and T all add a suffix to the noun, "his brightness," but Barb gives a similar interpretation of the sense of the line with a dative expression, "brightness of light is to him *(autǭ).*" This variation may suggest that the suffix reflected in the versions represents an interpretative tradition rather than a variant Hebrew Vorlage. None of the ancient translations give any support to attempts to emend the noun into a verb form (Albright, "Psalm," 13–14; Hiebert, HSM 38:17), and the comparison of *nōgah,* "brightness," to *'ôr,* "light, daylight, lightning," is not a

serious objection; while the two terms can be used in parallel (Isa. 60:3, 19; Amos 5:20; Hab. 3:11), they are not identical. The only question is what kind of light Habakkuk was referring to with this word.

[20]Hiebert suggests translating *'ôr* as "flame" rather than "light" based on Isa. 31:9 (HSM 38:17), a suggestion that effectively undercuts his emendation of *nōgah,* since the comparison "a brightness like fire" would present no problems. The translation "lightning," suggested by Eaton ("Origin," 148), is preferable, however, since *'ôr* is associated with lightning a few verses later in Hab. 3:11, and it clearly occurs several times with the meaning "lightning" in Elihu's similar portrayal of God's theophany in a thunderstorm (Job 36:30, 32; 37:11, 15).

[21]The feminine verb form *tihyeh* has occasioned suspicion, since its subject, *nōgah,* "brightness," appears by form to be masculine. None of the other biblical passages in which the noun occurs actually demonstrate that *nōgah* is masculine, however, and one cannot always depend on the form of a noun to indicate its grammatical gender. Moreover, the feminine form of the verb could be by attraction to the noun *'ôr,* which is feminine (Jer. 13:16; Job 36:22). Eaton correctly noted that this context requires the ingressive, assertive sense of the verb *hāyāh* ("Origin," 148).

[22]This line is an ancient crux, but the versions offer no support for emending the line. S's peculiar reading, "in the city of his hands," probably results from inner Syriac corruption, and the slight variations in LXX, Barb, and V do not suggest a variant Hebrew Vorlage. The MT literally reads, "there are two horns from his hand to him," i.e., "he has two horns from his hand." Both the term *qarnayim,* "two horns," and the phrase *miyyādô,* "from his hand," have been felt as very serious problems. Albright radically emended the whole verse ("Psalm," 12–14), and Hiebert treats this line as hopelessly corrupt (HSM 38:5, 17–18). Others treat *qarnayim* as "rays of light," based on the use of the denominative verb *qāran* in Ex. 34:29–35, and, while their translations vary in detail, the general sense assumed is "rays of light radiate from its/his side." Despite William Propp's strong case against the meaning "shine" for the verb *qāran* in Exodus 34 (*CBQ* 49 [1987]: 375–386; *BibRev* 4/1 [1988]: 30–37), one cannot dismiss the early exegetical tradition of the versions as easily as he does. Nonetheless, the traditional interpretation of Hab. 3:4, based on this assumed meaning of *qāran,* has seemed forced. Eaton has resolved this problem by an appeal to ancient Near Eastern iconography ("Origin," 148). Ancient Near Eastern representations of the storm god typically portray him with a stylized lightning bolt in his hand. Normally three prongs of the stylized "forked lightning" extend above his hand, while below his hand the bolt may be either forked or a single spear (*ANEP,* nos. 490, 500, 501, 531, 532, 538),

but two-pronged representations of lightning are also attested (*ANEP,* nos. 519–521, 703). The prongs extending above the hand of the storm god look like horns, and whatever the meaning of the verb *qāran,* an Israelite describing such a symbolic representation of lightning could very well refer to these prongs as *qarnayim,* "two horns." T's translation moves in the direction of this interpretation: "he revealed himself, and lightning flashes *(zīqûqîn)* went forth from his glorious chariot." That portrayal recalls the ancient representation that shows the storm god sitting in his chariot preceded by a goddess who stands upon the chariot team holding three-pronged lightning bolts in both her hands (*ANEP,* no. 689).

[23]MT has *wᵉšām,* "and there," but LXX's *etheto,* "he placed," and S's *nsym,* "he places," both presuppose a form of the verb *śûm/śîm,* "to place." V and T support MT, and Barb has a double reading showing both options: "There *(ekei)* the power of his glory was supported *(epestēriktai).*" Eaton's attempt to defend the MT reading by reference to Job 36:32 ("Origin," 148–149) produces an unconvincing interpretation for both passages. One should emend with LXX and P to either *wᵉśām* or *yāśēm.*

[24]The noun *ḥebyôn* gave the versions difficulty. LXX derives it from *ḥābab,* "to love," and translates it as *agapēsin,* "love." Barb may represent the word with *doxa,* "glory," in its very free rendering "the power of his glory." S's "in the countryside" makes no sense. The later Greek translations, V, and T all derive the noun from the verb *ḥābāh,* "to withdraw, hide." The noun probably means "hiding place" and refers to the veil or envelope of dark clouds and gloom within which God hides his glory (see Ps. 18:12).

[25]The Hebrew word *dāber* means "plague," but it is personified here as the proper name for a demon of plague who travels in Yahweh's royal entourage. LXX and Theodotion read the Hebrew word as *dābār,* "word," but this is obviously a misreading. Barb and the other Greek translations translate *dāber* more appropriately with a number of different Greek terms for "death" or "pestilence." S and V translate the term as "death," and T renders "the angel of death."

[26]The term *rešep* was the proper name for a West Semitic god of pestilence, and the Hebrew use of the term for "flame" or "spark" probably derives from this god's association with fever. The god is envisioned here as another member of Yahweh's entourage of servants. Thus V's rendering as *diabolus* is not far from the mark, but the Greek translators had trouble with the word *rešep.* The Alexandrian group of LXX manuscripts offers the very peculiar rendering *en pedilois,* "in sandals": "and he shall go forth, his feet in sandals." Vaticanus and Sinaiticus have *eis pedia,* "into the plain," perhaps based on a misreading

of *ršp lrglyw* as *lšpl rglyw* (see Rudolph, 234). Barb and the later Greek translations translate the word with various terms for bird or winged creature, and S follows suit. The thought may be that vultures or birds of prey follow in the wake of Death, who precedes Yahweh.

[27]Literally, "at his feet," but the sense is that just as Plague precedes Yahweh, Fever follows him. Barb catches the sense quite well with its rendering, "at his feet shall follow . . . ," as do Syh and Arm with their rendering, "behind him."

[28]Hebrew *waymōded* is analyzed as a polel converted imperfect from a root *mwd,* cognate with Arabic *māda,* "to be in strong motion." T gets the sense right, and LXX errs only in translating the verb as a passive. Barb, V, and S all derive the form from the root *mdd,* "to measure," but this does not offer an acceptable parallel for the following verbs that reiterate or second the thought.

[29]LXX has a passive and V an active form, but both assign the verb the meaning "dissolve" or "melt," perhaps based on a derivation from *ntk* rather than *ntr.* Barb's odd *exeikase,* "he made like," may be a corruption of *ezētase,* "he investigated," which presupposes a derivation of the verb from the root *twr.* Rudolph, following Driver, suggests a derivation from *ntr* III, which would give a stronger meaning, "he tore apart" (p. 234), but "startle" seems to fit the context as well or better. The qal of *ntr* occurs in a similar theophanic passage where the meaning clearly seems to be "to start, jump in fright" (Job 37:1): "Yes, at this my heart trembled and started from its place." Driver's attempt to tie in this occurrence with the meaning of Akkadian *nutturu* ("Difficult Words," 71) is not convincing.

[30]LXX's reading, "the mountains were shattered *with violence (bią),*" presupposes Hebrew *'oz,* "strength" (cf. Ex. 14:21), rather than MT's *'ad,* "eternity." Barb has a double translation of the verb. Neither reading offers a superior text to the MT. The Hebrew *hrry 'd//gb'wt 'wlm* are a common parallel pair in early Hebrew poetry (Gen. 49:26; Deut. 33:15).

[31]LXX has "melted."

[32]This line and the next have been widely emended, either out of a general aversion to tricola or on the assumption that this line should express a thought parallel to the two preceding lines and thus required a verb. The most compelling emendation has been that of Albright, who attaches *tḥt 'wn* of the next line to this line, removes the word division to get a passive form of the verb *ḥt',* deletes the following *r'yty,* and ends up with reading *hlkwt 'wlm l tḥt'n,* "Eternal orbits were shattered" ("Psalm," 11, 15). This may very well represent the text of the ancient hymn Habakkuk adapted, but it is very doubtful that it represents the text as the prophet adapted it for his vision. Though the versions had

difficulty construing this line, they give almost no support for emending it. Barb ends the line with an extra verb, inserting it just before the final *lô,* which Barb takes with the following line: "The eternal ways will be altered *(alloiōthēsontai).*" It is difficult, however, to regard this as anything more than an exegetical expansion to ease the problem of construal (cf. Eaton, "Origin," 149).

[33]Barb's reading *autou heneka seisthēsetai hē oikoumenē,* "On account of him/this the world will be shaken," appears to presuppose the Hebrew *lô tēḥat 'iyyin* (Hiebert, HSM 38:21), but this can hardly be original. If one preserves the MT, several options are open. Rudolph construes *taḥat 'āwen* with the preceding line, understands the preposition as meaning "on account of," and translates the line, "Those are his ways from of old as punishment for iniquity" (p. 231). This produces an excessively long line, and Rudolph must treat it as a later gloss. It also forces him to take *rā'îtî* as the first word of the following line, which he ends after *yirgᵉzûn,* and that division produces another awkwardly long line. Eaton construes the line as extending from *taḥat* through *yirgᵉzûn,* understands the preposition in the sense "burdened, weighed down beneath," and translates the line, "I see the tents of Kushan sore burdened" ("Origin," 145, 150). His line is even longer than Rudolph's and quite impossible. As Hiebert has demonstrated (HSM 38:22–23), agreement in gender between subject and predicate as well as the normal poetic conventions require the following stichometric division of the next two lines:

'hly kwšn yrgzwn	The tents of Cushan quiver,
yry'wt 'rṣ mdyn	The curtains of the land of Midian.

That means that our line, if it is an original poetic unit of Habakkuk's vision, must be delimited as *tḥt 'wn r'yty.* One can translate the line, taking *r'yty* as an unmarked relative clause, either as "because of the iniquity that I saw" or "instead of the iniquity that I saw." As it stands, the line refers back to Habakkuk's complaint in 1:3, and it serves as the protasis to the following two lines. Compare the similar construction with *taḥat* in Isa. 60:15:

> Whereas *(taḥat)* you have been forsaken,
> And hated, with no one passing through,
> I will make you an everlasting pride,
> A joy forever.

[34]The parallel pair River//Sea is a traditional pair, representing alternative names for a single cosmic enemy of Baal in the Ugaritic (and presumably Canaanite) mythology. In the Ugaritic texts *nhr,* "River," is normally singular in this usage, and the normal Hebrew plural for river is *nᵉhārôt,* not *nᵉhārîm,* so the form here has probably been construed

as a plural only secondarily. The mimation on the end of this form may be a misunderstood enclitic *mem,* or, less likely, a dual referring to the cosmic sources of the deep (see Hiebert, HSM 38:23).

[35]LXX and Barb read a second-person verb form here because of the following vocative, but the delayed subject of the verb is *'appekā,* "your anger," in the next line (Hiebert, HSM 38:23). The qal of *ḥārāh,* "to burn," either takes *'ap,* "anger," as its explicit subject, or it is implicit in an impersonal construction with *lᵉ* + the person: "(anger) burns to PN." The qal never takes a personal subject.

[36]Yahweh is clearly a vocative, as the following second-person forms show. The presence of the divine name, however, is no justification for deleting this line as a gloss, contra Van der Woude (p. 62).

[37]Since the second line is simply a restatement and completion of the same question begun in the first line, Albright ("Psalm," 11) and Hiebert (HSM 38:23) correct the interrogative *'im* to *hᵃ,* as in the first line, but this hardly seems necessary (see Eaton, "Origin," 150–151). Even less convincing is the widespread deletion of *'m bnhrym* in this line as a secondary gloss, thus turning the climactic tricolon into a simple bicolon (cf. the judicious remarks of Hiebert, 23–24).

[38]The verb *rākab* in normal biblical usage means "to mount" rather than "to ride." See Hiebert (HSM 38:24, 154 n. 52) and the literature cited there.

[39]Barb appears to reverse the order of "horses" and "chariot," and Humbert adopts this reversal because warriors in the Near East normally mounted the war chariot rather than the horse (p. 61). However, the other versions support MT, and the order of the pair in the MT is its normal order in poetry (Isa. 2:7; Joel 2:4–5; Micah 5:9 [10]; Nahum 3:2; but cf. Jer. 4:13; Hag. 2:22). Also, the lines have better balance with the order in MT. Hiebert explains the difficulty in the bicolon as an example of "imagistic parallelism," a common phenomenon in biblical and Ugaritic poetry, in which the poet refers not "to two separate acts but to a single act described with two related images" (HSM 38:24).

[40]MT and V read the plural, but one does not expect Yahweh to mount a plurality of chariots, and the corruption would be very easy to explain by the mechanical influence of the plural ending on its preceding parallel, "your horses." LXX has a singular noun, but it is a collective, so it is weak support for the emendation, but S has a clear singular. It also removes the suffix from the *nomen regens* to its more normal position on the *nomen rectum,* but this is probably a stylistic improvement rather than evidence of a different text. This would appear to be one of those rare examples where the suffix comes in the middle of a construct chain.

[41]Barb has a difficult relative clause at the end of this line, *ho proebēs,* "which you went before." Rudolph has explained the *ho* as a small circle

originally intended to mark the position for *proebēs* to be inserted as a marginal correction on *anebēs,* "you mounted" (p. 235). Barb has no term corresponding to the first word of the next verse, however, so Eaton reports a suggestion of Driver that *ho proebēs* represents a form of Hebrew *'ādāh,* "to advance," and is just a corruption of the *'eryāh* that begins the next verse ("Origin," 151).

[42]The form *'eryāh,* "nakedness," is a feminine noun from the root *'ārāh,* "to be naked, bare," used in place of the infinitive absolute. V and S, however, appear to treat the word as though it were from the root *'wr,* "to awake." LXX's *enteinōn* has been taken as evidence for Hebrew *dārōk,* "to string (the bow)," but it is probably just a free translation of the MT. A number of critics suggest emending the Hebrew to the piel infinitive absolute *'ārōh,* but while this is possible it is not necessary.

[43]The form *tē'ôr* is normally analyzed as a niphal imperfect 3 f. s. from *'wr,* "to be naked," a rare by-form of the root *'rh.* Barb, S, and V derive it from *'wr,* "to awake," and V turns it into an active form, perhaps *tᵉ'ōrēr,* with God as the subject and the bow as the object. It is best to correct the form to the active piel *tᵉ'āreh.* The corruption is easily explained by the defective orthography of the preexilic period (see Hiebert, HSM 38:25–26).

[44]The form *šᵉbū'ôt* has received many interpretations. The original reading of LXX was apparently *hepta* (= *šeba'*) "seven." V and T take it as the word for oath or covenant, and Barb and S read it as from the root *śāba'.* Barb's reading is particularly worthy of note, "You sated the arrows of his quiver." Modern explanations of the phrase have been even more numerous. Eaton, following Driver and Mowinckel, preserves the MT, analyzes the form as a qal passive participle, and translates the two lines as "Mightily awakened is thy bow, Adjured are the shafts with a word" ("Origin," 145, 151–152). Rudolph's objection that having Yahweh give such an adjuration to his weapons does not correspond with the prophetic view of God (p. 236) is less than convincing. Nevertheless, the reading *śibba'tā,* "you sated," following Barb, would seem to go better with the most likely reading of the preceding line (so also Hiebert, HSM 38:27).

[45]LXX takes *maṭṭôt* as "scepters," V and T as "tribes," and S and Barb as "arrows." In addition to the support from S and Barb, the meaning "shafts" or "arrows" is suggested by the parallelism with "bow," by the use of the verb *nāqab,* "to pierce," with *maṭṭāyw,* "his shafts," in Hab. 3:14, and the occurrence of *mṭ* in this sense in Ugaritic (*CTA* 23.37, 40, 44, 47; 3.2.15–16). The evidence for the masculine plural in both Ugaritic and Hab. 3:14 suggest that one emend the consonantal text from *mṭwt* to the masculine plural construct *mṭy.*

[46]The real crux in the line is the last word *'ōmer,* "speech, word."

LXX, V, T, and S all seem to represent the MT, though the translation is loose, and one should note that both S and T add a 2 m. s. suffix. Barb departs radically from MT with its *tēs pharetras autou,* "of his quiver." Unless one follows the interpretation of Driver, Mowinckel, and Eaton, the reading of the MT offers no intelligible meaning and must be emended. If one follows the lead of Barb, several options are open. LXX uses *pharetra* to translate a number of different Hebrew terms in the Old Testament: *tᵉlî,* "quiver" (Gen. 27:3), *yeter,* "bowstring" (Ps. 11:2 [LXX 10:2]; Job 30:11), *'ašpāh,* "quiver" (Isa. 22:6; 49:2; Lam. 3:13), and *šeleṭ,* "quiver" (Jer. 51:11 [LXX 28:11]; Ezek. 27:11), and *mišmār,* "watch" (Jer. 51:12 [LXX 28:12]). (The lexicons give the meaning of *šeleṭ* as "small shield," but the Akkadian cognate *šalṭu* supports the translation of LXX, *AHW,* 1151.) The closest graphically to MT's *'ōmer* is *mišmār,* but if that is what Barb read, it offers no help for emending the text. Hiebert emends to *'ašpātᵉkā* (HSM 38:7), but an emendation to *yeter* or *mêtār* is preferable orthographically, and semantically "bowstring" fits the context as well as "quiver."

[47]LXX and S read a passive verb with "earth" as the 3 f. s. subject. That would link this line with the following line as a part of nature's reaction to the appearance of the divine warrior, and Hiebert, who prefers this division, reads the niphal *tibbāqa'* here (HSM 38:28–29). MT has an active verb form with a 2 m. s. subject, and this is supported by V and Barb, though Barb adds a gratuitous second verb: "You will scatter the rivers, and you will shake the earth." Reading an active 2 m. s. verb form here would link this line with the preceding two lines, where Yahweh is also the subject. It is the preferable division, because it is only in the next line that nature is said to have seen Yahweh. Thus nature's reaction to the theophany should follow the next line, not anticipate it.

[48]Keller interprets *nᵉhārôt* not as "rivers" but as "lightning bolts," since "rivers" are the enemies of Yahweh, not his weapons (p. 172). The sense, however, is similar to that found in Ps. 74:15, where the deity cleaves open springs and wadis as a result of his victory over the powers of chaos. Compare also the passage in the *Enuma elish* where Marduk creates the water courses from parts of Tiamat's body (*Ee* V, 54–55).

[49]LXX reads "peoples," but this does not fit the context, which concentrates on nature's reaction to the theophany (Humbert, 63).

[50]Reading *'ābôt* with Ps. 77:18 and the Murabba'at manuscript. The MT has "A downpour *(zerem)* of water passed by *('ābār).*" Barb, V, and S reflect MT, but LXX takes *'br* as a nominal form.

[51]Reading the polel perfect *zōrᵉmû* with Ps. 77:18 [17] and the Murabba'at manuscript. Barb, V, and S reflect MT, but LXX translates the form with a participle, "scattering *(skorpizōn)* the waters of the way," which suggests a Hebrew reading *zōreh.*

[52]The major difficulty at the end of this verse and the beginning of v. 11 is the asyndetic juxtaposition of "sun" with "moon." The word *šemeš* does not go well with v. 11: (1) that would result in a line with two subjects unconnected by a conjunction; (2) this compound subject would precede a singular verb; and (3) it would form a plural antecedent for the singular suffix on *zᵉbūlōh.* On the other hand, it does not go well with v. 10. Even if the image of the sun with outstretched hands is common in Near Eastern iconography (HSM 38:31), it makes little sense in this context, where the storm cloud has covered the face of the heavens. In this context the sun is surely hidden by the clouds, so any imagery used of the sun should reflect that fact. Thus the subject of the verb *nāśā'* must be the Deep, which raises up its waves against Yahweh as in the primordial cosmogonic battle (cf. Ps. 93:3). So S and V. Barb appears to omit this line apart from the opening *rôm,* "on high," which Barb takes with the preceding line.

[53]"Its hands" refers to the waves of the Deep. LXX's *phantasias* presupposes a misreading of *yādêhû* as *yōreh* (see Hab. 2:19).

[54]Barb takes this adverb with the preceding line, but it gives better poetic balance when one takes it with this line.

[55]The awkward *šemeš,* which goes well neither with the preceding nor with the following line, can be best explained with B. Margulis on the assumption that part of a line fell out by haplography: *rwm ydyhw nś' ⟨dm ngh 'wr⟩ šmš yrḥ ʿmd zblh* (*ZAW* 82 [1970]: 424). Barb, which appears to have omitted part of the preceding line, supports the restoration: *phōs to lampron tou hēliou epesche,* "he withheld the bright light of the sun." Hiebert objects to the translation of *epesche* as "withheld" or "stopped," arguing that it must mean "held out," because of the adversative *de* in the next line (HSM 38:31), but the argument is unconvincing. The word *de* can be used as a simple copulative: *to de pheggos tēs selēnēs estathē,* "and the brilliance of the moon was stayed." Barb clearly implies the darkening of the light of the heavenly bodies. Moreover, that is expected as a normal feature of Yahweh's theophany. The day of Yahweh is a day of darkness and clouds without the light of sun, moon, or stars (Isa. 13:9–10; Joel 2:2; 3:4 [2:31]; 4:15 [3:15]; Amos 5:18–20; Zeph. 1:15).

[56]MT's *zᵉbūlāh* should be read as *zᵉbūlōh.* The final *h* represents the older use of *h* instead of *w* as the mater for the 3 m. s. suffix, *-ô.*

[57]The sense of the idiom *lᵉ'ôr,* "for light," and *lᵉnōgah,* "for brightness," is the same as that found in Isa. 60:19. Since the sun and the moon have been blotted out by Yahweh's thick clouds, the light that remains is furnished by God's lightning. Hiebert misses the sense of the idiom because of his misinterpretation of the preceding lines (HSM 38:32).

[58]The subject of the verb is God's arrows, his lightning (cf. Ps. 77:18

[17]). So MT and LXX. Barb, V, and S all presuppose a different construction: "In/At the light of your arrows, they go." If one adopts this construal, the most natural antecedent for the subject of the verb "go" would be sun and moon, but neither sun and moon nor any of the other alternatives suggested fit well in the context (see HSM 38:31).

[59]For MT's *ḥ^anîtekā,* "your spear," LXX has "your weapons," and Barb "your sword." The later Greek translations, V, and S all have words for spear.

[60]LXX's *oligōseis,* "you will make small," results from misreading *tiṣʻad* as *tiṣʻar.* The confusion of *d* and *r* is quite common in most periods of the Hebrew script. Barb's *egerthēsēi,* "you will be roused," apparently misread the Hebrew as *tēʻôr,* the niphal imperfect from *ʻwr.* The MT is supported by V and S, and the parallelism with *dwš,* "to trample," confirms it as the correct reading.

[61]S and T have the infinitive here, but LXX, Barb, and V support the reading of MT.

[62]In contrast to the previous line, MT here appears to construe the preposition plus nominal form, *l^eyēšaʻ,* as a substitute for the hiphil infinitive construct, since it is followed by the direct object marker. LXX, Barb, S, and T all take it in that fashion. V and Aquila construe the direct object marker as a preposition, but this simply confirms the *'ēt* as present in their Vorlage. The use of a nominal form with the force of an infinitive is well attested (Eaton, "Origin," 154; GKC 115d; Rudolph, 237), so there is no justification for Hiebert's emendation of *'t* to *ʻm* (HSM 38: 34–35). On the other hand, the direct object marker is rare in old poetry, so the *'t* probably arose out of an original *lyšʻt mšḥk* that was misread under the influence of the similar form in the preceding line.

[63]LXX and Barb have a plural here, but the other Greek translations, V, S, and T all have the singular. The plural may reflect a tradition of interpretation that wished to avoid the idea that God must save the Messiah, or it may have been influenced by a passage like Ps. 105:15, where the anointed ones refer to the patriarchs, as Eaton points out ("Origin," 154). Moreover, as Eaton also notes, LXX often renders a Hebrew singular with a plural in this chapter: *erga* (v. 2), *chersin* (v. 4), *kopōn* (v. 7), *hoplōn* (v. 11), *desmous* (v. 13), *kephalas* (v. 14).

[64]Reading *bāmat,* the 3 f. s. construct form of *bāmāh,* with Hiebert (HSM 38:36). The word *rō'š,* "head," was probably introduced into the line from v. 14 as a variant for *bāmat,* "back," and these variants resulted in a conflate text with both words. Since *bāmat* would no longer make sense following *rō'š,* this conflate text led to the corruption of *bāmat.* MT's "head from the house of the wicked" can hardly be original. The context with the following *y^esôd,* "base," *ṣawwā'r,* "neck," and *rō'š,*

"head," call for a noun designating a part of the body. In such a context, both "head" in the sense of leader and "house" are inappropriate. For the motifs in this text, one should compare the Near Eastern accounts of the storm god smiting the dragon of chaos. The LXX reading, "you threw death against the heads of the wicked," may suggest a Hebrew text such as *mḥṣt r'šy mwt rš'*. Barb's reading, "you shot full of arrows the heads of arrogant men," may presuppose a Hebrew text such as *mḥṣt r'šy mty rš'*. Either reading could be seen as a corruption of the conflate reading *mḥṣt r'š bmt rš'*.

[65]The form *'ārôt* is the piel infinitive absolute from the verb *'rh.* LXX, V, and S translate as though one had a 2 m. s. perfect verb form, and on this basis Hiebert emends to *'ērîtā* (HSM 38:40). This is possible but not necessary; the use of the infinitive construct form in place of the "normal" form of the infinitive absolute, *'ārēh,* need not be a late error. LXX's *exēgeiras,* "you awakened," mistakenly derived the form from *'wr.* Barb's translation, "unto the abyss of the sea they shall go down," is very difficult to explain. It may be a targumic rendering of the MT (Eaton, "Origin," 154).

[66]The word *y^esôd* normally means "foundation" or "base," but it can be used figuratively of humans (Job 14:19; cf. 22:16; Prov. 10:25). Semantically it is similar to the Akkadian *išdu,* which also means "foundation," but which can be used figuratively of humans. The Akkadian word is used specifically to refer to the bottom part of the anatomy of Tiamat, the Babylonian sea monster (*Ee* IV, 129), and that would appear to be the sense of *y^esôd* in this passage. LXX's *desmous* is due to a misreading of *yswd* as *'swr,* "bond, band."

[67]Apart from Barb, all the versions render this word as "neck." Rudolph's emendation to *ṣûr,* "bedrock" (p. 237), assumes that the imagery in the verse is architectural, but the parallels with the Near Eastern mythological texts and the continuation in the next verse suggest that one is dealing with parts of the body of the conquered foe. MT requires no emendation.

[68]So LXX, S, and T. Barb's *exedikēsas,* "you avenged," probably resulted from a hearing error in which Hebrew *nāqabtā* was misunderstood as *nāqamtā.* V's *maledixisti,* "you cursed," simply misunderstood the verb as *nāqab* II.

[69]MT has no suffix on *rô'š,* but pronominal suffixes are often omitted with parts of the body in Hebrew where English usage would require them. The more serious question is that of the division of the line. All of the ancient versions read *rô'š* as in construct with the following word *p^erāzāyw:* LXX, "the heads of the princes;" Barb, "the chiefs of the sinners;" V, "the head of his warriors;" S, "the heads of his princes," and

T, "the warriors of the heads of the camp of Pharaoh." If one reads *pᵉrāzāyw* with this line, however, the line appears overly long (Hiebert, HSM 38:44).

[70]MT has "his," and it is supported by V, S, and T, though T is thinking specifically of Moses' rod, with which he split the sea. If MT is correct, it might imply that God turned back the enemy's weapons so that the enemy's own arrows pierced his head (Eaton, "Origin," 155). Barb has "your," however, and though this is the easier reading, it also seems the most probable. In other passages where God conquers the sea monster, it is God's sword, his hand, his might, or his wisdom that accomplishes this feat (Isa. 27:1; Job 26:12–13; Ps. 74:13).

[71]For the meaning "shafts" or "arrows," see v. 9 and note 45 above. Barb's "with your power" is probably an interpretative translation influenced by a passage like Ps. 74:13. LXX's *en ekstasei,* "in astonishment," may reflect a reading *bmṭw,* in which *mṭw* was derived from the root *mwṭ,* "to totter, shake" (Eaton, "Origin," 155).

[72]The three lines in brackets are impossibly corrupt. A literal rendering of the MT yields no meaning acceptable in the context, and any attempt to achieve such involves a high degree of subjective emendation. The translation offered above is simply an attempt to suggest the general direction in which one would expect an appropriate restoration of the text to go, based on the parallels with other biblical and nonbiblical accounts of the storm god's defeat of the sea dragon. Psalm 74:13–14 has been particularly influential in this restoration.

[73]The precise meaning of *pᵉrāzāyw* is disputed. It has been associated with Hebrew *pᵉrāzôt,* "the open land," which has suggested the meaning "villager, peasant, serf," and it has also been associated with the Arabic *faraza,* "to muster, choose," which has suggested the meaning "leader" (*HALAT,* 908). In any case it must refer to the supporters of God's enemy.

[74]Reading the piel *tᵉsā'ēr.* MT has the qal *yis'ᵃrû,* "his followers stormed," but in a cosmogonic context that has been describing Yahweh's crushing of his enemy, one does not expect any further mention of the enemy's struggle. LXX reads a passive form, "they were shaken," which is better, but it is difficult to construe with the following infinitive. Barb and S apparently misread MT's *ys'rw* as *ys'dw.*

[75]Reading *lahᵃpîṣēm* in place of MT's *lahᵃpîṣēnî,* "to scatter me." MT's first-person suffix is quite improbable. Not only is the necessary antecedent lacking, one expects Yahweh, who comes in the storm clouds, to do the scattering. Note the connection between his storm wind and the driving away or scattering of his enemies in other passages (Isa. 40:24; 41:16; Jer. 13:24; 18:17; 23:19; 25:32; Zech. 7:14; Ps. 83:16 [15]). Barb omits the word in its translation. LXX separates the initial *lh* as

the preposition plus suffix and then treats the remainder of the word as a form of *pṣh* to yield, "They will be shaken *at it, they will open* their bridles." Neither treatment offers much help for understanding the original text.

[76]Reading *bᵉmistār* from the end of the following line. Compare the passage in *Ee* IV, 132, where the north wind carries away the blood of Tiamat to a secret place. MT's *'ᵃlîṣūtām,* "their exultation," though it is supported by the versions other than LXX, makes little sense. The meaning "throat," suggested by Driver and supported by Eaton ("Origin," 155–156) on the basis of the peculiar LXX reading, "their bridles," is hardly an improvement. Eaton's suggested translation of the end of the verse beginning with this word shows that his understanding of the lines yield neither contextual sense nor good poetry: "Their throat craving to devour//The poor in the darkness" ("Origin," 146).

[77]Reading *kᵉma'ᵃkāl,* based on the parallel with Ps. 74:14. MT's "as though to eat the poor in secret" does not fit the context, though it has the support of the versions.

[78]Reading *lᵉ'amlᵉṣê yām,* based on the suggestion for the reading of Ps. 74:14 (*HALAT,* 800). Perhaps the corruption developed in the following way. The original reading, *l'mlṣy ym,* was misdivided as *l'm lṣyym,* as in Ps. 74:14. Then the initial *l* was lost by haplography due to the final *l* of the preceding word, and *'m* was corrupted to *'ny.* At this point, *bmstr* and *lṣyym,* now corrupted into *'lyṣtm,* were transposed, resulting in the present incoherent text.

[79]There is no need to emend this line. The idiom *drk b* means "to tread upon" (Deut. 1:36; 11:24–25; Josh. 14:9), *sûseykā* is an instrumental accusative, and the image is that of the victor trampling on his conquered foe, as in Deut. 33:29 and *Ee* IV, 129 (Eaton, "Origin," 156; Hiebert, HSM 38:47).

[80]MT does not have the preposition *b,* and it is also lacking in LXX, Barb, and S, which adds the copulative *w.* T and V do have the preposition, however, and, since V normally follows the MT very closely, the *b* is probably original. Its restoration provides better parallelism and balance to the lines. The word *ḥomer* is probably to be taken as a nominal form from the verb *ḥāmar* II, "to foam, surge" (*HALAT,* 317). LXX and Barb connect it to that root, but treat it as a verbal form. V's "mud" and T and S's "heap" appear to be influenced by the Exodus story, but neither meaning seems appropriate here. For the imagery, see Ps. 46:4.

[81]LXX's *ephylaxamēn,* "I kept watch," presupposes a reading *šāmartî,* and Barb's *etaxamēn,* "I stationed myself," though it could be attributed to the same reading understood in the light of Hab. 2:1, probably presupposes *śamtî,* since Greek *tassein* normally renders Hebrew *śîm* in the minor prophets. Both readings are simple corruptions

of MT's *šāma'tî,* which points back to the use of the same verb in Hab. 3:2. V, S, and T also support MT's superior reading.

[82]LXX's rendering of *ṣllw* as a noun for prayer, "from the sound of the prayer *(proseuchēs)* of my lips," apparently derives the word from Aramaic *ṣl'*. S omits the word, but appears to understand the passage in similar fashion. Barb also omits the word, but has "your lips," which gives a different meaning altogether. MT's verbal form is supported by V, and it provides an excellent parallel to the preceding line.

[83]LXX, Barb, S, and T have "trembling" rather than "rottenness." Since LXX often uses *tromos,* "trembling," to translate Hebrew *ra'ad* or *r^e'ādāh* (Ex. 15:15; Isa. 33:14; Pss. 48:7 [6]; 55:6 [5]; Job 4:14), this rendering may suggest a variant text. V supports MT, however, and the parallel usage of *rāqāb,* "rottenness," with bones in Prov. 12:4 and 14:30 confirms its reading.

[84]Read the dual *'^ašūray,* "my steps," as the subject of the verb in place of MT's awkward relative pronoun *'^ašer.* LXX's reading, "and beneath me my stance *(hexis)* was troubled," supports the correction, which clarifies an otherwise obscure text.

[85]Reading *tirgoz,* 3 f. s. form of the verb, in order to agree with the dual subject (HSM 38:50–51). LXX, V, and S all have third-person forms over against MT's first person. Only Barb and T support it.

[86]The MT reading *'ānûaḥ* is supported by LXX and V. Barb's *phylaxeis* may represent *tannîaḥ* and T's *dšbqny* presupposes some form of *nwḥ,* but S's reading *dbdq ly,* "which he showed me," is puzzling (Eaton, "Origin," 157). Most critics want to emend the text to some form of *'nḥ,* "to groan," but often for the wrong reason. Hiebert comments that "the act of resting is hardly appropriate in this context of emotional intensity" (HSM 38:52), but that is because he regards the whole chapter as an ancient poem and fails to recognize the turning point in the composition. Rudolph correctly recognizes the logical structure of the chapter, but the limited attestation of *nwḥ* in the sense required leads him to emend the text to *'āz 'ôḥîl,* "now I will wait . . ." (p. 238). The emendation is probably unnecessary. Though there is a dispute about the original text, the MT of 1 Sam. 25:9 uses *nwḥ* in the sense of "to cease speaking while waiting for an answer." Daniel 12:13 uses the verb of resting while awaiting a set time in the future. In Daniel the usage appears to imply resting in death, but this may be a secondary development of an earlier idiom that simply meant to wait quietly.

[87]For the rendering of the idiom *l^eyôm* in this passage, compare the similar usage in other prophetic texts where one is waiting for a set time in the future (Isa. 30:8; Jer. 12:3; Zeph. 3:8).

[88]MT's *y^egûdennû* is the qal impf. 3 m. s. with 1 c. pl. suffix of *gwd,* "to attack," used in an unmarked relative clause. Barb's *ton laon sou,*

"your people," is simply an exegetical rendering of the MT. LXX's *paroikias mou,* "of my sojourning," presupposes a misreading of the Hebrew as *mgwryny.* S's *wḥwyny,* "and he informed me," presupposes the reading *wygydny.* There is no reason to emend the MT.

[89]All the versions other than Barb preserve the *kî,* and Barb's omission probably reflects an exegetical failure to recognize the meaning of *kî* here rather than providing evidence of a variant text. Contra Hiebert (HSM 38:53), the conjunction serves a clear concessive function here (cf. BDB, 473b).

[90]LXX and Barb translate as though the verb were *pārāh* rather than *pāraḥ,* but that may reflect no more than a very slight freedom in translation. V and S support MT, and no emendation is required.

[91]The precise meaning of *šᵉdēmôt* is disputed; it may refer to cultivated terraces rather than fields in general (L. E. Stager, *JNES* 41 [1982]: 111–121).

[92]Many critics repoint the MT to obtain a passive form of the verb, but the verb with indefinite subject can function as the equivalent of the passive, so such emendation is unnecessary.

[93]MT's *miklāh* is an incorrect spelling for *miklā',* "sheepfold." LXX's *brōseōs,* "food," probably presupposes an inferior reading *mm'kl.*

[94]Barb's "gave me strength" is interpretative.

[95]MT is supported by V, S, and T. Barb's *asphaleis,* "secure," is interpretative, and LXX's *eis synteleian,* "unto completion," presupposes some form from *klh.*

[96]LXX omits the suffix on *bmwty,* but V, S, and T have it, and it is found in 2 Sam. 22:34 and Ps. 18:34 [33]. Barb gives an interpretative rendering, "and on the necks of my enemies he makes me tread." Hiebert suggests the final *-y* is not the pronominal suffix, but an old genitive case ending frozen in an archaic stereotyped phrase (HSM 38:56). In related passages elsewhere, *bāmôtê/bomᵒtê* occurs as the plural construct before *'ereṣ,* "the high places of the earth" (Isa. 58:14; Amos 4:13; Micah 1:3), and *yām,* "the back of Sea" (Job 9:8). The reference to the surefootedness of deer in the preceding line suggests that the image is that of walking on the heights, but Barb's interpretation suggests a double entendre. Habakkuk's surefootedness will allow him to experience the triumph over his enemies.

[97]The meaning of *mᵉnaṣṣēaḥ* is not certain, though it occurs frequently as a heading in the Psalms (some 55 times). The translation "leader" or "overseer" is suggested by the three occurrences in 2 Chronicles (2:1, 17; 34:13). LXX, V, and T treat the term either as an infinitive or a participle from the Aramaic root *nṣḥ,* "to conquer," but both V and T have a secondary interpretation that connects it with singing or instrumental music. The text underlying Barb is unclear.

[98]The suffix on *ngynwty* is treated as 3 m. s. by LXX and S, but 1 c. s. by T and V. Mur 88 has the final *-y*. The precise significance of the ending is problematic. It is also found in Isa. 38:20.

Commentary

Chapter 3 begins and ends with rubrics similar to those found in the Psalms, and, at three points in the text, the as yet unexplained rubric *selāh* occurs (vs. 3, 9, 13). Much of the chapter is marked by archaic poetry that differs stylistically from the poetry of the rest of the book, and the chapter is not included in the Qumran commentary on Habakkuk. These considerations have led a number of scholars to regard the chapter as an independent composition that has been secondarily attached to the book of Habakkuk, but the arguments remain unpersuasive. The absence of the chapter in the Qumran commentary may have many explanations, but it is extremely doubtful that it bears witness to a Hebrew manuscript tradition lacking the chapter. Habakkuk 3 is included in the Murabbaʻat text and in the Greek scroll found at Qumran in 1952 (Barthélemy, VTS 10 [1963]). The archaic features in the poetry are concentrated in vs. 3–15, and they can be adequately explained by the prophet's use of older texts, as we shall see. The superscription, subscription, and musical rubrics do suggest that this chapter was at some point used in worship—it is included as an independent text in the LXX's collection of Songs *(ǭdai)*—but just as the headings and rubrics in the Psalms are generally regarded as later additions to the text, so they should be regarded in the case of Habakkuk. They were presumably added when the text came to be used in communal worship (Rudolph, 240).

Once the rubrics are removed as secondary insertions, the text actually begins in v. 2, which fits very well after 2:20. Yahweh's second response to Habakkuk, which began in 2:1 and continued in his citation of the *hôy*-sayings to be spoken by the oppressed nations (2:6ff.), ends in 2:20 with the affirmation that Yahweh is still in his holy temple. To this affirmation and its demand that the whole earth keep silence before God, Habakkuk responds that he had heard about Yahweh's former awesome deeds, but he requests that God bring these former deeds to life again in his own time (3:2). In other words, Hab. 3:2 continues the pattern found earlier in the book of prophetic lament followed by divine response followed by a renewed lament. Despite God's instructions to Habakkuk in 2:2–20, the prophet is still not prepared to rest his case.

God's third response to Habakkuk comes in 3:3–15. These verses contain a number of archaic features that suggest the adaptation of an ancient hymn that celebrated Yahweh's march from his ancient home in the southern mountains to destroy the enemies of his people in Syria-Palestine. The portrayal in these verses of Yahweh's march and the resulting convulsions both in nature and among the nations closely resembles the treatment of the same motif in a number of archaic poems (Deut. 33:2–5; Judg. 5:4–5; Ps. 68:8–9 [7–8]; cf. Ex. 15:14–16). These archaic poems all celebrate God's march from the south as a mighty work done by God in the past, and it may be to such songs about God's prior acts that the prophet refers in 3:2, when he says he has heard the report about God. It is even possible that Habakkuk was listening to a variant form of the hymn embedded in 3:3–15, one that celebrated God's past actions just as the parallel texts cited, when that hymn became the catalyst for his prophetic vision. Prophetic visions in the context of the temple or communal worship are well attested both in Israel (Num. 23:3ff., 14ff., 29ff.; Isa. 6; Jer. 14:10ff.; 2 Chron. 20:5–17; Luke 1:11–20) and the surrounding cultures (ARM X, 7:5–6; 8:5–7; 10:5–6; 50:22–23), and music was sometimes a catalyst for the onset of prophetic inspiration (2 Kings 3:15). At any rate, the present text of Hab. 3:3–15, in contrast to the parallels, no longer celebrates Yahweh's march as a past event, but describes this event as it is happening, as a visionary experience. In short, Hab. 3:3–15 contains Yahweh's last response to Habakkuk, and that response is the vision promised in 2:2–3.

Habakkuk 3:16 is linked to 3:2 by the repetition of the verb "I heard," and indicates both the conclusion of the vision and the prophet's response to it. That response includes the typical reaction of terror in the presence of Yahweh's majesty, but it also indicates the prophet's willingness at last to await the fulfillment of the vision as he had been instructed in 2:3. Habakkuk 3:17–18 backs up the prophet's statement of acceptance of God's instruction with a vow to trust in the vision's reliability (cf. 2:4), even in a worst-possible-case scenario, and 3:19 ends the chapter with a typical statement of confidence.

In other words, apart from the secondary rubrics, the chapter is a unified piece that forms an integral part of the argument of the larger book of Habakkuk. Without it, the book remains a fragment with no resolution of the prophet's laments, and with no vision for the prophet to record as he had been commanded to do (2:2). There is no justification for treating Habakkuk 3 as an independent piece or for denying its traditional attribution to Habakkuk.

[3:1] Though this superscription is a secondary addition to the chapter, its characterization of the following text as a prayer *(tᵉpillāh)* of Habakkuk is accurate in the sense that the text corresponds in many respects to a particular genre of Israelite prayer. If the earlier addresses of Habakkuk could be classified as individual laments followed by an oracular response, this final address bears a striking resemblance to an individual prayer of thanksgiving. It begins with an invocation of Yahweh and the statement of the prophet's request. The prophet then reports the vision he experienced as the oracular response to that request. In the light of that positive oracular response, Habakkuk ends his prayer with a vow and a statement of confidence.

[2] Just as in numerous communal laments, where the psalmist and his community reflect on the accounts preserved in the cult of Yahweh's glorious works of old (Pss. 44:2 [1]; 77:6–21 [5–20]; 143:5), Habakkuk acknowledges that he has heard of Yahweh's work, and he asserts that those ancient stories have filled him with awe. God's mighty power revealed in those ancient deeds is no longer evident in the present, however, and Habakkuk prays that God will renew his work, that he will demonstrate it in the very near future; he also asks that, in the process, God will remember to show mercy, presumably to his own oppressed people.

The expression "when the years draw near" picks up on God's promise to Habakkuk in 2:3. Yahweh had promised that the vision *(ḥāzôn)* would testify concerning a fixed point in the future and that the appointed time would not pass without the vision being fulfilled. When that time for the fulfillment of the vision draws near, Habakkuk asks Yahweh to once again display his mighty work as in the glorious days of old. This use of *qārab,* "to draw near," is very similar to that in Ezek. 12:23, where it also refers to the approaching term for the fulfillment of a prophetic vision *(ḥāzôn).*

The imperative Habakkuk uses in the first line of his request is quite striking: *ḥayyêhû,* "revive it/bring it back to life." Because the figure is so striking and not semantically parallel to the imperfect that seconds it in the following line, *tôdîaʿ,* "make it known," one may be tempted to correct *ḥayyêhû* to *ḥawwêhû,* "declare it." Such a temptation should be avoided, however. The imperative formulations of requests in laments often use striking imagery; one need only think of the appeal to God in Ps. 44:24 [23]: "Rise up! Why do you sleep, my lord? Wake up! Do not be angry for ever!" Moreover, Habakkuk's request is not that God should talk about his work, but that he should once again perform it so that it will become transparent to the eyes of the world; for this sense of "to make it known" the expression "to revive it" forms an excellent parallel.

Habakkuk's appeal to God to remember to show mercy could be read as just another way of saying, "Renew your work," but it can also be read as qualification of that request. After all, there was a disturbing ambiguity in the concept of God's work. As his earlier word to Habakkuk had revealed, it was Yahweh's work *(pōʿal)* that had brought the Babylonian oppressor down upon hapless Judah in the first place (Hab. 1:5–6). The older prophetic tradition also knew of God's strange work *(maʿăśeh)* of judgment on his own people (Isa. 28:21), and only an impious fool would want to hurry that along (Isa. 5:19; cf. Jer. 17:15–16). Thus, while asking for the fulfillment of the promised vision, the prophet qualifies it with the request that it be accompanied by mercy. He wants a renewal of God's work, but his early work of deliverance as in the exodus and conquest, not that of his more recent work against Jerusalem (Hab. 1:5; cf. Isa. 10:12).

The ambiguity in the expression *bᵉrōgez,* "in agitation," supports this fuller reading of the text. One could take this to mean either "in (your) wrath" or "in (our) turmoil." The prophet may have intentionally omitted the suffix to create a double entendre based on this resulting ambiguity. When you renew your work, let your wrath, which has brought such turmoil upon us, be tempered by the memory of your mercy, so that your new work, the fulfillment of the vision, will mean our salvation.

[3] Verse 3 begins the description of this renewed work of Yahweh. It describes God's march to Palestine from his ancient home in the southern mountains, a very popular motif in archaic Hebrew poetry (Deut. 33:2–5; Judg. 5:4–5; Ps. 68:8–9 [7–8]; cf. Ex. 15:14–16), but unlike his archaic models, which portray this as a past event, Habakkuk portrays God's march as though it were happening in the present, before his very eyes. Note Habakkuk's use of the imperfect over against the perfects (Deut. 33:2; Ex. 15:10–16) or infinitive constructions followed by perfects (Judg. 5:4–5; Ps. 68:8–9 [7–8]) in the older texts. It is true that imperfects often represent a simple narrative tense indistinguishable from the perfect in Hebrew poetry, particularly archaic poetry, when the two tenses are used interchangeably in parallel lines. Normally, however, the opening verbs indicate clearly enough whether the action is set in the past or the present-future, and the imperfects that open Hab. 3:3 clearly set the action in the present-future. This difference from the older models suggests that Habakkuk is reporting a visionary experience (cf. Rudolph, 241; Eaton, "Origin," 164–165).

The two terms used to designate the deity contribute to the awe-inspiring quality of the vision. The normal word for God is the plural *'ᵉlōhîm,* but Habakkuk uses the relatively rare singular form *'ᵉlôah,* common only in Job, which contains the vast bulk of the word's occurrences in the Bible (41 out of 57). He also uses the epithet *qādôš,* "the Holy One," which emphasizes the radical and dangerous otherness of God, his separation and elevation over all possible rivals (cf. Isa. 6:3 and the widespread use of the epithet in the Isaianic corpus).

God is said to come from Teman and Mount Paran. Teman, which occurs in the inscriptions from Kuntillet 'Ajrud, probably designates a general area in southern Edom, in the Transjordan (Gen. 36:34; Jer. 49:7, 20; Ezek. 25:13; Amos 1:12; Obadiah 9). The location of Paran is more disputed, some scholars placing it south of Canaan and west of the Arabah on the basis of references in the P source (Num. 12:16; 13:3, 26), but there are archaeological difficulties with this location; others, basing themselves on presumably older sources (Gen. 14:6; Deut. 33:2; cf. Judg. 5:4), place it east of the Arabah, in the general region of Teman (Hiebert, 84–88). Though the precise location of Moses' mountain of God, Mount Sinai/Horeb, is plagued by similar problems, it also lay somewhere in the same general area to the far south of Canaan, and the religious traditions associated with it are probably only a part of a larger tradition associated with this whole southern area.

God's march from these regions is accompanied by phenomena that further underscore his majesty. Unlike the Exodus tradition of God's appearance on Mount Sinai, which speaks quite specifically of the phenomena of a heavy cloud, thunder, lightning, fire, smoke, and the shaking of the whole mountain (Ex. 19:16–18), or the Exodus tradition of God's guidance through the desert, which speaks of a pillar of cloud and fire (Ex. 13:21; passim), Habakkuk uses quite general terms for majesty and glory to designate the phenomena that accompanied God's march from Teman. Nevertheless, the verbs used with these nouns and the light imagery in the following verse suggest that Habakkuk had in mind meteorological phenomena similar to those mentioned in the Exodus traditions. The verb *kissāh* suggests a storm cloud has covered the sky, turning the light into darkness (Ex. 24:15–16; 40:34; Num. 9:15–16; 17:7 [16:42]; Ezek. 32:7; Ps. 147:8), and *mālᵉʾāh* implies that this phenomenon has filled the whole horizon, leaving no area unaffected (cf. Ex. 40:34–35; 1 Kings 8:10–11; Isa. 6:1; Ezek. 10:3). Both verbs are in the perfect, but, rather than describing a past event, they seem to be describing the scene as it is developing in Habakkuk's visionary experience. That is, it is past only in terms of the narrative sequence of the vision. One could smooth out the English by rendering the perfects as narrative present tenses—"God comes from Teman . . . his majesty covers the heavens"—but that would obscure the contrast for the English reader, and it seemed better to preserve the contrast, even at the expense of English style.

[4] Despite the difficult cruxes in this verse, it can be interpreted without radical emendation, if one keeps in mind both the literary conventions of Israelite descriptions of God's coming in a thunderstorm (note esp. Ps. 18:8–16 [7–15]; Job 36:27–37:5, 15–22; Ezek. 1:4–28) and the iconographic conventions associated with the storm god in the broader regions of Syria-Palestine. In the continuation of Habakkuk's vision, after the skies have been covered over by God's majestic storm cloud, there is a sudden brightness like lightning, and in that momentary brilliance God is revealed. He stands there in the cloud in the conventional iconographical form in which Syro-Palestinian storm gods were typically portrayed; two prongs of the lightning bolt that he holds, presumably the same bolt whose brilliance revealed him, extend upward from his hand. Then just as suddenly the brilliance is gone. The figure vanishes in darkness. God has put back the envelope of gloom that hides his glorious strength.

That both *nōgah,* "brightness," and *ʾôr,* "lightning," are original and that they are related to the phenomenon of lightning find confirmation in their reappearance together in Hab. 3:11. The term *nōgah* also appears in another theophanic context that has striking similarities in thought to Hab. 3:4, the doubly transmitted hymn of deliverance attributed to David (2 Sam. 22:8–16 and Ps. 18:8–16 [7–15]). After v. 12 of that hymn has described how God has placed *(yāšet)* darkness and thick clouds as his hiding place or screen round about him, v. 13 describes how from the brightness *(nōgah)* before him coals of fire blazed, and this is followed by thunder and lightning (vs. 14–15). The conception seems to be that God himself is present in brilliant light and blazing fire at the center of the storm cloud (cf. Ezek. 1:4–28), but the intensity of his presence, his face as it were, is veiled and obscured by an envelope of darkness and thick clouds. Yet his glory cannot be completely hidden. From the brightness of his presence lightning bolts blaze forth, and in their brilliant but flickering light, God's veil is momentarily pierced, and some hint of the awesomeness of that fiery presence within is revealed.

The second line of Hab. 3:4 develops this thought with imagery drawn from the traditional iconography of the storm god in the regions of Syria-Palestine. The line, "he has (lit. "there is to him") two prongs (projecting) from his hand," clearly portrays Yahweh. Since both *nōgah* and *'ôr* appear to be feminine nouns, the antecedent of the masculine singular suffixes on "from his hand" and "to him" cannot be "brightness" or "lightning." They can only refer back to God, the antecedent of the similar masculine singular suffixes in the preceding verse. In the sudden brilliance described by the first line of the verse, Habakkuk catches a glimpse of Yahweh's form just as Ezekiel saw a form in his vision (Ezek. 1:26–28). There is actually nothing unusual about a prophet seeing the figure of God in a visionary experience; note the examples of Isaiah (Isa. 6:1–4), Micaiah ben Imlah (1 Kings 22:19), and even Jeremiah (Jer. 1:9). The form Habakkuk sees has two prongs *(qarnayim)* extending from his hand. This is an apt description of the standard representation of the Syro-Palestinian storm god. He is usually portrayed standing, one hand grasping a lightning bolt as a weapon, and the end of the stylized lightning bolt that extends above the hand forks into two or more prongs that closely resemble horns. This appears to be what the prophet saw, and Habakkuk's dependency on such iconography should be no more surprising than Ezekiel's dependency on traditional Near Eastern iconography for his vision of God. The imagery of visions, after all, like the imagery of dreams, arises from the scenes and symbols familiar to one in his or her cultural context. The implication of Habakkuk's glimpse of God, however, is that Yahweh is poised, weapon in hand, to strike down the wicked oppressors of whom Habakkuk had complained. The *deus absconditus* has revealed himself, however briefly, as a pledge of his coming intervention.

The third line, which should be compared to Ps. 18:12 [11], has God put back in place *(wᵉśām* or *yāśēm;* cf. *yāšet)* the covering that hides *(ḥebyôn;*

cf. *sitrô, sukkātô)* his strength. In other words, the divine glory in the heart of the storm is again veiled in his envelope of darkness and thick clouds. Yahweh's return to hiddenness is no less a sign of his grace than his brief unveiling, however. No human can stand more than a glimpse of God's unveiled glory and live (Ex. 34:18–23).

[5] Habakkuk then mentions members of Yahweh's military entourage, who both precede and follow him in his march against his enemies. As Hiebert has pointed out, the mention of a military retinue is an extremely common feature of the description of great gods throughout the ancient Near East, and these military assistants are often mentioned in pairs (HSM 38:93). Note particularly the description of Adad's appearance in the Epic of Gilgamesh (Tablet 11:96–100; *ANET,* 94):

> With the first glow of dawn,
> A black cloud rose up from the horizon.
> Inside it Adad thunders,
> While Shullat and Hanish go in front,
> Moving as heralds over hill and plain.

Plague is often mentioned as a weapon used by Yahweh against his enemies (Ex. 5:3; 9:15; Lev. 26:25; Num. 14:12; Deut. 28:21; 2 Sam. 24:15; Jer. 14:12; etc.), and 2 Sam. 24:16 comes close to identifying Plague with the *mal'āk hammašḥît,* "the destroying angel" (cf. Ex. 12:23; 2 Kings 19:35; Isa. 37:36). At any rate, the presence of Plague and Fever in Yahweh's entourage points again to Yahweh's intention to punish his enemies.

[6] Yahweh's appearance with his terrifying retinue convulses both the natural world and its human inhabitants. His standing up to do battle shakes the earth, and his mere glance causes the nations to jump in fright. The ancient mountains are shattered and sink down in his presence. These motifs are common features of biblical theophanies (Ex. 15:14–16; Judg. 5:4–5; Joel 2:10; Amos 1:2; Micah 1:3–4; Nahum 1:3–5; Zech. 14:4–5; Hag. 2:6–7; Pss. 18:8 [7]; 46:7; 68:9 [8]; 97:4–5; 144:5), but they derive from earlier theophanic conceptions common to most of the peoples of Mesopotamia, Syria, and Palestine (cf. J. Jeremias, *Theophanie,* 78–85). For the motif of the god's glance terrifying the enemy, see *Ee* IV, 67–68: "As he (Marduk) gazes, his (Kingu's) plan is confused; his thought is scattered and his action disorganized."

The last line of this verse, in the form in which Habakkuk transmitted it, suggests that Yahweh was once more taking the routes that he had taken in days of old. Just as Israel's ancient hymns celebrated Yahweh's march from the southern mountains to assist his people, so Habakkuk in his vision sees Yahweh renewing that pattern of action. In short, Yahweh was about to intervene to save his people from their enemies just as he had done in those great days of the past.

[7] Thus instead of the trouble and iniquity that Habakkuk had complained about seeing in 1:3, now in his vision he sees other nations in terror before the march of the divine warrior. Cushan and Midian are to be located fairly far south along the route that Yahweh must take on his march from the southern mountains to Palestine. They are not the objectives of God's march any more than Edom or Moab was his objective in the events celebrated in Ex. 15:14–17, but, just as Edom and Moab were terrified by his passage then, so Cushan and Midian are terrified by Yahweh's passage in Habakkuk's vision. The positive implication of this scene for Habakkuk is not that Cushan and Midian will be destroyed, but that their reaction to God's passage shows that God is prepared to attack his real enemy, the Babylonian oppressor. Even if Cushan and Midian do not draw Yahweh's attention as the object of his attack, however, they are hardly portrayed here as Israel's associates and friends (contra Hiebert, HSM 38:96–97). They are simply portrayed as nomads encamped along the line of march of a terrifying army, fearful that it may turn its attention to them.

[8] Babylon has not been explicitly mentioned in the vision, however, so Habakkuk questions God on his objective. Against whom was God angry? Against what enemy had he mounted his war chariot? The mention of River and Sea, the cosmogonic enemy of Yahweh in the paradigmatic mythical pattern borrowed from the Baal cycle of Canaanite mythology, suggests that Habakkuk's query concerns the fundamental significance of this new intervention of Yahweh. The point of the questions is not to suggest that God's anger is really directed at Babylon, rather than the natural world. The point of the questions is to identify Babylon with the primeval powers of chaos and thus to suggest that this new march of Yahweh is a fundamental reenactment of Yahweh's primeval victories from which there emerged an ordered world under God's kingship (cf. Ps. 74:12–17). The questions, if answered affirmatively, contain the promise for Israel of renewed national life under their divine king (cf. Isa. 51:9–11).

[9] Habakkuk does not answer the questions explicitly, however. Instead, he uses them to expand his description of Yahweh as the divine warrior. God is portrayed as a typical charioteer, whose main weapon is the bow. The first two lines of this verse are full of textual difficulties, but the image in the first line seems to be that of the charioteer taking his bow from its carrying case on the chariot (see Hiebert, HSM 38:26; Yigael Yadin, *The Art of Warfare in Biblical Lands* [New York: McGraw-Hill Book Co., 1963], 4–5, 39–40, 88–89, 199, 212, 214–215, 240–241). The image in the second line is that of the arrows finding their mark and being sated on the blood of their victims. The imagery of the third line is hardly typical of an ordinary charioteer, however. Yahweh's splitting open of the earth with rivers recalls the motif in which the cosmogonic warrior, after having subdued the waters of chaos, reorders them as manageable sources of water

for the benefit of his structured world (Ps. 74:15; *Ee* V, 54–55). It is a reminder of the cosmogonic significance of Yahweh's coming intervention.

[10] This cosmic imagery is continued in v. 10. The writhing of the mountains and the rainstorm is a constant feature of theophanic texts. One reason for this is that, very early in pre-Israelite thought, the struggle between chaos and order was personified in the physical phenomena of a thunder storm over the coastal sea, the storm god representing the forces of order, the sea those of disorder. Israel borrowed this language from its neighbors, and, since God's victory over chaos was the theophany par excellence, such imagery became standard for all theophanies. The portrayal of the Deep in the last half of the verse is that of the still rebellious waters of chaos rising up against Yahweh in a vain attempt to cross over their appointed bounds (Jer. 5:22; Pss. 93:3–4; 148:4–6; Job 38:8–11; Prov. 8:27–29; cf. Isa. 17:12–14).

[11] Again there are very serious textual difficulties, most of the first line of this verse having been lost by haplography. Nevertheless, the imagery is that of the sun and moon being darkened by Yahweh's storm clouds. They blocked out the light of the heavenly bodies, and, in the ensuing darkness, the only light is that provided by lightning flashes, regarded as God's arrows or the glint of his spear (Ps. 77:17–19 [16–18]).

[12] The actual goal of Yahweh's march is indicated in this verse. Yahweh's anger is directed against the nations, and, as the following verse shows, specifically those nations who had oppressed his people. God's trampling of these human enemies is not set in opposition to his trampling of the sea, however, as Rudolph argues (p. 245), for then it is difficult to explain Habakkuk's resumption of the mythological metaphor in vs. 13b–15. Rather, these human enemies are identified with the mythological representatives of chaos precisely to underline the cosmic significance of Yahweh's coming intervention.

[13] Yahweh's intervention was for the salvation of his people and God's anointed one, the Davidic king. Since the vision refers to a set time in the future, there is no reason why Habakkuk need have had a particular Davidide in mind. One could as easily think of Jeremiah's ideal Davidide of the future (Jer. 23:5–6; cf. Rudolph, 245). Habakkuk probably did have a particular enemy in mind, however. The Chaldeans, or Babylonians, about whose oppressive dominion the prophet had complained earlier in the book and whom he had characterized as *rāšā'*, "wicked" (Hab. 1:12–17), must have been foremost in his mind when he spoke of the wicked one from whom Israel and its Davidic king must be delivered. Nonetheless, he does not explicitly mention the Babylonians here, and, in fact, he describes this wicked one in the imagery of the ancient myth, not as a human, but as a sea dragon (Hiebert, HSM 38:38). Just as Baal in the Ugaritic myth (*CTA* 4.16–17, 24–25), Yahweh smites first the back and then the head of his opponent (cf. *Ee* IV, 97–104, 128–132), and just as Marduk in the Babylonian myth (*Ee* IV, 135–138), Yahweh splits his opponent open from bottom to top.

[14] The extensive corruption in this verse makes any discussion of it somewhat problematic. The first line portrays Yahweh as riddling his enemy's head with arrows, but the following lines are quite obscure. My reconstruction and translation presuppose that they deal with Yahweh's treatment of the sea dragon's supporters (cf. *Ee* IV, 106–126). He scatters them, and uses them as food for his sea creatures (cf. Ps. 74:14).

[15] Having defeated his enemy and his helpers, Yahweh drives his chariot over the carcass of Sea and tramples it with his chariot horses (cf. *Ee* IV, 103–104, 128–129). Note that the enemy here is clearly identified with the personified Sea of the ancient myth. The gesture is symbolic of Yahweh's total defeat of his enemy and, in the context of Habakkuk's vision, a clear promise that God would destroy the Babylonian oppressor, the contemporary embodiment of those ancient powers of chaos.

[16] The verb *šāma'tî,* "I heard," points back to the use of the same verb in 3:2, and together they provide a kind of bracket around Habakkuk's vision, which begins in v. 3 and ends in v. 15. Verse 16 is no longer a part of the vision but is now a description of the prophet's reaction to the visionary experience. Despite the promise of deliverance that it contained for Habakkuk's people and its king, the prophet's vision of the majestic power of the divine warrior remained a terrifying experience (cf. Isa. 21:3–4), as any visionary experience tended to be regardless of the content of the vision (Job 4:12–16); the first four lines of Hab. 3:16 express that terror in terms of somewhat stereotypical physical reactions. The prophet's stomach grows queasy, his lips quiver, perhaps implying the chattering of his teeth (Rudolph, 238), and he feels his legs go weak.

Nonetheless, even in his terror, the prophet recognizes the promise implicit in the vision, and the response of his will to the vision is precisely what God demanded in Hab. 2:3. In light of the vision, Habakkuk is willing to cease from his complaints and to wait quietly for the vision's fulfillment, for the day of judgment to come upon the Babylonian oppressor.

[17–18] Far from being a secondary gloss or another lament, v. 17 is simply an expansion on Habakkuk's decision to patiently wait for the fulfillment of the vision. Formally, it is the protasis of a vow, whose apodosis comes in v. 18. Come what may, even if all outward signs point to God's absence (v. 17), Habakkuk vows to steadfastly walk in the light of the vision and not to lose hope (v. 18). Habakkuk may have chosen to illustrate the apparent absence of God through crop failures and the loss of livestock rather than through specific references to Babylonian oppression, because Babylonian oppression was already a fact of life, and he wanted to paint a worst-case scenario. Even if, in addition to Babylonian oppression, the crops fail and no livestock remain, still Habakkuk will trust in God to overcome these powers of chaos. Despite God's apparent absence, the prophet will continue to exult and rejoice in Yahweh as the God who brings about his salvation.

[19] The vow is followed by a statement of confidence that is typical of individual prayers of thanksgiving and that uses traditional hymnic imagery. Habakkuk uses a word for strength not otherwise attested in such predications about God (*ḥêlî,* "my strength, my army"), but the identification of the deity as the psalmist's strength is a common feature in the Psalms. Note especially the use of the synonym *'uzzî,* "my strength," as a predicate for God (Ex. 15:2; Pss. 28:7; 118:14). The prophet may have chosen the more unusual word *ḥêlî* for the sake of a double entendre. In contrast to the Babylonian oppressor who worshiped his military might as a god (1:11), Yahweh was Habakkuk's army. The second metaphor, that of making the psalmist's feet as nimble and surefooted as the hinds of the mountains, is also attested in earlier hymnic material (2 Sam. 22:34; Ps. 18:34 [33]). The prophet has clearly borrowed from Israel's hymnic tradition to express his confidence in God's ultimate salvation, but in so doing he expressed a profound truth about eschatological existence. In the certainty of that coming salvation, Habakkuk appears to say, one is both able to stay on the path, as precarious as it may seem, and, what is more, to experience in the interim some foretaste of that coming victory over the powers of evil.

After this closing statement of confidence, the prayer and the book are concluded with a musical rubric.

Zephaniah

Zephaniah

INTRODUCTION

The oracles collected in the book of Zephaniah have undergone a compositional editing that makes the collection extremely difficult to break down into the original independent units. It is clear, however, that the larger compositional structures within the book have been fashioned out of smaller, independent oracles, presumably given originally in an oral setting.

There is considerable discussion on the appropriate division even of these larger compositional structures within the book. Paul R. House *(Zephaniah: A Prophetic Drama)* has recently suggested that the book as a whole be read as a "prophetic drama" and that one divide it into three acts (1:2–17; 1:18–3:5; 3:6–20), each of which may be further divided into multiple scenes. House's analysis, however, seems seriously flawed. The characterization of the book's genre as prophetic drama is rendered problematic by the lack of any historical evidence that dramas were ever staged in ancient Israel, and House's appeal to "closet drama" or "literary drama" (p. 106) does not resolve this difficulty. Western culture is certainly familiar with written dramas that were never intended to be staged, but these closet dramas presuppose the earlier existence of staged dramas, and it is questionable if this secondary adaptation of stage dramas would have developed apart from that earlier genre. House's analysis also assigns too much importance to the variation between first- and third-person narration in these oracles. This is the key that allows him to claim that the drama's framework is built on seven sets of speeches containing a dialogue between Yahweh and the prophet (pp. 56–57). Such variation between first- and third-person narration is quite common in most prophetic material, and it seldom provides reliable criteria for distinguishing between the voice of God and the voice of the prophet, much less for analyzing a composition's structure. This is clear even from House's own translation of Zephaniah, where other, apparently nonstructural, third-person references to God occur in the material House assigns to Yahweh's narration (1:5, 6, 17; 2:10; 3:9, 12). Finally, one should note that House lumps the *hôy*-oracle against Jerusalem in 3:1 with the preceding material against Assyria and Nineveh in 2:13–15 as a continuation of the same speech. That goes against the normal conventions in the use of *hôy*-oracles. Except when they occur in a series, *hôy*-oracles almost always begin a new unit. Isaiah 1:4 might be an exception, but Isa. 1:4 introduces no shift in subject matter. In contrast, the radical shift in subject matter at Zeph. 3:1 suggests that this example of Zephaniah's use of the *hôy*-oracle presents no exception to the normal conventions governing the genre, and thus any close compositional tie to the preceding material is highly dubious.

This commentary also suggests that the book of Zephaniah is composed of three main compositions following a standard superscription (1:1), but the breaks are located at different points. Zephaniah 1:2–2:3 announces Yahweh's terrifyingly thorough judgment on Jerusalem and Judah. It opens with a threat of destruction on the Judean syncretists (1:2–6); urges silence before Yahweh, who has prepared Judah's faithless leaders and leading citizens to be sacrificed (1:8–13); announces the approach of the terrifying day of Yahweh against his sinful people (1:14–18); and concludes with an admonition to the poor and humble to seek Yahweh while there is at least a faint hope of escape from this terrible judgment (2:1–3). The second composition contains a collection of oracles against the foreign nations (2:4–15). It begins with an oracle against Philistia (2:4–7), includes an oracle against Moab and Ammon (2:8–10), cites a fragment against Ethiopia (2:12), and then concludes with a climactic oracle against Assyria, Judah's main enemy in Zephaniah's time (2:13–15). The third composition begins with an announcement of judgment against Jerusalem and ends with the promise of its transformation and salvation (3:1–20). It opens with a *hôy*-oracle against the rebellious and polluted city, whose surprising failure to learn from God's punishments will lead to its further punishment at the hand of the nations (3:1–8), but that judgment is intended to produce a transformation of the city and its surviving populace, so that the inhabitants will serve God with one accord (3:9–13). Once this transformation has taken place, the city may rejoice, for its period of judgment will have come to an end, and it can look forward to the restoration of its fortunes under Yahweh, its divine king (3:14–20).

Outline

I. Superscription (1:1)

II. Judgment against Judah and Jerusalem (1:2–2:3)
   A. Threat of destruction on Judean syncretists (1:2–6)
   B. Yahweh's sacrifice is prepared (1:7–13)
   C. The day of Yahweh is near (1:14–18)
   D. Seek Yahweh while there is still a chance (2:1–3)

III. Oracles against the foreign nations (2:4–15)
   A. Against Philistia (2:4–7)
   B. Against Moab and Ammon (2:8–10)
   C. Against Ethiopia (2:12)
   D. Against Assyria (2:13–15)

IV. Judgment and deliverance of Jerusalem (3:1–20)
   A. *Hôy*-oracle against Jerusalem (3:1–13)
      1. Judgment on the city (3:1–8)
      2. Its transformation (3:9–13)
   B. A call for Jerusalem to rejoice in its salvation (3:14–20)

Text

The text of Zephaniah is in relatively good condition. It has its text-critical problems, like many other prophetic books, but they are comparatively minor. Moreover, there are few secondary additions to the book. There is an explanatory gloss in 1:3, there appears to have been a secondary transposition of verses at 2:4–5, and there are two late universalizing glosses at 2:11 and 3:10. Apart from these few examples, the rest of the material in the book appears to be original. It is possible that some of the oracles against the foreign nations have been shortened in the editorial process, and there may have been some rearrangement of the originally independent oracles in the editorial formation of the compositional units in the book, but these changes were part of the composition of the book, not late, secondary alterations to the composition. In general, the book may be taken as a clear statement of the message of Zephaniah.

Date

The superscription dates the book to the reign of Josiah, and, despite the attempt of Smith and Lacheman to date the book as late as 200 B.C. (*JNES* 9 [1950]: 137–142), there is no good reason to doubt the correctness of the superscription's historical information. Moreover, Zephaniah's portrayal of the rampant syncretism and rapacious behavior among the royal and religious officials in Jerusalem (1:4–6, 8–9; 3:3–4) suggests that these oracles come from early in Josiah's reign, well before his famous religious reform began in 622 B.C. (2 Kings 22:3–23:25). The oracles make no mention of the person of the king himself, probably because at the time of Zephaniah's work Josiah was still just a boy, king in name, but actually under the control of royal officials (2 Kings 22:1). It is difficult to say just what influence external political realities may have had on Zephaniah's conviction that Yahweh's terrifying day of judgment was at hand. The evidence for a Scythian invasion during this period is tenuous at best, and even if an Egyptian attack on Philistia by Psammeticus during this period could be firmly established, it is unclear what impact that would have had on Judah (cf. Cazelles, *RB* 74 [1967]: 24–44). Zephaniah's theology, while it addresses internal Judean problems, seems far more rooted in Judah's earlier prophetic tradition than in a close observation of external political developments.

The Prophet and His Message

Relatively little is known about the prophet Zephaniah, but his message has much in common with the earlier prophetic tradition. His proclamation of the Day of Yahweh as a day of judgment on God's own people is dependent on the earlier work of Amos and Isaiah, and his understanding of the impending judgment on Jerusalem as a refining judgment to transform God's royal city corresponds very closely to Isaiah's use of the Zion Tradition. Just as Isaiah did, he proclaims God's judgment on Jerusalem's ruling classes with a vengeance, but, also as Isaiah, he sees that judgment as performing a positive function: God's ultimate goal in judgment is the transformation of his people, the creation of a poor and humble people in whose presence the righteous God can live, and this righteous remnant will one day rejoice in God's restoration of the fortunes of Zion.

COMMENTARY

I. The Title: 1:1

1:1 The word of Yahweh, which came to Zephaniah the son of Cushi, son of Gedaliah, son of Amariah, son of Hezekiah,[1] in the days of Josiah the son of Amon, king of Judah.

Textual Notes

[1]A few Hebrew manuscripts and the Peshiṭta have Hilkiah instead of Hezekiah, while a late corrector of Codex Siniaticus and the Ethiopic read Zedekiah, but there is no reason to prefer either of these readings to the MT.

Commentary

The title contains three elements: (1) It designates the content of the book as the word of Yahweh; (2) it identifies the prophet through whom this word of Yahweh came; and (3) it specifies the historical context in which this word was originally spoken. The same form of the title may be found in Hos. 1:1, while slightly variant forms are found in Joel 1:1 and Micah 1:1. Joel lacks the dating, while Micah adds an additional element further specifying the contents of the prophetic word: "which he saw concerning Samaria and

Jerusalem." The titles in the other prophetic books are less similar in form, though many of the same elements appear in variant formulations.

Each of these three elements found in the title of Zephaniah is important for an adequate understanding of the book. The title claims for the book the status of divine revelation; the words that follow are not mere human words, but words given to the prophet by Yahweh himself. Therefore they deserve a careful hearing.

The second element places the responsibility for this claim squarely on the prophet who first spoke these words. It is possible that the practice of attaching the name of the prophet to his oracles derived from the legal responsibility that a prophet bore for his words. At least in Mesopotamia, it seems clear that the prophets were held legally accountable for their messages. This seems to be what lay behind the practice at Mari of enclosing a clipping of the prophet's hair and of the fringe of his or her garment along with the prophetic message (*ANET,* 623 n. 10. See André Finet, "Les symboles de cheveu, du bord du vêtement et de l'ongle en Mésopotamie," *Eschatologie et cosmologie,* Annales du Centre d'Étude des Religions 3 [Brussels: Free University of Brussels, 1969], 101–130, esp. 124–125). It may also be the reason why the name of the prophet or prophetess responsible is attached to each of the oracles in the Neo-Assyrian collection of oracles concerning Esarhaddon (*ANET,* 605). The test given in Deut. 18: 21–22 for determining a true prophet presupposes the prophet's accountability for his words and therefore some record of which prophet said what. In its present form, it is a generalized theological test that the people as a whole may apply, but it may derive from an earlier practice of the royal court keeping a record of prophetic oracles.

The genealogical information attached to the prophet's name in Zeph. 1:1 is intended to identify the particular Zephaniah in question. The name Zephaniah means "Yahweh-Has-Hidden/Protected" (Ps. 31:20–21). Sabottka's understanding of the name as "Zaphon-Is-Yah" (pp. 1–3), seems less probable; personal names that equate Yahweh with another divinity or even with a sacred mountain are hardly well attested in the Israelite onomasticon. LXX's vocalization of the name as Sophonias does not support Sabottka's analysis, but probably understands the verbal element in the name as an imperative **ṣupun* > *ṣᵉpōn,* "Hide/Protect-O-Yahweh." Zephaniah appears to have been a very common Judean name in the late preexilic and exilic period. Four different Zephaniahs appear in the Old Testament: the prophet; a priest contemporary with Jeremiah (2 Kings 25:18; Jer. 21:1; 29:25, 29; 37:3; 52:24); and two others (Zech. 6:10, 14; 1 Chron. 6:21 [36]). A four-generation genealogy for identification purposes is rather unusual, however, and this has provoked a debate over the reason for including the extra names in this list. The two most common explanations are that (1) Zephaniah was of royal blood, that his ancestor Hezekiah was none other than the Judean king of the same name, or (2) that the editor wanted to make clear that the prophet was of native Judean stock despite his father's name, Cushi, which means "the Ethiopian." Though neither explanation can be entirely ruled out, neither is compelling. The Hezekiah in Zephaniah's genealogy is not designated as king, and the early church fathers seemed to know of no Jewish tradition that made such an identification. Indeed, the textual corruption in the Syriac text would not have been possible had such a tradition been widely known in the Syrian church. Whether the name Cushi implied anything about the bearer's nationality, or whether it was just a nickname, like our Tex, given for any of a variety of reasons, cannot be determined. Moreover, the genealogy in Jer. 36:14, which ends with a Cushi, makes the assumption that the ancient editor would have been bothered by a Cushi in Zephaniah's ancestry rather dubious.

The third element reminds us that the prophetic word is not a universal proposition, but a word spoken in a particular historical context. Whoever attached the title to the following collection of oracles—whether the prophet himself, a disciple, or a later editor—apparently believed that a knowledge of the historical context was essential to a genuine understanding of the oracles themselves. He dates Zephaniah's prophetic activity to the reign of Josiah; the internal evidence of the oracles suggest, as we have argued in the introduction, a more precise setting during the early years of Josiah's reign, when the actual power was in the hand of the boy-king's regents and before his religious reform.

II. The Day of Yahweh: 1:2–2:3

Zephaniah 1:2–18 represents a compositional unit, but there are indications that it is made up of originally independent oral pronouncements.

1. Yahweh's Impending Judgment: 1:2–6

1:2 I will gather up[1] everything
From upon the face of the earth,
Says Yahweh.
3 I will gather up[1] man and beast;
I will gather up[1] the birds of the sky
And the fish of the sea.
[Those who cause the wicked to stumble.][2]
I will cut off mankind
From upon the face of the earth,
Says Yahweh.

4 And I will stretch out my hand against Judah,
And against all the inhabitants of Jerusalem,
And I will cut off from this place
The last vestige[3] of Baal,
The name of the pagan priests,[4]
5 And those who bow down on the roofs
To the host of heaven;
And those who bow down to Yahweh,[5]
But swear by Milkom;[6]
6 Those who turn back from following Yahweh,
Who do not seek Yahweh
Or inquire of him.

Textual Notes

[1]The precise analysis of the Hebrew construction here remains a subject of debate. As it is pointed, the Hebrew must be analyzed with Gerleman (*Zephanja,* 2) as the qal infinitive absolute of *'sp,* "to gather," followed by the hiphil jussive of *swp,* "to bring to an end." The same construction is found in the MT of Jer. 8:13: "Gathering them up, I will bring them to an end." The LXX appears to have a different text in Jer. 8:13, however, and it is quite unusual in such a grammatical construction for the infinitive absolute and the finite verb to be derived from two different verbs. Gerleman cites the *'ādôš yᵉdûšennû* of Isa. 28:28 as a parallel (p. 3), but most scholars regard *'ādôš* as a textual error. Because of this difficulty with the construction, Rudolph corrects *'āsēp* to *'ōsēp* and interprets it as a qal imperfect 1 c. s. of *'sp,* thus keeping the same verb for both the infinitive and the following finite verb (p. 261). My translation follows Rudolph's analysis and emendation, but even if the MT's pointing were correct, the translation would differ only slightly; the general sense of the passage would remain the same. Other suggestions will be discussed in the notes.

[2]RSV emends the text to read "I will overthrow the wicked," but MT actually has "and those who cause the wicked to stumble." The line is missing in the LXX and is probably a late gloss that sees the animals mentioned in the preceding line as creatures that led the wicked astray into idolatry.

[3]The LXX reads *ta onomata tēs Baal,* "the names of Baal" *(=šᵉmôt habba'al),* rather than *šᵉ'ār habba'al,* "the remnant of Baal," but this is probably due to corruption from the following *šēm hakkᵉmārîm,* "the name of the pagan priests." Name, *šēm,* and remnant, *šᵉ'ār,* are well attested as parallel terms (Isa. 14:22; and with *šᵉ'ērît* in place of *šᵉ'ār,* 2 Sam. 14:7).

[4]The Hebrew contains the additional phrase *'im hakkōhᵃnîm,* "with

the priests," but the LXX omits this phrase. The term *hakkōh^{a}nîm* was probably introduced into the text as a gloss on the unusual word *hakk^{e}mārîm,* and this in turn necessitated the introduction of the preposition *'im* in order to make sense of *hakkōh^{a}nîm* syntactically. The term *k^{e}mārîm* occurs in only two other passages in the OT (2 Kings 23:5 and Hos. 10:5), and in both cases it gave the Greek translator trouble. The LXX of Hos. 10:5 does not translate the word; it reflects a text redivided as follows: *wkmryw 'lyw.* The translator apparently read it as *k^{e}mô mārû 'ālāyw,* "just as they rebelled against him," or possibly he simply repointed *wkmryw* as the preposition *k^{e}* plus the masculine participle with suffix *ûk^{e}mōrāyw* (Rudolph, 196). In 2 Kings 23:5, the Greek translator simply transliterated the word as *chōmareim.* Some minuscules translate it as *iereis* (bi[mg]o c^{2}e^{2}Syroh[mg]) and two (g,246) preserve both the translation and the transliteration in slightly garbled form. Thus a gloss on *hakk^{e}mārîm* would not be unexpected. Sabottka, following van Hoonacker, keeps the Hebrew text and translates the phrase as "den Namen der Gözenpriester aus den Priestern" (p. 18), but this explanation must assume an unusual meaning for *'im,* "with," and seems less likely than a simple gloss.

[5]The Hebrew contains an additional participle, *hannišbā'îm,* which would require a translation such as, "And those who bow down, who swear to Yahweh." LXX omits the first participle, *hammištaḥ^{a}wîm,* which would result in the translation, "And those who swear by the LORD." One of the two participles would appear to be an expansion. The first could be due to the influence of the preceding *hammištaḥ^{a}wîm;* the second could be due to the influence of the following *hannišbā'îm.* Two considerations support the deletion of *hannišbā'îm:* (1) the verb *hštḥwh,* "to bow down," is normally construed with the preposition *l^{e}* to indicate the object of worship (as in the preceding phrase *w^{e}'et-hammištaḥ^{a}wîm . . . liṣbā' haššāmāyīm,* "and who bow down . . . to the host of heaven"), but the verb *nšb',* "to swear," is normally construed with the preposition *b^{e}* to indicate the name by which one swears (as MT has in the following phrase, *wehannišbā'îm b^{e}malkām,* "and who swear by their king"); (2) it is unusual to have the same verb repeated in two parallel lines.

[6]The reading *milkom* follows S and V; MT and LXX have "their king," *malkām.* The reference is clearly to a pagan god worshiped alongside Yahweh, but whether that god was the Ammonite Milkom or the Canaanite Molech, as Irsigler suggests (pp. 31–35), is impossible to decide. Both deities are mentioned in the account of Josiah's reform (2 Kings 23:4–5, 10–13).

Commentary

Zephaniah 1:2–6 contains the announcement of Yahweh's impending judgment against Judah and Jerusalem because of their religious syncretism, but, like many such announcements of God's judgment against his people (Amos 1:2–2:6; Micah 1:2–5), it begins with a word of judgment against the whole world (vs. 2–3). As Franz Hesse (*ZAW* 65 [1953]:49) and others following him have pointed out, this pattern is based on the conception that Yahweh's theophany, with its cosmic disturbances, will bring destruction upon all Yahweh's enemies (cf. Hab. 3:3–15). The new twist introduced by the prophets is the thought that God's own people could be among those enemies (Rudolph, 265), but the prophets typically introduce this thought only after capturing the interest and approval of their audiences by a prior announcement of God's impending judgment on the heathen world (Kapelrud, *Message,* 20). Thus the mixture of universal judgment and a particular judgment on Judah and Jerusalem in Zeph. 1:2–6 is neither unparalleled nor particularly surprising, and this mixture provides no justification for the judgment common in older critical commentaries that vs. 2–3 be considered a secondary insertion in the text.

[1:2] The oracle begins with Yahweh's solemn assertion that he is about to gather up everything from upon the face of the earth. The root *'āsap,* "to gather in/up," is often used in the sense of "destroy" or "take away" (Hos. 4:3; Pss. 26:9; 104:29; Job 34:14; Hab. 2:5; cf. Ezek. 34:29). The same 1 c. s. qal impf. form (see textual note) is repeated twice more in the next verse. This extensive wordplay on the root probably has some significance. T. H. Gaster suggested there was an allusion here to the autumn festival of *'āsîp,* "ingathering" (*Myth, Legend, and Custom in the Old Testament* [New York: Harper & Row, 1969], 679; cf. Ex. 34:22), and it is quite conceivable that Zephaniah proclaimed his message to the people when they had assembled to celebrate this feast. The feast would not be what they expected; it was Yahweh who was going to do the gathering in (Kapelrud, *Message,* 22).

Sabbotka repoints the two initial verbs as *'ōsēp 'ᵉsōp* (1 c. s. qal impf. of *ysp* + qal inf. const. of *'sp*), "I will again gather in" (pp. 6–7), and finds an allusion here to the flood story (p. 10). The repointing and derivation of the initial verbal form from *ysp,* "to do again," is unnecessary, and it is also unconvincing, since the Genesis flood did not destroy the fish of the sea (Rudolph, 261), but the verse probably does allude to the flood story. The expression *m'l pny h'dmh,* "from upon the face of the earth," which occurs twice in Zeph. 1:2–3, occurs three times in the flood story (Gen. 6:7; 7:4; 8:8), and Zephaniah's specification of what was to be cut off from upon the face of the earth (v. 3) is very similar to the formulation in Gen. 6:7 (see below).

The expression *nᵉʾûm yhwh,* "says Yahweh" (lit. "oracle of Yahweh") is a common formulaic expression in prophetic material. Its function is to claim divine authority for the prophetic word. The formula tended to be inserted at random in prophetic oracles, so it is not a reliable guide for detecting seams between oracles. Here it is inserted between the opening statement of the oracle and its closely connected elaboration in the next verse.

[**3**] This verse specifies what is meant by the *kōl,* "everything," of v. 2. Genesis 6:7 specified the creatures who were to die in the flood as *mēʾādām ʿad-bᵉhēmāh ʿad-remeś wᵉʿad-ʿôp haššāmāyîm,* "humans together with beasts, creeping things, and birds of the heavens." Zephaniah's formulation *ʾādām ûbᵉhēmāh . . . ʿôp-haššāmayîm ûdᵉgê hayyām,* "humans and beasts . . . birds of the heavens and fish of the sea," omits any specific reference to the creeping things, but it includes fish (cf. Hos. 4:3; Ezek. 38:19–20), which are never mentioned in the Genesis flood story and so were presumably unaffected by that judgment. In this regard, the impending judgment announced by Zephaniah is characterized as more inclusive even than the primeval flood (cf. also Jer. 4:23–27, where the judgment is portrayed as a return to primeval chaos).

Nevertheless, while the impending judgment will be even more inclusive than the primeval flood, the real target of Yahweh's wrath, just as in the earlier flood, is not the dumb creatures of nature but sinful humanity. This is made clear by the repetition in slightly altered wording of the judgment against mankind. The other creatures are caught up in this judgment willy-nilly, through no fault of their own, merely because of their solidarity with mankind (cf. Gen. 3:17–19; Rom. 8:19–22) as creatures subordinated to human authority by divine decree (Gen. 1:26, 28; 9:1–3; Ps. 8:5–9 [4–8]). The glossator who added the line "and those who cause the wicked to stumble" misunderstood this point and tried to provide an explanation for the judgment on the nonhuman creatures. In his view these creatures stood under judgment because they had tempted the wicked to honor them as gods, as idols fashioned in the image of these creatures. This is a basic misunderstanding that detracts from the point of the oracle, which is to focus on human culpability.

[**4**] That focus is sharpened in v. 4, where the prophet turns from mankind in general to announce God's judgment on Judah and Jerusalem in particular and then, sharpening the focus even more, on particular groups in Judah and Jerusalem. The idiom *nṭh yd ʿl,* "to stretch out the hand against," is often used of God's initiation of judgment against his enemies (Isa. 14:26–27; Ezek. 14:13; 16:27; 35:3; cf. Isa. 5:25; 9:11, 16, 20 [12, 17, 21]; 10:4; Jer. 21:5) and normally suggests a hostile intent in contrast to the related expression *šlḥ yd ʿl,* "to stretch out the hand toward," which may express positive intent (1 Chron. 13:10). The difference between the two

expressions should not be overdrawn, however; the idiom *nṭh yd ʿl* can be used with a human subject (Ex. 7:19; 8:1 [5], 12 [16]; passim; Job 15:25; cf. Humbert, *VT* 12 [1962]: 383–395).

Many critics delete the expression "from this place" as a prose gloss that unduly restricts Zephaniah's words to the holy places in Jerusalem. Irsigler agrees and suggests that the gloss is due to deuteronomic influence (see Deut. 12:3; Irsigler, 108), but it is not at all clear that the expression *hammāqôm hazzeh,* "this place," carries any such restriction. The expression can be used to refer to a holy place, but it has a much broader usage that can include a specific territory or country (Jer. 16:2–3, 9; 22:11–12; cf. Van der Woude, 91). In the context in Zeph. 1:4, the expression can only refer to the broader territory of Judah and Jerusalem mentioned in the first part of the verse. Metrical arguments provide no firm ground for deleting the phrase, and as Van der Woude has pointed out, a late glossator would be unlikely to want to restrict idolatry specifically to Jerusalem (p. 91). The thought is rather that God would cut off from both Judah and Jerusalem the idolatrous practices that offended him.

There are several expressions used with the verb *hakrît,* "to cut off," to indicate a total destruction. Some involve antithetical pairs to encompass the whole: *ʾādām ûbᵉhēmāh,* "man and beast" (Ezek. 14:13, 17; 25:13; 29:8); *ṣaddîq wᵉrāšāʿ,* "righteous and wicked" (Ezek. 21:8 [3]); *ʿōbēr wāšāb,* "the one who passes by and the one who returns" (Ezek. 35:7); *rōʾš wᵉzānāb,* "head and tail," in parallel with *kippāh wᵉʾagmôn,* "palm frond and rush" (Isa. 9:13 [14]); and *ʿāṣûr wᵉʿāzûb,* "the shut up and the released" (1 Kings 14:10; 21:21; 2 Kings 9:8). Others are complementary rather than antithetical: *ʿôlāl miḥûṣ baḥûrîm mērᵉḥōbôt,* "the child from the street, the young men from the squares" (Jer. 9:20 [21]); *ʾîš wᵉʾiššāh ʿôlēl wᵉyônēq,* "man and woman, child and suckling" (Jer. 44:7); *ʿēr wᵉʿōneh,* "protector and one who answers" (Mal. 2:12; see Rudolph's discussion in KAT XIII/4, 269); *pesel ûmassēkāh,* "idol and graven image" (Nahum 1:14); and *šēm ûšᵉʾār wᵉnîn wāneked,* "name and remnant and offspring and descendant" (Isa. 14:22). Whether by antithesis or by complementarity, however, all these expressions underscore the totality of the destruction.

The expression *šᵉʾār,* "remnant," like the related *šᵉʾērît,* when used in parallel with *šēm,* "name," refers to someone's descendants who can carry on his name and memory (Isa. 14:22; 2 Sam. 14:7). What Zephaniah means when he speaks of Yahweh cutting off "the remnant of Baal" and "the name of the pagan priests" is that Yahweh's destruction will be so thorough that it will leave both Baal and his priests without descendants or adherents to preserve their memory after the judgment is passed. It does not imply that either has already been reduced in number or influence; hence it cannot be used to date Zephaniah after Josiah's reform.

Sabottka corrects *šᵉʾār* to *šᵉʾēr,* "flesh, blood relative, blood relationship," and translates the phrase *šᵉʾēr habbaʿal* as "family of Baal," which he understands as "the worshipers of Baal" who were conceived of as the god's relatives (p. 16). Irsigler supports Sabottka (p. 17 n. 52), but their whole case rests on the mistaken assumption that there is a radical difference in meaning between *šᵉʾār* and *šᵉʾērît* and that the MT cannot simply mean that Baal and his priests will be exterminated. To make his case, he must also emend *šᵉʾār,* "remnant," to *šᵉʾēr,* "flesh," in Isa. 14:22, but, contra Sabottka (p. 16), the Syriac translation of this verse hardly justifies his emendation.

Baal is an epithet that means "Lord," and, as such, it could be used to refer to a number of different deities. During early periods of Israelite history, it was widely used even as a epithet for Yahweh (see 2 Sam. 5:20), a practice that Hosea said must stop (Hos. 2:18–19 [16–17]). It was especially used, however, as the common designation for the great Canaanite storm god Hadad under any of his various local manifestations, and it is probably this deity, perhaps in its Phoenician form, to which the prophet here refers.

The word *kᵉmārîm,* "priests," is only used for pagan or idolatrous priests in the OT (2 Kings 23:5; Hos. 10:5), but its cognates are attested in Canaanite *(kumiru),* Akkadian *(kumru),* and Aramaic *(kumraʾ)* as ordinary words for priest. Its extremely rare occurrence in biblical Hebrew is probably responsible for the explanatory gloss using the ordinary word for priest that ultimately produced the peculiar MT reading *ʿim-hakkōhᵃnîm,* "with the priests." One should note that Josiah did away with these pagan clergy in his religious reform (2 Kings 23:5).

[5] Yahweh's threat to cut off all memory of the Canaanite Baal and his cultic personnel is extended in this verse to the Judeans who worshiped other pagan deities. The *ṣᵉbāʾ haššāmāyīm,* "host of heaven," refers to the sun, moon, planets, and stars (Deut. 4:19; 17:3). These were always considered deities in Canaanite culture, but cultic devotion to these heavenly bodies does not seem to have become widespread in Judean culture until the Assyrian period, especially during the reign of Manasseh and his successors (2 Kings 21:1–7). The heavenly bodies played an important role in Assyrian religion, and it is likely that their growing prominence in syncretistic Judean piety was largely because of the strong Assyrian influence on Judah during this period when the Assyrian imperial power was at its peak, extending deep into Egyptian territory. Josiah suppressed this practice during his reform (2 Kings 23:4–5), but it had become deeply rooted in popular piety. This practice was soon revived after Josiah's death, and Jeremiah saw it as a major religious problem (Jer. 8:2; 19:13). The worship of *mᵉleket haššāmayīm,* "the queen of heaven," against which Jeremiah also raged, was probably a part of this same phenomenon (Jer. 7:18; 44:15–25). With the exception of the sun and moon, these heavenly bodies were normally visible only at night, so worship of the astral deities was normally carried out at night on the rooftops where one could get a more unobstructed view of the night sky (Jer. 19:13; 32:29).

If the text is correct, the next line refers to those who continue to worship Yahweh but at the same time take oaths in the name of other gods. Some critics suggest emending *yhwh* here to *yrḥ,* "Yareah," the name of the Canaanite moon god (so *BHS*). This would fit the context of the prophet's condemnation of idolatry much better than the somewhat jarring mention of Yahweh, and the verse so rendered would lead more smoothly into v. 6, but the correction is not necessary. Worship of the national god Yahweh continued unabated even during the most idolatrous and syncretistic periods of Judah's existence.

The correct reading and identification of the pagan god in whose name the Judeans were swearing is problematic (see the textual notes). Milkom was the Ammonite god (1 Kings 11:5, 33; 2 Kings 23:13), while the reading "their king" would be a reference to the Canaanite Baal, sometimes referred to as Molek (Rudolph, 266). Whichever reading one chooses, the syncretism involved in this action is obvious. 2 Kings 23:1–15 gives some indication how widespread such syncretistic practices had become by the time of Josiah's reform sometime later than Zephaniah.

[6] This unit concludes the list of those Judeans whom Yahweh will cut off from the land. The idiom *nswg m'ḥry,* "to turn aside from," means to prove faithless, to treacherously desert one to whom one had a commitment (Isa. 50:5; 59:13; Jer. 38:22; Pss. 44:19 [18]; 78:57). The verb *baqqēš,* "to seek," when used with a god as the object, originally meant to approach the deity with a request or prayer (2 Sam. 12:16; 21:1) and *dāraš,* "to inquire," when used with a god as the object, originally meant to go to the god for an oracle (Gen. 25:22; Ex. 18:15; 1 Kings 14:5; 22:4–8), but oracular response to prayer was so much a part of the religious culture that the terms could be used synonymously (Deut. 4:29; Isa. 65:1; Jer. 29:13; Pss. 24:6; 105:3–4; 1 Chron. 16:10–11). Eventually, both terms came to refer to religious devotion to a deity in a more general sense. Nevertheless, the idea that one found direction for one's life through such religious devotion always seems to have been retained in the meaning of the expressions.

To whom is Zephaniah referring with these expressions? Most critics assume he is referring to the same syncretists mentioned in the preceding verses, and for this reason many of them delete the verse as a gloss. Keller says that it merely explains that worshiping other gods is tantamount to deserting Yahweh (p. 189). On the other hand, Rudolph argues that the verse refers to a separate group, not those who are devoted to pagan gods, but those who are not devoted to any god at all, who trust in their own ability to direct their lives, i.e., to the same people Zephaniah mentions in 1:12 (p. 266). Rudolph may have overstated his case; those who do not seek direction for their lives from Yahweh could include the Judean adherents of these deified heavenly bodies, who sought oracles from these deities rather than from Yahweh (Jer. 8:2; cf. 2 Kings 1:2–6, 16), as well as those who simply trusted in their own plans and ignored oracles altogether (cf. Isa. 31:1). Nevertheless, Rudolph is correct in his judgment that v. 6 is not simply a repetition of v. 5. It offers a new thought by shifting the reader's attention from Judah's sinful devotion to other gods to Judah's neglect of Yahweh and the people's failure to seek direction from him. Verse 6 should not be deleted.

2. Yahweh's Sacrifice Is Prepared: 1:7–13

1:7 Be silent before my Lord Yahweh,
For the day of Yahweh is near,
For Yahweh has prepared a sacrificial feast,
He has consecrated his guests.
8 And on the day of Yahweh's sacrifice,
I will punish the officials,
And the king's sons,
And all those who wear foreign apparel.
9 And I will punish every one who leaps[1] over the threshold[2]
in that day,
Those who fill the house of their lord[3] with violence and deceit.
10 And there will be on that day, says Yahweh,
The sound of crying from the fish[4] gate,
And wailing from the second district,
And a great shattering from the hills.
11 Wail,[5] O inhabitants of the "Mortar"![6]
For all the tradespeople[7] have perished,[8]
All who weigh silver[9] have been cut off.
12 At that time
I will search Jerusalem with lamps,[10]
And I will punish the men[11] who are thickening[12] on their lees,[13]
Who say in their hearts,
"Yahweh will not do good nor will he do harm."
13 And their wealth will be for plunder,
And their houses for desolation.
They will build houses and not live in them,
They will plant vineyards and not drink their wine.

Textual Notes

[1]LXX translates *hdwlg* with the adverb *emphanōs,* "openly;" V renders *omnem qui arroganter ingreditur,* "everyone who arrogantly en-

ters;" and S translates with *ḥṭwp'*, "the rapacious ones." All these translations take the verb as describing a manner of approach that suggests evil intentions. As Gerleman says, "Whoever comes in this manner has evil intentions, comes in order to rob and to plunder" (*Zephanja,* 11). T's "all those who walk in the laws of the Philistines," on the contrary, interprets the verb and its dependent phrase as a reference to the pagan religious rite mentioned in 1 Sam. 5:5 in the idiom *drk 'l mptn,* "to tread upon the threshold." This also seems to be the interpretation of Symmachus, who translates *hdwlg* with *epibainontas,* "(those who) tread upon," the verb used in 1 Sam. 5:5. The other occurrences of the Hebrew verb in the Bible show that *dlg* means "to leap" or "to skip," and they give no indication that any hostile intention is inherent in the meaning of the verb (2 Sam. 22:30 = Ps. 18:30 [29]; Isa. 35:6; S. of Sol. 2:8; cf. Sirach 33:33 [31]).

[2]LXX translates *'l-hmptn* with *epi ta propyla,* "upon the gateways," and V has *super limen,* "upon the threshold." S apparently took the phrase as parallel with *'l kl-hdwlg* and saw *hmptn* as another participle; it renders the phrase as *wbzwz',* "and the plunderers." Gerleman (pp. 9–10), Sabottka (pp. 39–40), and others have argued that *mptn* is not a threshold or doorsill but a stepped podium; however, Donner (*JSS* 15 [1970]: 42ff.), Rudolph (p. 262), and Irsigler (pp. 45–47) have argued persuasively for the traditional rendering. Note esp. Ezek. 46:2 and 47:1.

[3]LXX and V have "house of their lord God," which indicates that they interpreted the MT as referring to the temple in Jerusalem. S has *byt mdnyhwn,* "the house of their storerooms."

[4]LXX's "gate of those who pierce *(apokentountōn),*" arose from the misreading of *haddāgîm,* "of the fish," as *hōrᵉgîm,* "of slayers" (see Ezek. 21:16 [11]; Hos. 9:13).

[5]The hiphil imperative m. pl. and perfect 3 m. pl. are identical in form, but in this context one would expect the perfect to be preceded by *wᵉ-*.

[6]The "Mortar" is a district in Jerusalem. It apparently received its name because it was in a hollow and resembled the shape of a mortar. T identifies it with the Kidron Valley, but Rudolph locates it somewhere in the western part of the city (p. 268).

[7]LXX, V, and S translate *kn'n* as though it referred to the land, and T's periphrastic rendering, "all the people whose deeds resemble the deeds of the people of the land of Canaan," assumes the same literal meaning. Nevertheless, the parallelism indicates that *kn'n* is used here in the sense "merchant" (cf. Isa. 23:8; Ezek. 16:29; 17:4; Hos. 12:8 [7]; Zech. 14:21). Aquila has *metabolōn,* "of traders."

[8]LXX derived *ndmh* from *dmh* I, "to be similar," and ended up with the very awkward translation "because all the people became like Ca-

naan." V's *conticuit,* "became silent," and S's *twr,* "to be dazed," from *dmh* II are not much better. The parallel with *nkrtw* shows that the verb must be derived from *dmh* III, "to destroy, be destroyed."

[9]The form *nāṭîl,* derived from the verb *nāṭal,* "to weigh," is a *nomen agentis* meaning "the weigher, the one who weighs" (Rudolph, 263); "the weigher of silver" is another expression for the merchant, since in the absence of standard coinage silver was taken in exchange by weight. Apart from S, the versions took *n*ᵉ*ṭîlê* as a passive form and ended up with slightly different readings. LXX has "those who are lifted up *(epērmenoi)* by silver," i.e., haughty because of wealth. V has "those who are involved *(involuti)* with silver," i.e., loaded down and entangled by it. T has "all those who are rich in silver."

[10]LXX and S have the singular, but V supports MT. T expands the text to avoid attributing the action directly to Yahweh: "I will appoint investigators and they will investigate the inhabitants of Jerusalem as those who investigate with a lamp."

[11]Rudolph suggests inserting *haššaʾ*ᵃ*nannîm,* "who are at ease," either after or in place of *hʾnšym,* "the men," based on the parallel in Jer. 48:11 (p. 263). The insertion would ease the excessively long line by allowing one to divide it as follows: "I will punish the men who are at ease//Who are thickening on their lees." The loss of *haššaʾ*ᵃ*nannîm* would be easily explained by haplography. There is no textual support for the insertion in the versions, however.

[12]The image is drawn from that of wine maturing undisturbed on its lees, as V saw (cf. Isa. 25:6; Jer. 48:11). S and LXX agree in rendering the participle as "those who despise," but it is unclear how they arrived at this meaning. Biel (in Johann F. Schleusner, *Novus thesaurus philologico-criticus: sive, Lexicon in LXX et reliquos interpretes graecos ac scriptores apocryphos Veteris Testamenti,* vol. III [Leipzig: Weidmann, 1820], 273) has conjectured that LXX's *kataphronountas* is a corruption of *kataphorountas,* "who are lethargic," which would be a fair rendering of MT.

[13]LXX mistakenly derived *šimrêhem,* "their lees," from *šmr* I, "to guard, keep," and thus translated the term as "their ordinances *(phylagmata),*" i.e., the ordinances they were supposed to keep. S apparently read *šōm*ᵉ*rêhem* but understood it as a plural of majesty referring to God, "their watchman." T catches the sense with its "who are resting unconcerned on their money."

Commentary

[1:7] Verse 7 switches from direct address by Yahweh to a word of admonition by the prophet, but the transition is made easier by the third-person references to Yahweh in vs. 5–6. The cry *has* or *hās,* "be silent!" though used in other contexts where immediate silence was required (Judg. 3:19; Amos 6:10; 8:3), was apparently widely used as a liturgical cry to silence the gathering community prior to the beginning of communal worship (Hab. 2:20; Zech. 2:17 [13]), and it is that liturgical usage that the prophet is imitating here. The audience was to keep silence because the day of Yahweh was at hand and the sacrifice was ready to be offered.

This mention of the day of Yahweh and his sacrifice introduces a new theme and justifies the treatment of v. 7 as the beginning of a new unit, rather than as the end of the preceding unit, but there is no radical break in the text, and one could regard the threats in vs. 2–6 as leading up to the announcement in vs. 7ff. (Rudolph, 266). Some critics have suggested transposing v. 7 to just before v. 14 in order to bring it into closer proximity to this other material on the day of Yahweh, but if v. 7 originally belonged there, it is difficult to explain its present position except by the assumption of a conscious compositional intent. If that is so, one should interpret the present text as it stands.

The concept of the day of Yahweh was apparently well known in both Judah and Israel; it appears to have been an expectation cultivated in the Yahwistic liturgy that Yahweh would, at some set day, intervene dramatically in history to destroy his enemies. The liturgical presentation of the concept must have portrayed Yahweh's enemies as identical with the enemies of his people, because it is clear from Amos that the Israelites had positive expectations concerning this day (5:17–20). Amos turned the concept on its head by suggesting that Israel could also be numbered among God's enemies, but there is little reason to think his message changed the basic attitude toward this concept in Judah. Long after Amos, similar positive expectations were still associated with the concept in Judah, since God's judgment on Babylon could be announced in terms of the day of Yahweh (Isa. 13:5–9). Zephaniah follows Amos in using the concept to announce God's judgment on his own people, but Zephaniah's negative use of the concept would not have been immediately apparent to his Judean audience. In Zephaniah's Judah, just as in Amos's Israel, the positive expectations still dominated the conception, so the implications of Zephaniah's announcement of the nearness of the day of Yahweh would have been initially heard as a positive or, at worst, an ambiguous announcement.

Zephaniah continues to play on this ambiguity when he announces Yahweh's preparation for a sacrificial feast. If Zephaniah spoke these words in the temple complex on the occasion of the autumn feast of ingathering, when the people had come to the temple to participate in one of the three major sacrificial festivals of Yahweh, his announcement might have been understood initially to refer to the rites in that festival. The Judeans would not eat the sacrificial meal Yahweh was preparing, however, for the implication of Zephaniah's words is that Judah would be the sacrifice (cf. Isa. 34:6–7; Jer. 46:10)! Yahweh's guests, consecrated by him to eat the sacrifice (see 1 Sam. 16:5 for this practice) would not be the Judeans, but either the foreign armies he would bring against Judah (Isa. 13:3–5) or the birds and beasts of prey who would feed on the corpses of the dead (Ezek. 19:17–20).

[8] The expression *wᵉhāyāh bᵉyôm zebaḥ Yhwh,* "and it will come to pass on the day of Yahweh's sacrifice," is an editorial link probably added when v. 7 was placed in its present position. It provides the transition from the third-person announcement of Yahweh's sacrifice (v. 7) back to Yahweh's first-person announcements of the judgments he was about to mete out (vs. 4–6, 8b). Kapelrud (p. 30) and Irsigler (p. 96) think the function of this expression is to displace the expected intervention to the distant future, and Kapelrud suggests that the motivation for its insertion was to reassure the contemporary princes and officials that the prophet's words were not really directed against them, but against a situation in the distant future. The insertion of this expression was an attempt on the part of the early editors to avoid persecution for their part in preserving the prophetic message (Kapelrud, 19). Neither point seems convincing. The expression leaves the exact time of Yahweh's intervention indefinite, but, in juxtaposition with the statement, "the day of Yahweh is near" (v. 7), it can hardly imply the distant future, and it is hard to imagine government officials so easily placated by a mere cosmetic touch to Zephaniah's damning message. The function of the expression is to provide an editorial transitional link, nothing more, and it could have been added by the prophet in his compositional work as easily as it could have been added by a later editor.

Yahweh threatens the officials, royal princes, and all the others who wear foreign apparel. Sabottka takes *hammelek,* "the king," in this verse to refer to the god Baal-shamem. He interprets "the sons of the king" as simply referring to the adherents of this god, and he suggests that the *śārîm,* "officials," were cultic officials, not political functionaries (pp. 36–37; cf. Jer. 48:7). Sabottka's interpretation seems farfetched and improbable, however. The king himself is not placed under judgment in this oracle, presumably because Josiah was still just a child and not really in control of the government; he was only eight at the time of his enthronement (2 Kings 22:1). That also suggests that the expression *bᵉnê hammelek,* "sons of the king," be taken not as referring to the actual sons of Josiah, the reigning king, but as a general designation for male members of the royal family, princes (cf. Rudolph, 267).

One could interpret the prophet's objection to foreign apparel as an attack on Judah's loss of self-identity as the people of Yahweh. Defenders of traditional culture often regard the importation of foreign styles in clothing as both a sign and a cause of corruption in the society's fundamental values, and conservative reform movements are often somewhat xenophobic in restoring traditional modes of dress. (One need only look at radical Islamic fundamentalism in modern Iran to see this tendency at work.) On the other hand, it is possible that there is a more directly religious concern in the prophet's words. Special clothing was sometimes worn in the worship of Baal (2 Kings 10:22), and it may be that Zephaniah's reference to foreign apparel is concerned more specifically with this kind of religious syncretism, in which foreign apparel was donned for religious purposes.

[9] Religious syncretism seems to be the target of the first line of v. 9. Though the meaning of the expression *kol haddôlēg 'al-hammiptān,* "everyone who leaps over the threshold," is hotly disputed (see the textual notes), the practice to which the expression refers appears to be identical with the Philistine religious custom mentioned in 1 Sam. 5:5: "Therefore the priests of Dagon and all those who enter the temple of Dagon do not step on the threshold of Dagon *(lō' yidrᵉkû . . . 'al miptān Dāgôn)* in Ashdod until this day." The avoidance of stepping on the threshold is a widespread superstitious practice rooted in the belief that all sorts of evil spirits are congregated near the doorway, and to step on the threshold would allow them the opportunity to slip in (see Rudolph, 268). Zephaniah attacks this practice because of its foreign origin in the cult of gods other than Yahweh.

The expression *bayyôm hahû',* "in that day," which is inserted here between the two objects of the verb "I will punish," is clearly a secondary insertion. It disturbs both the regularity in the length of the poetic line and the syntax.

The second line of the verse implies a connection between "leaping over the threshold" and "filling the house with violence and deceit." There is a certain ambiguity in the expression *bêt 'ᵃdōnêhem,* "house of their lord," which leaves it uncertain whether "their lord" refers to the human king or to the deity and whether "house" in the expression refers to the temple or to the royal palace. If the phrase "violence and deceit" refers to wealth obtained by injustice, the difference in meaning will not be great, regardless of how one resolves this ambiguity, since the preexilic Judean temple complex in Jerusalem was attached to the royal palace (2 Kings 16:18; Ezek. 43:6–9) and the crown controlled the treasures deposited in the temple as well as the treasures of the palace (1 Kings 14:26; 15:15, 18; 2 Kings 12:18 [19]; 16:8; 18:15). If "violence and deceit" refers specifically to the continuation of the horrendous religious abuses instituted by Manasseh (2 Kings 21:4–7), however, the reference is probably to the temple. In either case, the point would seem to be that pagan religious mores, no matter how silly or unimportant they may appear, reflect and bring with them a far deeper and more pervasive corruption of Yahweh's religious and ethical demands than surface appearances may indicate.

[10] Verse 10 is also introduced by a compositional editorial link, but it is necessary in order to connect vs. 9–10; unlike the insertion in v. 9, it is probably an original part of the present compositional unit. The formulaic *nᵉʾūm Yhwh,* "says Yahweh," indicates that one is still dealing with divine speech, and it is also an original part of the composition.

The following three lines mention different noises coming from three different districts of Jerusalem. All the noises—*ṣᵉʿāqāh,* "a cry or calling out in distress"; *yᵉlālāh,* "a wailing"; and *šeber,* "the sound of breaking or collapsing structures" (Isa. 30:13–14)—suggest something very unpleasant is happening in and to Jerusalem. For the geographical location of these districts, see the discussion in E. Vogt, *Bib* (1967): 337–358. They all apparently lay in the northern part of the city, where Jerusalem was most vulnerable to attack by a hostile army. The fish gate was located in the north wall (Neh. 3:3; 12:39) and was probably so named because the fish merchants from the coast set up a fish market there (Neh. 3:16). The second district was a part of the new city that was built up northwest of the temple complex, and the hills probably refer to parts of the ridges west of the Tyropoeon Valley.

[11] The inhabitants of the Mortar are called upon to join in this wailing because of the loss of economic activity in the city. That suggests that the Mortar was a part of the city dedicated to the activity of tradesmen and merchants, and the name suggests that it was located in a depression, perhaps somewhere along the northern course of the Tyropoeon Valley.

[12] Once again the slightly varied temporal expression *wᵉhāyāh bāʿēt hahîʾ,* "and it will come to pass at that time," functions as an original editorial link in the compositional unit to ease the otherwise abrupt transition from vs. 10–11 to v. 12. The connection between vs. 10–11 and v. 12 is in no way an artificial editorial connection, however; there is an underlying continuity in thought. The people threatened in v. 12 are the wealthy, precisely those who have profited from all the economic activity whose end was threatened in vs. 10–11.

Yahweh's threat to search Jerusalem with lamps suggests how thoroughly he will search out his enemies upon whom he plans to take vengeance. As Amos had indicated earlier (Amos 9:3), there can be no hiding from Yahweh's search and no escape from his judgment. Jeremiah later used the same motif of searching through the streets of Jerusalem in a different way (Jer. 5:1–6). While Zephaniah has Yahweh searching Jerusalem for the unrighteous and finding them, Jeremiah searched the city for a single righteous person and came up empty.

Those threatened by Zephaniah are identified as being like well-aged wine, long undisturbed in their tranquillity. They had been secure so long in their wealth, despite their means of obtaining it, that they no longer took seriously any thought that Yahweh might affect the outcome of business or politics. They were self-sufficient, self-made men, and God was no factor in their calculations (cf. James 4:13–17). Like those mentioned in v. 6, they neither sought nor inquired of God, for they were convinced that God neither helped nor hindered a person in reaching his goals.

[13] God's imminent judgment would soon sweep away that illusion. Their wealth was about to be plundered and their houses left desolate. The elaborate homes and rich vineyards they had worked so hard to acquire would no longer be theirs to enjoy. Elliger treats the last two lines of this verse as a later insertion influenced by Amos 5:11 (p. 65), and Irsigler concurs (p. 106), but their logic reflects a wooden literalism that is unconvincing. If the nature of the threatened judgment remains somewhat veiled and mysterious in vs. 7–12, the imagery of this verse clearly implies that the judgment coming upon Jerusalem would take the form of conquest by a foreign power, who would plunder its wealth and redistribute its properties.

3. The Day of Yahweh: 1:14–18

1:14 The[1] great day of Yahweh is near,
It is near and approaching very quickly.[2]
The noise[3] of the day of Yahweh is bitter,
There a warrior will cry out.[4]
15 That day is a day of wrath,
A day of affliction and distress,
A day of devastation and desolation,
A day of darkness and gloom,
A day of cloud and dark overcast.
16 A day of horn blowing and battle cry
Against the fortified cities,
And against the lofty corner towers.
17 I will bring distress upon the people,[5]
And they will walk like the blind,
Because they sinned against Yahweh;
Their blood will be poured out[6] like dust,
And their flesh[7] like dung.
18 Neither their silver nor their gold
Will be able to save them
On the day of Yahweh's wrath.
And in the fire of his passion
The whole land will be consumed;
For he will make an end, a terrifying one,[8]
Of all who inhabit the land.

Textual Notes

[1]LXX begins the verse with *hoti,* "because," but this is secondary and unattested in the other versions.

[2]The form *mahēr* should be analyzed as a piel infinitive absolute used adverbially. For the parallelism, compare Jer. 48:16.

[3]All the versions read *qwl* as "voice" or "sound."

[4]While the preceding line gave the versions no difficulty, this one did, and the difficulty seems to have been centered in the rare word *ṣōrēaḥ.* This verb is clearly attested in Isa. 42:13, however, where the parallelism with *hryʿ* shows that the meaning must be something like "to cry out" or "to shout," and that general range of meaning is confirmed by the well-attested Akkadian cognate *ṣarāḫu,* "to cry out, lament" (*AHW,* 1083). The versions do not suggest a significantly different Hebrew Vorlage. LXX's reading of the two lines *phōnē hēmeras kyriou pikra kai sklēra, tetaktai dynatē,* "the sound of the day of the Lord is bitter and harsh, it is set up as strong," appears to presuppose the reading *wṣr hūśam gbwr.* The final *ḥ* on *ṣrḥ* has been read as *h* and attached to the following word. The *w* on *wṣr* might suggest an original *wᵉṣāraḥ.* V's *tribulabitur ibi fortis,* "the strong man will suffer tribulation there," may suggest the reading *ṣr*[*h*] *šm gbwr* with the total loss of the *ḥ.* S's *mryr wqšʾ wʿšyn,* "bitter, and harsh, and strong," appears to read *mr wṣr*[*ḥ šm*] *gbwr.* T's *ql ywmʾ dʿtyd lmyty mn qdm ywy dbyh mrr wṣwḥ tmn gybryʾ mtqṭlyn,* "the sound of the day which is about to come from before the Lord is one in which one will be bitter and cry out, there the warriors are being killed," while periphrastic, supports the MT. Aramaic *ṣwḥ* is a good equivalent for *ṣrḥ.* The versions give no support for the emendation of these lines to *qal yôm yhwh mērāṣ wᵉḥāš miggibbôr,* "the day of Yahweh is swifter than a runner and faster than a warrior" *(BHS).* Moreover, despite its seductiveness, such an emendation would produce an unnecessary repetition of the thought in the two preceding lines. MT is probably correct. At most one might propose the slight correction of *ṣōrēaḥ* to *wᵉṣāraḥ.*

[5]The translation of *lāʾādām* as "the people" (cf. JPSV) rather than as "mankind" is based on the exegetical judgment that Zephaniah is referring to the human inhabitants of Judah, not humanity in general. He is using the vocabulary of v. 3 with its contrast between the rest of creation and human beings, but in the meantime the judgment has been focused on Judah and Jerusalem, so the reference should be to the humans in this restricted area.

[6]LXX read the verb as active, "he will pour out," but that would involve a switch from first to third person with the same subject, so MT is the better text.

[7]The Hebrew word *l^eḥûm* is attested only here and in Job 20:23, where its meaning is unclear. The versions all understand the word in Zeph. 1:17 as "flesh" or "corpse," and that fits with the Arabic cognate *laḥm* as well as with the context. Rudolph objects that one does not "pour out" flesh (p. 264), but one does not "pour out" dung, either. If this line had its own verb, one might expect its verb to be more appropriate to both the subject and the term of comparison, but, since it depends on the preceding line for the verb, this slight semantic incongruity is hardly surprising. The image is that of lumps of the decaying flesh of corpses left strewn upon the ground like so many piles of dung (cf. 2 Kings 9:37; Jer. 9:21 [22]).

[8]The versions differ on the precise connotations they assign to the niphal participle *nbhlh.* LXX and V understand it in the temporal sense of "speedy," but S takes it in the qualitative sense of "troubling, disturbing." The meaning "hasten" appears to be a late development under Aramaic influence. The older meaning is clearly "to be disturbed by fear, to be terrified, to be frightened out of one's wits" (Gen. 45:3; 2 Sam. 4:1; Isa. 13:8; 21:3; Ezek. 26:18), and it is the meaning appropriate in this context.

Commentary

Verses 14–18 pick up the motif of the day of Yahweh first introduced in v. 7 and develop it in far greater detail. This is the third rhetorical unit in the larger composition that extends from 1:2 through 2:3. It may once have existed independently of its present compositional placement, and in that earlier existence it may have functioned quite differently. Taken as an independent unit, vs. 14–18 could be read as a very universal announcement of the day of Yahweh against human beings in general, as an announcement of judgment against the whole world. There is nothing in these verses themselves that indicates precisely who is on the receiving end of this judgment. Taken in isolation, these verses could be read as an announcement of judgment on Judah's enemies as easily as they can be read as a judgment on Judah (cf. Isa. 13:1–16; Obad. 15). In their present context following vs. 4 and 10–12, however, there can be no doubt as to the target intended.

[1:14] Verse 7 announced that the day of Yahweh was near; v. 14 repeats that announcement but heightens it by adding that it is not only near, but approaching very quickly. Zephaniah then goes on to characterize the day as one whose sound is bitter. It will be a day on which the warrior will "cry out," but the significance of that "outcry" is somewhat ambiguous. The use of the verb *ṣrḥ* in Isa. 42:13 suggests that it designates the scream or battle cry of the warrior who has worked himself up into a killing rage. If used in that sense here, the warrior who cries out is presumably part of the enemy army. Isaiah 42:13 employs the hiphil stem, however, while the qal is used here, and it is possible that the qal has a slightly different meaning. One could interpret the expression in Zephaniah as referring to a cry of lament or despair that even the Judean warrior will resort to when he sees the hopelessness of Judah's situation. In either case, the "outcry" is a terrifying sound to the inhabitants of Jerusalem. Since the preceding section has already indicated that Jerusalem will bear the brunt of Yahweh's punishment on that day, the announcement no longer retains any ambiguity. The day of Yahweh will not be a happy day for Jerusalem and Judah.

[15] For the inhabitants of Judah and Jerusalem, it will be a day to feel God's wrath (cf. Isa. 13:13; Lam. 2:22), a day to experience affliction and distress, a day to see one's land and city devastated and left desolate. As Amos indicated to Israel years before (Amos 5:18–20), it will be a day of darkness and gloom and heavy overcast skies without any brightness. It will be a day whose clouds have no silver lining.

[16] Instead of any hopeful sound, it will be a day to hear the sound of battle directed against Judah's fortified cities and strong corner towers.

[17] Verse 17 has Yahweh speak again in the first person, though in the middle of the verse and again in the following verse Yahweh is referred to in the third person. This variation is fairly characteristic of prophetic oracles and provides no reliable criteria for literary criticism or even for the too neat distinctions that are sometimes drawn between the words of the prophet and the words of Yahweh.

God threatens to bring such distress on the human inhabitants of the land that they will lose all sense of direction for their lives. They will be left to stumble around in the dark like blind people (Deut. 28:29; Isa. 59:10). This judgment is still focused on the people of Judah and Jerusalem; to read it as a statement of universal judgment is to pay insufficient attention to the larger context in which these words are embedded.

The reason for this judgment is that the people have sinned against Yahweh. Many critics delete this line as a later gloss because it states the obvious, separates material that belongs together, and refers to Yahweh in the third person immediately after Yahweh has spoken in the first person (Rudolph, 263–264). One may wonder whether any of these arguments carries conviction. The interchange between first and third person is a very shaky reed to lean on, and the so-called separation of related material is hardly significant; it certainly involves no syntactical problems. It is not clear that what the line states was as obvious to the ancient audience as it is to the modern; even if it was, that might not have been sufficient reason for omitting it. It may be that the line was a part of this general material on the day of Yahweh (vs. 14–18) before this unit was given its particular focus by its inclusion in the larger compositional whole. If so, the absence of this larger context would have made this line far less obvious or redundant than it now seems. One should note that the day of Yahweh material directed against Babylon in Isaiah also refers to human sin as the reason for God's judgment (Isa. 13:9, 11).

The last two lines of the verse not only point to the slaughter of the inhabitants of Judah and Jerusalem by the attacking army, they also underscore the utter disdain the enemies will feel for their unfortunate victims. The Judeans' blood will be poured out as though it was as worthless as dust, and their corpses will be left moldering unburied on the ground as though they were as unworthy of attention as excrement (2 Kings 9:37; Jer. 9:21 [22]).

[18] Against an enemy with so little human feeling, a hidden treasure of silver and gold will not buy safety for the conquered Judeans. It is not that the enemy is not interested in money (cf. Isa. 13:17), since they will plunder the Judeans' wealth (Zeph. 1:13); it is rather that they will take the money and still not spare the lives of those who reveal its location to them (see, by contrast, Jer. 41:7–8 for the idea involved in these lines).

The real reason for this merciless treatment, however, is Yahweh's burning anger. His anger is so inflamed that he will make a complete and terrifying end of the whole land and all its inhabitants. Rudolph regards the last four lines of this verse as a later gloss, since they imply a total destruction of the land and the inhabitants, while earlier verses in the compositional unit spoke only of certain groups that would be punished: idolaters and syncretists (vs. 4–5), practical atheists (vs. 6, 12), political officials (vs. 8–9), and merchants and tradesmen (v. 11). Thus Rudolph argues that these last lines presuppose the Babylonian exile and must be a later gloss (p. 270). If these verses once existed independently of the present compositional unit, however, this universal orientation would be no more surprising than the universal orientation found in 1:2–3. It is only Zephaniah's working of 1:14–18 into the larger compositional unit that has focused the judgment on Judah and Jerusalem, and these traces of that original universal outlook now function to underscore how thoroughgoing the judgment will be. The language is hyperbolic, however, as all language of total judgment or annihilation tends to be, and it was understood as such, for the possibility was still held out that one might survive the judgment, as the following section indicates.

4. The Possibility of Escape: 2:1–3

2:1 Gather yourself together[1] and be gathered,[1]
O nation undesired,[2]
2 Before you are driven away[3]
like the passing chaff,[4, 5]

Before there comes upon you
the fierce anger of Yahweh,
Before there comes upon you
the day of Yahweh's anger.
3 Seek Yahweh, all you humble of the land,
Who have done his command,[6]
Seek righteousness, seek humility;[7]
Perhaps you will be hidden in the day of Yahweh's anger.

Textual Notes

[1]The derivation and meaning of the two imperative forms *hitqôšᵉšû wāqôššû* is disputed. LXX, V, S, and T take the first verb as meaning "come together, assemble." LXX and S render the second verb as "be bound," while V has "congregate" and T has "come and draw near." These versions are apparently connecting both verbs with the denominative root *qšš* from the noun *qaš,* "stubble." The root is well attested in the polel in the meaning "to gather stubble," and LXX and S apparently understood the hithpolel and qal here as commanding the gathering of the people under the figure of stubble. Their translation of the second verb as "be bound" is not tied to another root, but to the consideration that, after one has gathered up stubble, the next thing one does is to tie it into bundles. The figurative sense of the verbs is not as clearly indicated in V and T, but there is little question that they assume the same derivation. Rudolph speaks for many modern scholars when he asserts that "since in Hebrew there are several common words for 'assemble,' there hardly existed a need to employ in a general sense such a specific word for 'gather' " (p. 271). This objection is groundless, however, if the prophet is using a quite specific figure, if he is intentionally comparing the people to stubble. That appears to be the case, and, as Irsigler has noted, the traditional derivation from *qšš,* "to gather stubble," is supported by the occurrence of *mōṣ,* "chaff," in the next line (p. 61). For more elaboration on the figure, see the commentary section.

None of the alternative interpretations of the line carries conviction. The emendations such as *htbwššw wbwšw,* "shame yourself and be ashamed," or *htqdšw wqdšw,* "consecrate yourself and be consecrated," are not convincing, since they produce such clear texts that one wonders why anyone would have turned them into the present forms (cf. Rudolph, 271). Two other derivations for the verbal root should also be mentioned. Sabottka takes *qwš* as a by-form of the root *yqš,* "to lay snares," and finds an ironic command in the line (p. 62), but by-forms are too easily invoked without compelling reason, and as Rudolph notes (p. 271), Sabottka's irony does not fit the context. Rudolph's own solution to the crux is to suggest a derivation from a root *qwš,* attested in

Arabic, meaning "to have a crooked back" (p. 271). Based on this root, he translates the line as "Stoop down and bend your backs" (p. 271). Quite apart from the fact that Arabic derivations are always somewhat suspect, this rendering does not fit the context particularly well either. Contextually it offers no improvement over the traditional derivation of the verb forms.

[2]The verb *kāsap* occurs only twice in the qal (Ps. 17:12; Job 14:15) and four times in the niphal conjugation (Gen. 31:30; Ps. 84:3 [2]; Zeph. 1:1). In the qal, construed with the preposition *l* to introduce the object, the verb means "to long for, desire." In Gen. 31:30 and Ps. 84:3 [2] the niphal is used in the same construction with the same meaning. On the basis of that common meaning for the two conjugations, one might translate *haggôy lō' niksāp* in Zeph. 1:1 as "O nation without longing" or "O indifferent nation" (see Irsigler, 62). This may be the understanding that lies behind T's *'m dr' dl' ḥmyd lmtb l'wryt',* "O scattered people who do not desire to return to the law." On the other hand, one could take the niphal participle here as a passive and understand the whole expression as another way of saying *haggôy 'ᵃšer yhwh lō' kāsap/niksap lô/lᵉkā,* "O nation for whom Yahweh does not long." This understanding is probably presupposed by V's *gens non amabilis,* "unloveable nation," and it is supported by the strikingly parallel expression *lō' ruḥāmāh,* "not pitied," in Hos. 1:6. The thought would be that Judah is about as attractive to Yahweh as loose straw scattered in the field.

It is less clear how LXX and S arrived at "undisciplined nation." Rudolph suggests the derivation of *niksāp* from **kāsap* I, "to break in pieces," and assumes the niphal means "to be contrite, inwardly broken" (p. 271). It is doubtful whether either the Greek or the Syriac translators were aware of such a root, however. They may have been influenced by the late Hebrew and Aramaic meaning of the root, "to be ashamed, frightened." The undisciplined nation was the one that had never been shamed or frightened by discipline. On the other hand, in the light of Prov. 3:11–12, which equates Yahweh's discipline with his love, their "undisciplined nation" may simply be an interpretative rendering of "unwanted nation."

[3]The first two lines of v. 2 appear to be quite corrupt. MT's text for the first line, *bṭrm ldt ḥq,* "before the giving birth of the decree," could be understood with Rudolph as a striking figurative expression for "before God brings the decree of judgment to fulfillment" (p. 272), but this rendering does not go well with the comparison in the next line. The difficulty is well illustrated by V's *priusquam pariat iussio quasi pulverem transeuntem diem,* "before he brings forth the day by decree like passing dust." Though this translation presupposes a text almost identical to the MT, the comparison in the second line does not work. T also reflects

MT, but it must paraphrase to smooth out the rough connection between the two lines: "Before there come out upon you the decree of the house of judgment and you become like chaff. . . ." LXX's *pro tou genesthai hymas,* "before you become," and S's identical reading may be based on a misreading of the MT *ldt ḥq* as *ldtkm.* In any case, both simplify the text and offer no basis for correcting the MT.

The emended text underlying the translation offered in this commentary is *bṭrm l*⟨'⟩ *tdḥq*⟨*w*⟩. It presupposes that the first line should continue the figure begun in 1:1 and continued in the second line of 1:2. It also presupposes that the temporal idiom *bṭrm l'* + imperfect, which introduces the next two bicola, should also introduce this bicolon. The precise sequence of corruptions that led to the present text is uncertain, but it probably began with the failure to recognize the negative, perhaps because of a writing without the *aleph* (*l-* is the normal orthography for the negative in Ugaritic [*UT,* 425] and Old Aramaic [*DISO,* 133], and the *aleph* is sometimes also omitted in Hebrew [cf. Deut. 3:11; 1 Sam. 2:16; 20:2]). This led eventually to the wrong division of the following verb into two discrete words and the transposition of the initial *t* and *d.* The original verb should be analyzed as *tiddāḥ*^{e}*qû,* the niphal imperfect 2 m. pl. of *dāḥaq,* "to thrust, crowd, oppress," used here in the sense attested in Arabic, "to drive away." Such a meaning would fit well with the figure of the people as ungathered and unbundled straw in danger of being blown away like chaff.

[4]Reading *k*^{e}*mōṣ ʿōbēr.* LXX's "like a passing flower" probably presupposes an early misreading of *kmṣ* as *knṣ* in its Vorlage; *m* and *n* may be confused in the old Canaanite script, and LXX renders *nṣ* with *anthos,* "flower," in Sirach 50:8. However, LXX's reading of the participle *ʿōbēr,* "passing," instead of MT's perfect *ʿābar,* is probably correct. Its adjectival position following the noun points to the participle, V also reads the participle, and the same participial expression is found in Isa. 29:5. MT's reading as a perfect is probably the result of the corruption in the first part of the verse, but it is poetically and grammatically awkward. If the verb were intended to parallel the temporal infinitive construction in the first line, "Before the decree bring forth//before the day pass as the chaff" (so KJV), one would expect the imperfect, not the perfect. The perfect is only used one time with *b*^{e}*ṭerem* in the Hebrew Bible, and that is to refer to events in the distant past (Prov. 8:25). One could construe the MT as "Before the decree bring forth the day like chaff which passes by," but such a construal would turn poetry into prose.

[5]MT's isolated *yôm,* "day," at the end of the verse creates all sorts of difficulties for the syntactical construal of the verse. LXX and S omit it, V makes it the object of the infinitive, and T adds another term of comparison: "like the chaff from the threshing floor which the wind

blows away and like dew which passes away from before the day." Isaiah 17:13's *kᵉmōṣ hārîm,* "like the chaff of the mountains," suggests that the MT conflated two variants: *kmṣ ʿbr,* "like the passing chaff," and *kmṣ hrym,* "like the chaff of the mountains," > *kmṣ ʿbr hrym* > *kmṣ ʿbr ym.* LXX and S reflect a nonconflated Hebrew text.

[6]LXX and S omit the relative, read the verb as an imperative, and omit the pronominal suffix on the noun. The word order in this line differs from that in the preceding and following lines, however. The three imperatives in those lines precede the object, while the object in this line precedes the verb. The difference in word order suggests that MT offers the better text. It is supported by V and T.

[7]LXX appears to have omitted the first of the identical imperatives in this line, while S has omitted the second. LXX also misread *ʿᵃnāwāh,* "humility," as *waʿᵃnûhā,* "and answer it/them." MT is clearly the superior text.

Commentary

This final rhetorical unit in the larger composition offers at least a slight possibility of escape to those who are willing to seek it. In this Zephaniah resembles Amos (Amos 5:4–6; 14–15) and especially Joel, who, after announcing the day of Yahweh with its hostile army that would leave no remnant (Joel 2:1–3), nonetheless goes on to urge his audience to repent in the vague hope that Yahweh might leave a blessing behind for his people after all (Joel 2:12–14).

[2:1] The two verbs that are used to urge the people to assemble are very unusual in that they are normally used to refer to the gathering together of straw. The point of the assembly is to seek Yahweh's favor (see v. 3 below), but the use of these verbs suggests that, at the moment, the people of Judah and Jerusalem are about as precious in God's eyes as a lot of loose straw left lying scattered in an already harvested field. This negation of the bonds of love that one expects to characterize Yahweh's attachment to his chosen city and elect people is further underscored by the epithet that the prophet assigns the nation. To address Judah as "O nation undesired" is to indicate that Yahweh's passionate love for his people has been replaced by his fierce anger. They are no longer the apple of his eye, just worthless stubble to be dispensed with.

[2] Given their precarious loss of esteem in God's affections, the people are called upon to assemble and do something to correct the situation before it is too late. Otherwise, like the passing, windblown pieces of straw to which they are compared, they will be driven away from the presence of Yahweh. They must act before Yahweh's fierce anger comes upon them, before the dreadful day of Yahweh arrives.

[3] What they are to do is to seek Yahweh. That expression normally means to approach the deity with prayers or supplications, but Zephaniah further defines the kind of religious approach to Yahweh that Judah's desperate situation demands. It is a religious devotion to Yahweh that involves the serious attempt to live righteously and humbly before him, and that is neither careless about obedience nor haughty in human self-sufficiency. Such an approach to Yahweh may offer some hope, but Zephaniah does not extend that hope to everyone. It is only the humble who have tried to do God's will to whom the prophet offers this possibility of escape, and it remains just that, only a vague possibility. God's day of judgment will come upon the whole land bringing his terrifying punishment, but the humble who have tried to obey him, if they seek him in humility and in a renewed pursuit of righteousness, may find shelter and a hiding place in that day. The promise holds out no more than a possibility—only the judgment is certain—but, given the terrifying nature of the judgment, any course of action that offers the faintest possibility of protection in that day is worth pursuing.

II. Oracles Against the Nations: 2:4–15

2:4 For Gaza will become deserted,
And Ashkelon a desolation.
Ashdod they will drive out at noontime,
And Ekron will be uprooted.
5 Hey, inhabitants of the seacoast,
Nation of the Kerethites!
The word of Yahweh is against you,
O Canaan,[1] land of the Philistines.
And I will destroy you, leaving no inhabitant,
6 And the seacoast will become pastures,[2]
Encampments[2] for shepherds and folds for flocks.
7 And it will be a portion[3] for the remnant of the house of Judah,
By the sea[4] in the daytime[5] they will pasture,
In the houses of Ashkelon in the evening they will lie down,[6]
For Yahweh their god will visit them,
And restore their fortunes.[7]
8 I have heard the reproach of Moab,
And the taunts[8] of the Ammonites,
With which they have reproached my people,
And gloated over[9] their[10] border.
9 Therefore as I live, says Yahweh of Hosts, the God of Israel:
Moab will become like Sodom,
And the Ammonites like Gomorrah,
A possession[?][11] of weeds[12] and a salt pit,[13]
And a desolation forever.

The remnant of my people will plunder them,
And the rest of my nation will dispossess them.
10 This is what they will receive for their pride,
Because they reproached and gloated
Over the people[14] of Yahweh of Hosts.
11 [Yahweh will be awesome[15] over them,
Indeed,[16] he will cause all the gods[17] of the earth to waste away,[18]
And there will bow down to him, each one in its own place,
All the coastlands of the nations.]
12 You also, you Ethiopians,
Will be slain by my sword,[19]
13 And his hand will stretch out over the north,
And he will destroy Asshur,
And he will turn Nineveh into a desolation,
Desert, like the steppe.
14 And flocks will lie down in its midst,
Every wild creature of the meadow.[20]
Both the jackdaw[21] and the hedgehog[22]
Will spend the night on its capitals,[23]
The great owl[24] hoots[25] in the window,
The raven[26] [croaks][25] on the threshold,
For he stripped its cedarwork bare.[27]
15 Is this[28] the exultant[29] city
That dwelt in security,
That said in its heart,
"I am, and there is no one else"?
How has it become a desolation,
A lair for the wild animals?
Everyone who passes by it
Whistles and waves his hand.

Textual Notes

[1]The ancient versions had no problem with the apposition between Canaan and the land of the Philistines, but a number of modern scholars do. Gerleman translates the line as a nominal clause, "the land of the Philistines is a merchant land" (p. 30). Rudolph emends to *'aknī'ēk,* "I will subdue you" (p. 277). Neither change is convincing.

[2]LXX's rendering, *kai estai Krētē nomē poimniōn,* "and Crete shall become the pasture of shepherds," presupposes a Hebrew text without *ḥebel hayyām,* "the sea coast," and with the order of *n^{e}wōt* and *k^{e}rōt* reversed: *whyth* [*ḥbl hym*] *krt nwt r'ym.* V omits *krt,* but S and T follow MT. S has a double translation of *krt,* rendering it both as "Kerethites" and as "house (of pasture)": "and the seashore will become dwellings, the Kerethites a house of pasture for the folds of the flock." It is possible

that either *nwt* or *krt* should be deleted as a dittography of the other word, but I have kept both words, transposing *krt* to first position on the basis of the LXX. Rudolph's more radical emendation to *wᵉhāyīt nᵉwōt rōʿîm,* "and you will become pasture for shepherds" (p. 277), is also possible.

[3]LXX and S read *ḥebel hayyām,* "seacoast," which would yield, "And the seacoast will be for the remnant. . . ." V and T lack it, and it seems more likely that the author is playing on the ambiguity of the word, which literally means "cord" or "line." The *ḥebel hayyām,* "the seacoast, line of the sea," mentioned in v. 6 will become a *ḥebel (naḥᵃlāh),* "a portion of inheritance, line of inheritance," for Judah in v. 7.

[4]Though it is supported by the versions, MT's *ʿᵃlêhem,* "upon them," is problematic, since there is no clear antecedent for the masculine plural pronominal suffix. Correct MT to *ʿal hayyām,* "by the sea," with Rudolph (p. 277), following Wellhausen (p. 153).

[5]One expects a parallel for the temporal expression *bāʿereb,* "in the evening," so restore *yômām,* "in the daytime," which was lost by haplography after *hayyām* (Rudolph, 277).

[6]LXX inserts "from before the sons of Judah," but none of the other versions have this phrase, and it is clearly secondary. It may derive from a corrupt vertical dittography of the earlier *bēt (> bᵉnê) yᵉhûdāh.*

[7]All the versions understand the expression *šûb šᵉbût* to mean "to restore the captivity," but the expression has the more general meaning, "to restore the fortunes." See Joseph A. Fitzmyer, *The Aramaic Inscriptions of Sefire* (Rome: Pontifical Biblical Institute, 1967), 119.

[8]LXX's *kondylismous,* "blows with the fist," is based on the misreading of *gdwpy* as *grwpy* and the association of *grwpy* with *'egrōp,* "fist."

[9]The idiom *hagdil (peh) ʿal,* "to make great (the mouth) against," means "to gloat over" (see Jer. 48:26, 42; Ezek. 35:13; Pss. 35:26; 38:17 [16]; 41:10 [9]; 55:13 [12]; Job 19:5).

[10]LXX has "my borders," but that is by attraction to the suffix on "people" in the preceding line. MT is correct. "Their border" in this context means the territory of the Judeans.

[11]The precise meaning of *mimšāq* is not known, and the versions were obviously guessing. LXX's "Damascus" appears to be based on the explanation of *mešeq* in Gen. 15:2. V has *siccitas,* "dryness," S has a verb, "will be destroyed," and T reads *mašmēṭ,* "abandoned(?) land."

[12]The word *ḥārûl* probably refers to a particular weed, but its precise identification is unknown. LXX's *ekleleimmenē,* "abandoned," may be reading a form of the verb *ḥādal,* "to cease," (so Rudolph, 277), or it may be translating the sense of the expression (cf. its rendering in Prov. 24:31). V has "thorns," T has "salt-weeds," and S has "their plants."

[13]The meaning of *mikreh,* "pit," is also disputed, but T supports this

meaning as a place where salt is dug. LXX and V have "piles of salt." S reads a verb form.

[14]LXX omits "the people," but the other versions have it.

[15]LXX and S have "will appear." They obviously derived *nwr'* from *r'h,* "to see," rather than from *yr',* "to fear."

[16]Reading *kî* as the emphatic. LXX and V ignore it in their translation.

[17]LXX inserts "of the nations" and S changes "the gods" to "the kings," perhaps to avoid implying that there was more than one God of the earth (Rudolph, 278).

[18]MT has a perfect form, but all the versions read a future, so one should probably correct *rāzāh* to *yirzeh* or *yᵉrazzeh.* The piel is preferable, because the qal appears to be intransitive. The meaning "to cause to grow thin, waste away" is odd, however, and one could consider an emendation to *yirdeh,* "he will exercise dominion." LXX and S have "will destroy," but it is unclear what Hebrew text they were translating. V and T support a transitive imperfect from the root *rzh.*

[19]Taking the final *hēmmāh,* "they," as resuming the 2 m. pl. subject. The switch in person is attested elsewhere (cf. GKC, par. 141g–h) and requires no emendation. If one were to emend the text, the emendation of *ḥrby hmh* > *ḥrb yhwh,* "sword of Yahweh," seems far more likely than either of Rudolph's suggested emendations: *ḥarbêhēmmāh,* "by their sword," or *ḥereb kāhēmmāh,* "by the sword like them" (p. 278).

[20]MT's "every wild animal of a nation" is quite problematic. LXX's *tēs gēs,* "of the earth," while catching the sense of the expression, is based on the resemblance in sound between *gôy* and *gēs* rather than on a different Hebrew text. The word *ḥaytô,* "wild animal," is found elsewhere in construct with *'ereṣ,* "earth" (Gen. 1:24; Ps. 79:2), *ya'ar,* "woods" (Pss. 50:10; 104:20; cf. Isa. 56:9), and *śāday,* "field" (Ps. 104:11). Of these possibilities, *śāday* is probably the closest graphically, but one should also consider Rudolph's suggested emendation to *nāway,* "pasture, meadow" (p. 278).

[21]The *qā'at* is clearly an unclean bird of some kind (Lev. 11:13–18; Deut. 14:17) that was found in the steppe (Ps. 102:7 [6]) and among ruins (Isa. 34:11), but the precise identification is unclear. LXX's "chameleon" is clearly wrong, but Aquila's "pelican," though it is supported by V, S, and T, does not seem probable either, since one does not expect a seabird in a desert ruin. Theodotion's "swan" is also improbable for the same reason.

[22]All the versions understand *qippōd* as "hedgehog." Modern lexicographers also suggest "owl," "ruffed bustard," or some other bird. Its presence on the capitals does not necessarily point to a bird, since in a ruined city many of the capitals would be lying on the ground.

[23]LXX's "in its coffered ceiling work," S's "in its houses," V's "in its thresholds," and T's "in the opening of its gate," all miss the precise sense of the Hebrew.

[24]The meaning of *qôl* in this context is disputed. LXX and S translate "wild animals," V has the normal "voice," and T has "there is the sound of the bird which is chirping in the window." Rudolph inserts *kôs* after *qôl* to get his translation "Listen! The screech-owl cries in the window" (p. 278). It is possible, however, that *qôl,* "voice," is itself the name for a particular bird, whose sound could be mistaken for a human voice, even if *qôl* is not listed among the unclean birds in Lev. 11:13–18 and Deut. 14:11–18. It may be a particular name for a bird listed under a name for a larger grouping. Since so little is known about the ancient Hebrew bird names, it is hard to justify textual emendation based on the absence of a known name for a bird. Van der Woude treats *qwl* as a noun meaning "rubbish," derived from the root *ql,* "to fall" (p. 124). He translates these two lines as "the rubbish will stick out the windows, ruins upon the thresholds" (p. 124). Both the meaning he assigns to *qwl* and the meaning he assigns to *yšwrr* seem problematic, however.

[25]The polel imperfect *y^{e}šôrēr* means "to continually sing," but the nature of the singing depends on the singer, and for an owl "to hoot" seems the appropriate rendering. LXX has *phōnēsei,* "calls," S has *nnhmn,* "roar," T has *dmnṣyp,* "which chirps," and V has *cantantis,* "of the singer."

[26]LXX and V's "raven" suggests that one emend MT's *ḥōrēb,* "dryness, devastation," to *'ōrēb,* "raven."

[27]This line has been a major crux. The traditional rendering takes *'ērāh* as the piel perfect 3 m. s. from *'ārāh,* "to be naked, bare." The translators of the versions did not know what to do with it. LXX's "a cedar is its rising" is gibberish, presumably based on the derivation of *'ērāh* from *'wr,* "to awake, rise up." V's *adtenuabo robur eius,* "I will cause its strength to waste away," presupposes the reading *'arzeh 'uzzah.* S has "its root was uncovered," and T has "its roof they destroyed." Rudolph makes the seductive suggestion that the two words are an onomatopoetic representation of the cawing of the raven (p. 279), but in the nature of the case, such a suggestion is hard to either demonstrate or refute. The line remains a crux.

[28]The sentence should probably be read as an unmarked question (so JPSV).

[29]LXX has "the city that despises," V, "the glorious city," S and T, "the strong city."

Commentary

Zephaniah 2:4–17 consists of a collection of oracles against various foreign nations. Verses 4–7 are directed against the Philistines, vs. 8–10 are against Ammon and Moab, v. 11 is an isolated verse that speaks of the nations turning to the worship of Yahweh, v. 12 targets Ethiopia, and vs. 13–15 are directed against Assyria. They have been shaped into a loose compositional unity, but there are indications that that unity is not the rhetorical unity of their original oral presentation. The oracles reflect no common form, and there are no recurring patterns to tie them together. Verses 5–7 take the form of a *hôy*-oracle, a type of oracle that is often found in series, but none of the other oracles assume this form. The only thing the oracles really have in common is the announcement of a future judgment on foreign nations. It is also possible that the compositional process may have trimmed some of the individual oracles; the oracle against Ethiopia, for instance, is surprisingly brief. The composition ends with the oracle against Assyria, which may reflect the intention to emphasize this oracle as the climax of God's judgment against the foreign nations, since Assyria was Judah's major enemy in the time of Zephaniah. The oracle announces the future destruction of Nineveh, a feature that demonstrates that this oracle and probably the composition as a whole dates prior to 612 B.C.

There has been an attempt to provide an editorial link between this composition (2:4–15) and the preceding composition on the day of Yahweh (1:2–2:3) through the placement of 2:4 with its initial *kî* at the beginning of the composition. If one reads this *kî* as causal, the following series of oracles would provide one reason for seeking refuge with Yahweh while there is still time (2:1–3): God's judgment on the day of Yahweh will be so universal that no matter where one flees, one will not be able to escape that judgment. The superficiality of this link is immediately obvious, however. Zephaniah 2:4–15 makes no mention of the day of Yahweh and contains no judgment against Judah; there is no integral connection to the preceding composition in 1:2–2:3 at all. For this reason Van der Woude (p. 115) takes the initial *kî* in 2:4 as an emphatic, "surely," rather than as the causal conjunction. Despite the parallel he cites for the use of the emphatic *kî* in introducing a new oracle (Isa. 15:1), his treatment of the word here appears dubious.

One should note that the whole structure of the oracle against the Philistines is peculiar. Where else in prophetic literature does one introduce an announcement of judgment against a people so abruptly, and then, immediately following this announcement, address the same people with a *hôy*-oracle? The pattern is without genuine parallel. Isaiah 1:2–3 offers an indictment prior to the *hôy*-oracle in 1:4; Habakkuk 2:18, even if its placement before the *hôy*-oracle in 2:19 is original, contains only interrogation.

Neither passage contains an announcement of judgment before the *hôy*-oracle directed at the same audience. This suggests that Zeph. 2:4 has been transposed from its original position as a part of the *hôy*-oracle in order to create the bogus link with 1:2–2:3. It probably came originally after v. 5, where it would fit very well:

2:5 Hey, inhabitants of the seacoast,
Nation of the Kerethites!
The word of Yahweh is against you,
O Canaan, land of the Philistines.
And I will destroy you, leaving no inhabitant,
4 For Gaza will become deserted,
And Ashkelon a desolation.
Ashdod they will drive out at noontime,
And Ekron will be uprooted.
6 And the seacoast will become pastures,
Encampments for shepherds and folds for flocks.
7 And it will be a portion for the remnant of the house of Judah,
By the sea in the daytime they will pasture,
In the houses of Ashkelon in the evening they will lie down,
For Yahweh their God will visit them,
And restore their fortunes.

It remains unclear whether the attempt to create the editorial link between 1:2–2:3 and 2:4–15 through this displacement of 2:4 from its original position was part of the original compositional arrangement of 2:4–15 or whether it represents a later, secondary editorial rearrangement. The superficiality of the editorial link suggests the latter, and therefore my verse-by-verse commentary will follow the presumed original order of the oracle.

1. The Oracle Against Philistia

[2:5] The oracle begins with the direct, second-person address of the threatened party so characteristic of *hôy*-oracles. Zephaniah first gets their attention with the exclamation and a couple of designations for the Philistines. He addresses them as the inhabitants of the seacoast, because the main Philistine centers were located in the coastal plain, and he refers to them as the nation of the Kerethites, because the Kerethites, a subgroup of the Philistines that apparently traced their origins to the island of Crete, were a dominant element in the Philistine population (1 Sam. 30:14; 2 Sam. 8:18 and passim; Ezek. 25:16). He then informs them that the word of Yahweh is against them and addresses them with two more designations before quoting Yahweh's direct words to them: "I will destroy you, leaving no inhabitant." He addresses them as Canaan, the land of the Philistines, because the Philistines were early settlers in Canaan (K. A. Kitchen, "The

Philistines," in *POTT,* 53–78; Trude Dothan, *The Philistines and Their Material Culture* [New Haven, Conn.: Yale University Press, 1982]), and they remained the dominant non-Israelite population that still occupied a significant portion of ancient Canaan that impinged directly on Judean territory. Their territory is reckoned as Canaanite in Josh. 13:2–4. The prophet's failure to mention the Phoenicians in his oracles against the foreign nations may suggest either that their relations to Judah at the time were friendly or that their remoteness from Judah made their relations relatively insignificant to Zephaniah.

Normally the designations attached to the addressee in a *hôy*-oracle also function to provide an indictment against the party addressed. They are usually uncomplimentary epithets or participial phrases that identify the addressee as a wrongdoer ("sinful nation," Isa. 1:4; "rebellious and polluted one," Zeph. 3:1; "you who amass what is not yours," Hab. 2:6). The epithets heaped upon the Philistines, however, do not constitute so obvious an indictment. Why is God angry with them? The reference to them as Canaan may suggest that their principal sin was in being where they were. The ancient conquest tradition that was promoted so strongly in the deuteronomic movement associated with Josiah's reform demanded that the people of Israel drive every Canaanite out of the land or risk having their faith subverted. As long as the pagan Philistines remained there, those deuteronomic demands remained unmet. Though the epithets do not touch on this point, there may have also been a more obvious political reason for Yahweh's anger with Philistia. Philistia appears to have remained loyal to Assyria, at least in resisting Egyptian incursions into Palestine, even after Assyria's growing weakness had become apparent (see H. Cazelles, *RB* 74 [1967]: 24–44).

Despite the stylistic feature of the direct address to the Philistines that characterizes this oracle, it is unlikely that the Philistines ever heard it. Though the Philistines are addressed in the second person, and the Judeans are referred to later in the oracle in the third person (v. 7), the Philistines are only the fictive audience; the real audience for whom the oracle was intended was Judean. The oracle was probably spoken originally to Judeans; its written circulation certainly envisioned a Judean readership. The announcement of judgment on the Philistines contained a promise to Judah, and it is as a promise to Judah for a better future that the oracle actually functions.

[4] In its original position after v. 5, v. 4 grounded Yahweh's final threat in the previous verse with a list of the major Philistine cities that would be destroyed. Of the five historically most prominent Philistine centers (Josh. 13:3), only Gath is missing, perhaps because it was under Judean control at the time (Rudolph, 279). Gath is also missing in Amos's oracles against Philistia about a century earlier (Amos 1:6–8), apparently having been conquered by some enemy not long before Amos delivered his message (Amos 6:2). Zephaniah enumerates the cities beginning with the southernmost, Gaza, and working progressively northward to the northernmost, Ekron. As Rudolph notes, this order of listing makes it doubtful that the enemy force envisioned as the agent in the destruction of Philistia could have anything to do with the Scythians, since a Scythian invasion, if it occurred at all, would have come from the north (p. 279). Egypt, which under Psammetichus I (664–610 B.C.) began reasserting its claims on Philistia following the weakening of Assyrian control (ca. 640 B.C.), is a far better bet. Herodotus, at any rate, refers to campaigns of this king against Ashdod and in the area of Ashkelon (I, 104–106; II, 157; see H. Cazelles, loc. cit.).

The prophet makes a wordplay on the names of two of the four cities in his announcement of the fate that will befall them. There is paronomasia with elements of both assonance and alliteration in his statement that Gaza will be deserted *(‘azzāh ‘^{a}zûbāh),* and the statement that Ekron will be uprooted *(‘eqrôn tē‘āqēr)* involves paronomasia that connects the city name with Hebrew verb of the same consonants *‘āqar,* "to root up." (For the phenomenon of paronomasia in the OT see the basic work of Immanuel M. Casanowicz, *Paronomasia in the Old Testament* [Boston: Norwood Press, 1894] and the more recent treatments in J. M. Sasson, "Wordplay in the OT," *IDBSup,* 968–970. Adele Berlin also touches on the phenomenon in her book *The Dynamics of Biblical Parallelism* [Bloomington, Ind.: Indiana University Press, 1985], 103–124). Ashkelon and Ashdod do not receive the same treatment, though in the case of Ashdod the prophet could easily have made a wordplay with the verbal root *šādad,* "to plunder." Instead, Zephaniah emphasizes a common element in the fate of all four cities: They are emptied of their Philistine inhabitants. The cities are deserted, left desolate; their citizens driven out, uprooted. The reference to noontime in the Ashdod judgment simply underscores how quickly the city has fallen that its inhabitants could be removed by midday, but the emphasis still lies on the removal of the population, not the prior act of conquest. This emphasis on the removal of the Philistine inhabitants reinforces the judgment that the major problem with the Philistines was that they occupied territory claimed by Judah.

[6] Verse 6 follows naturally on v. 4, for it continues the portrayal of the Philistine coastal plain as denuded of its human inhabitants. They will be gone, so the coastal plain will become a pastureland, a place for shepherds and their flocks.

[7] These shepherds are not just any shepherds, however; they are Judeans, for the coastland will be allotted to the surviving remnant of Judah. In the daytime they will pasture by the sea, and at night they will find shelter in the deserted houses of the former Philistine cities, because Yahweh will visit Judah and restore its fortunes.

Rudolph deletes the first and the last two lines of this verse as later, postexilic additions to the text, partly on the formal grounds of the cessation of the direct address (p. 280), but the evidence does not demand this conclusion. The only indication for the cessation of direct address is the expression "Yahweh their God," but if the prophet can have Yahweh refer to himself in direct address in the third person with the expression "the word of Yahweh" (v. 5), there is no reason why in addressing the Philistines about the remnant of Judah he could not refer to himself as "Yahweh their God." Van der Woude's observation that the expression occurs nowhere else in the book of Zephaniah (p. 118) is no argument against the authenticity of the line; each of the expressions "Yahweh of Hosts, the God of Israel" (2:9), "her God" (3:2), and "Yahweh your God" (3:17) occurs only one time in the book, but in a book of only three short chapters such statistics are meaningless.

Nothing in these suspect lines actually requires a postexilic date. Zephaniah expected a severe judgment on Judah and Jerusalem as his day of Yahweh oracles indicate, but he held out hope that the righteous might survive, so it is not surprising if in other oracles he should speak of the remnant of the house of Judah. The expression "to restore the fortunes" came to be interpreted with reference to exile and return, but its original meaning was far more general and implied no more than a restoration of lost status. Quite apart from any further judgment threatened by Zephaniah, Judah was already in need of a restoration of fortunes. Under Assyrian domination it had lost its former status as an independent kingdom, not to mention its long-past but never-forgotten glory years as the center of Yahweh's empire under David and Solomon. Yet within a few years of Zephaniah's prophecy, Josiah attempted to restore that former glory. As part of that attempt, Josiah extended Judean hegemony into Philistine territory as far as the Mediterranean Sea south of Joppa, where he clearly had control of Yabneh Yam and the area around it, as evidenced by the ostracon found there (*KAI,* no. 200). Given this historical setting and Zephaniah's apparent influence on the Josianic reform, one may well attribute these lines promising Judean expansion into Philistine territory to the prophet Zephaniah.

2. The Oracle Against Moab and Ammon

[8] The oracle begins with Yahweh's announcement that he has heard the Moabites and Ammonites making fun of his people and gloating over their territory. Although little is known about the relations between Judah and her two eastern neighbors in the period between 650–600 B.C., these words imply that Moab and Ammon had encroached on territory claimed by the Judean monarchy, and there is no reason to doubt such confrontations took place during this period. The relations between the small states in Palestine tended to shift back and forth from the friendship of allies to the hostility of bitter enemies and vice versa within a very short space of time.

[**9**] For Moab and Ammon to reproach Yahweh's people in this fashion was tantamount to making fun of Yahweh himself, for he was their God who had given them their territory. It is striking that nowhere in this oracle does God refer to his people as Judah. In his oath formula Yahweh refers to himself as "Yahweh of Hosts, the God of Israel." This designation occurs elsewhere only in the account of Yahweh's covenant with David (2 Sam. 7:27; 1 Chron. 17:24), twice in the book of Isaiah (21:10; 37:16), and numerous times in the book of Jeremiah (7:3, 21; 9:14 [15]; 16:9; 19:3; passim). It would appear to be a formulation stemming from the Zion theology in which the claims for Judah's state God to hegemony over all of Israel is maintained long after the northern state of Israel has ceased to exist, the remaining population of the northern territories has become only partially Yahwistic, and any commitment to the Yahweh of Jerusalem has become quite restricted. Despite all the indications of a lack of interest in the north, the Judean expectation for a reunification of Israel and Judah under Yahweh and his Davidic monarch in Jerusalem, attested as early as Isaiah (2:5; 10:20–21; 11:12–14; see my "Isaiah 2 and the Prophet's Message to the North," *JQR* 75 [1985]: 290–308), remained alive down into the exile (Ezek. 37:15–28). Prior to the Babylonian exile, Jeremiah spoke of the return of the northern tribes from their Assyrian exile, their restoration to their land, and their renewed devotion to Yahweh in Jerusalem (Jer. 30–31); Josiah apparently tried to create the hoped-for reunification of Israel and Judah in his religious and political reform. Thus Zephaniah's formulation suggests that Yahweh is still laying claim to his whole people and to all the territory he had once allotted to them.

Because Moab and Ammon made light of that claim, both would be laid waste like the proverbial Sodom and Gomorrah (Gen. 19:24–28; Deut. 29:22 [23]; Isa. 1:9; 13:19; Jer. 49:18; 50:40; Amos 4:11). Their ruined territory will be overgrown with weeds, but useful plants will not grow there, for the soil will be too salty, an area fit only for digging salt pits, and thus perpetually desolate. The following two lines suggest that the remnant of God's people will be responsible for this desolation of Moab and Ammon. They will plunder Moab and the Ammonites and dispossess them of their inheritance.

Rudolph thinks it strange that Israel would want to take possession of a perpetual desolation, and he uses this "surprising" conflict in the thought of the verse to dismiss the last two lines as a later, postexilic gloss (pp.

280–281), but one must question the legitimacy of Rudolph's application of hairsplitting logic to poetry that works with graphic and shifting imagery. The main thought in the last two lines is that Israel will drive Moab and Ammon out of their territories and take everything of value that belonged to them. There is no contradiction between this imagery and the portrayal of these conquered territories, following such a conquest, as wasteland.

[10] Verse 10 summarizes the two preceding verses by identifying the judgment in v. 9 as the just reward of Moab and Ammon for their arrogant gloating over God's people mentioned in v. 8. The speaker refers to Israel as "the people of Yahweh of Hosts" rather than as "my people" or "my nation," but in a final summarizing statement Yahweh could very well refer to Israel and himself in this fashion, so the verse could still be part of the divine oath with God as the speaker. Repetition or summarization is no necessary indication of secondary editing, and, though the verse is not as clearly poetic as the preceding lines, I am inclined to accept the verse as original. Rudolph regards it as a postexilic gloss that offers a polemical correction of vs. 8–9a; i.e., it is Israel's occupation of the territory of Moab and Ammon, not its desolation, that constitutes God's punishment of their pride (p. 282). But such an interpretation reads far too much into the opening demonstrative *zô't,* "this," depends on a very dubious reading of v. 9b, and seems utterly strained. Gloss or not, the verse is merely a recapitulating summary of vs. 8–9.

3. The Nations Turn to Yahweh

[11] Verse 11 stands in this series of oracles against foreign nations as an isolated and apparently misplaced fragment. Unlike the other oracles, it focuses on the religious conversion of the nations into worshipers of Yahweh rather than on Yahweh's punishment of the nations. It is not a natural continuation of the divine oath in the preceding verses, because this verse is clearly not formulated as divine speech. Why and when it was placed here is unclear. It is uncertain whether it originally occupied a more suitable place and where that might have been. Because it is an isolated fragment, it is also difficult to determine whether it should be attributed to Zephaniah.

Whatever the original antecedent of the expression "over them" in the first line, in the present context the pronoun must refer back to Moab and Ammon mentioned in the preceding verses. Yahweh will prove awe-inspiring to them; they will learn to fear and respect him. The view of Yahweh as *nôrā',* "awesome," to the other nations is a conception with very deep roots going back to the earliest periods of Zion's imperial theology (Pss. 47:3 [2]; 76:8, 13 [7, 12]), and the royal cult in Jerusalem elaborated this conception with a clear claim for Yahweh's superiority over the gods of the other nations (Pss. 89:8 [7]; 96:4; see my "The Religio-Political Setting of Psalm 47," *BASOR* 221 [1976]: 129–132). The prophet is simply developing this same Jerusalemite tradition when he says that Yahweh will cause all the other gods of the earth to waste away. One should note the clear parallel to Psalm 82, where God condemns the other deities to death (see my discussion in *JBL* 92 [1973]: 340–341; and "Zion in the Theology of the Davidic-Solomonic Empire," *Studies in the Period of David and Solomon and Other Essays,* ed. Tomoo Ishida [Tokyo: Yamakawa-Shuppansha, 1982], 97–98).

The result of Yahweh's awesome display of power over the gods of the other nations will be the turning of all the nations to Yahweh. Unlike other prophetic texts dependent on the Zion Tradition, which speak of the nations making a pilgrimage to Jerusalem to worship Yahweh or to inquire of him (Isa. 2:2–4; Micah 4:1–5; Zech. 14:16–19), this text speaks of each of the nations worshiping Yahweh in its own place (cf. Isa. 19:19–25; Mal. 1:14). The reference to the coastlands of the nations makes one think of the distant lands of the western Mediterranean, but the point is probably to underscore the universality of the worship of Yahweh. It will extend throughout the whole world, as that world was known to the ancient Judean prophet.

4. The Oracle Against Ethiopia

[12] This oracle against Ethiopia, which opens with the word *gam,* "even" or "also," could never have existed by itself, but it does not follow naturally on v. 11, another indication that v. 11 is intrusive. It would follow naturally enough after vs. 9 and 10, however, since then it would be comparing the fate of Ethiopia to that just announced for Moab and Ammon. Having just sworn an oath to punish Moab and Ammon, Yahweh now turns and addresses a similar threat to Ethiopia: "You Ethiopians will also be a victim of my sword."

The historical background for this oracle is not self-evident. An Ethiopian dynasty had not ruled Egypt since 664 B.C., when Psammetichus I took the throne and reintroduced Egyptian hegemony as the founder of the genuinely Egyptian Saite dynasty. Moreover, while Psammetichus appears to have done some campaigning along the coastal plain relatively early in Josiah's reign, there is no indication that he was allied with Assyria much before 616 B.C., and there is even less evidence that his contingents operating in Palestine and later sent to Assyria's assistance were composed largely of Ethiopian troops. We simply do not know what provoked this oracle.

5. The Oracle Against Assyria

[13] That the oracle against Assyria was originally independent of the preceding oracle is evident from the switch from first person to third. In the oracle against Ethiopia, Yahweh is the speaker, but in this oracle against Assyria, Yahweh is referred to in the third person. Nonetheless, the literary unit (2:4–15) created by the prophet or his editors was probably intended to reach its climax in 2:13–15. Assyria had been Judah's main oppressor since the time of Ahaz and remained such until well into Josiah's reign, so one could hardly think of any other foreign nation against whom Judah felt more enmity or whose fall would bring greater joy to Judah, as the book of Nahum amply demonstrates.

As Yahweh once stretched out his hand against his own people (Isa. 5:25; 9:11, 16, 20 [12, 17, 21]), so in the future he will stretch out his hand against the north and destroy Assyria. Though Assyria lay somewhat east of Judah as well as far to the north, the routes from Judah to Assyria ran almost due north for a considerable distance before one could reach a passable route eastward. The Arabian desert to the east prevented any direct route from Assyria or lower Mesopotamia, so any Mesopotamian enemy who marched against Judah would be experienced by the Judeans as an enemy out of the north. It is not clear whether Asshur in this verse refers to the country or to the city of Asshur, but the city would make an appropriate parallel to Nineveh. Asshur, the ancient capital of Assyria, remained important even after the capital was moved to Nineveh. Asshur was destroyed in 615 B.C., only three years before Nineveh itself fell in 612 B.C. Since the oracle views these events as future, it is clear that the oracle is earlier than the conquest of these cities. The thoroughness of the destruction of Nineveh is underscored by traditional imagery in which the once proud city is turned into a desolation, a wilderness.

[14] Verse 14 elaborates this motif by the conventional description of a ruined city as inhabited by flocks (cf. vs. 6–7) and wild animals (cf. Isa. 34:11–15). Flocks will rest in its ruins, and both birds and small mammals will make their homes in its once elegant buildings. The poignancy of this portrait of a destroyed and abandoned city was brought home to me when I observed just such phenomena in the ruins of Recife, a Hellenistic city in the Syrian steppe.

The last line of this verse is a crux and is probably corrupt. Both the text and translation are uncertain. As translated, the subject of the verb would presumably be Yahweh, but the action is more appropriate to his human agent in the conquest of Nineveh. One could well expect the conqueror of Nineveh to mine the ruins for any valuable material useful to him, and choice cedar woodwork that could be used in the conqueror's own building projects would certainly fit into that category.

[15] The vision of Nineveh in ruins, occupied only by birds and wild animals, provokes the prophet to question in astonishment, "Can this be the same exultant city that was so secure that it considered itself without rival? How could the great Nineveh have become such a desolation?" Nonetheless, this is the fate that awaits Nineveh. Its imperial splendor and noisy crowds will give way to the sullen stillness of the desolate steppe, a stillness broken only by the lonesome cry of a bird or the scurrying of a small animal. The only human sound that will be heard in it will be the scoffing or astonished whistle of the occasional traveler who accidentally passes by it.

III. Jerusalem's Judgment and Salvation: 3:1–20

It is extremely difficult to isolate the individual oracles in the third chapter of Zephaniah, as even a cursory look at the commentaries will indicate. Many different suggestions for dividing the material into individual units have been proposed, and none of them are entirely convincing. The reason for this is that a compositional unity has been imposed upon the whole chapter so that whatever elements in the chapter may have once existed as independent oracles have lost much of the clarity of their original contours. The boundary marks between these original units have been largely obscured by the compositional editing. A clear break does exist at v. 13, however, despite the fact that the thought in vs. 14–20 follows naturally on the preceding material. Verse 13 concludes with good closing line, and v. 14 opens with an imperative call to rejoice that is attested elsewhere as an introduction to a new oracle. That justifies splitting the treatment of the chapter into two units: Zeph. 3:1–13 and 3:14–20.

1. Judgment and Purification: 3:1–13

3:1 Hey,[1] rebellious[2] and polluted one,[3]
City who oppresses,[4]
2 Who[5] did not listen to any voice,
Who[5] did not accept discipline.
In Yahweh she did not trust,
To her God she did not draw near.
3 Her officials within her
Are roaring lions,
Her judges are wolves of the steppe,[6]
Who do not gnaw bones in the morning.[7]
4 Her prophets are impudent,[8]
Men of treachery.[9]
Her priests profane what is holy,
They do violence to instruction.

5 Yahweh is righteous in her midst,
He does not do iniquity.
Morning after morning he gives his judgment,
At twilight[10] he does not fail,
But the wicked person knows no shame.[11]
6 I cut off their nation;[12]
Their corner towers[13] were left desolate.
I turned their streets into ruins,
With no one to pass through.
Their cities were laid waste,
Without a person, without an inhabitant.[14]
7 I thought, "Surely you[15] will fear me,
You[15] will accept discipline,
And there will not be cut off[16] from her eyes[17]
All the punishment[18] that I brought upon her";
But[19] they very quickly[19] corrupted
All their deeds.
8 Therefore wait for me, says Yahweh,
For the day of my rising as a witness,[20]
Because it is my judgment to gather up nations,
To assemble kingdoms,
To pour upon them[21] my anger,[22]
All the fierceness of my wrath,
Indeed, in the fire of my passion
All the land will be consumed.
9 For then I will restore to their people[23]
A pure[24] lip
So that all of them may call upon Yahweh,
To serve him with one shoulder.
10 [From beyond the rivers of Ethiopia,
My supplicants, the daughter of my dispersed ones,[25]
Will bring my offering.]
11 In that day you will no longer be ashamed
Of all your deeds by which you rebelled against me,
Because then I will turn aside from your midst
The exultant ones of your pride,
And you will no longer be haughty
In my holy mountain.
12 And I will leave in your midst
A poor, humble people,
And the remnant of Israel[26]
Will take refuge in the name of Yahweh.
13 They will not do wrong,
And they will not speak falsehood,
And a tongue of deceitfulness

Will not be found in their mouth.
But they will pasture and lie down,
With none to disturb.

Textual Notes

[1]The particle *hôy* is an exclamation or vocative particle normally followed by the direct address of the person or group named or characterized immediately after the particle. Though no explicit second-person forms occur in this oracle until v. 7, the opening lines are probably to be understood in line with the normal pattern as direct address. For further discussion of the meaning and structure of the *hôy*-oracles, see the treatment of Hab. 2:6ff. in this commentary and see Delbert Hillers, "*Hôy* and *Hôy*-Oracles: A Neglected Syntactic Aspect," in *The Word of the Lord Shall Go Forth,* ed. Carol M. Meyers and M. O'Connor [Winona Lake, Ind.: Eisenbrauns, 1983], 185–188, and the literature cited there.

[2]MT's *mōr*^{e}*'āh* has traditionally been analyzed as qal active participle f. s. from *mārāh,* "to rebel" (so Theodotion). The expected form would be *mōrāh,* but a number of final *he* verbs are sometimes parsed by analogy with the final *aleph* verbs (GKC, par. 75rr). Verse 2 supports this derivation (Rudolph, 285), but the analysis as the denominative hophal participle f. s. from postbiblical *r*^{o}*'î,* "excrement," would yield "sullied," an excellent parallel to "polluted," so this derivation cannot be ruled out either. Sabottka's reading *m*^{e}*rî'āh,* "fatted," taken in the sense of "recalcitrant," seems far less probable (p. 102). LXX and S apparently identified the form as the hophal participle of *rā'āh,* "to see." V's *provocatrix,* "provoker," seems to be derived from *mārar,* "to be bitter" (Rudolph, 285). T's "who hastens" is less easy to explain.

[3]LXX, V, S, and T all mistakenly derived this form from the verb *gā'al* I, "to redeem." It is actually from *gā'al* II, a by-form of *gā'al,* which in the niphal means "to be defiled."

[4]MT's *hayyônāh* is the qal active f. s. participle from *yānāh,* "to oppress." LXX and V misunderstood it as *yônāh,* "dove," and that is probably also what lay behind Symmachus's *anoētos,* "foolish" (Hos. 7:11; Rudolph, 285). S's "city of Jonah" reflects its understanding that the city mentioned is Nineveh and is interpretative in the same way as its addition at the end of 2:15.

[5]These clauses with finite verbs following the participles after the vocative particle *hôy* should be construed as unmarked relative clauses as S has done. The oracle presumably begins as direct address to the city, but in the repetition of the syntactically conditioned third-person forms,

the consciousness of that direct address is temporarily lost, only to be picked up again by the second-person forms in v. 7.

[6]Reading *ʿ^{a}rābāh* following LXX in the light of Jer. 5:6 (cf. Hab. 1:8). The MT and the other versions read *ʿereb,* "of the evening," but that corruption was probably due to the expression *labbōqer,* "in the morning," in the next line. It spread from this passage to Hab. 1:8, but it failed to spread to Jer. 5:6 because the parallelism there between "a lion from the woods" and "a wolf from the steppes" protected the original reading.

[7]The meaning of this clause is a notable crux. The major difficulty lies in the verb *gāram,* which in its other attested occurrences appears to be denominative from *gerem,* "bone," and to mean, "to gnaw" (Num. 24:8; Ezek. 23:34 may be corrupt, but the image of one gnawing on an empty earthenware container to express the thought of drinking a cup to its last drop is by no means impossible). But if that is the meaning here, what does it mean to say that wolves of the steppe "do not gnaw bones in the morning"? Gerleman argues that it means they have eaten their fill of flesh and thus are not hungry; the point is to picture the luxury of the judges (p. 49). Sabottka, on the contrary, sees the image as reflecting the hunger of the wolves; he translates "who have had nothing to gnaw on since morning" (p. 101). LXX and V have "who do not leave behind until morning," and S and T have "who do not wait until morning." The LXX might suggest the ravenousness of the wolves "who leave no bone to gnaw until morning." The expression remains awkward, however, and Rudolph's emendation of *l' grmw lbqr* to *l' grw mhbqr,* "who are not even frightened of cattle," is suggestive (pp. 285–286). On the other hand, it is hard to understand the corruption of "steppe" to "evening" if the word "morning" were not already in the text. Rudolph's suggestion that the corruption proceeded in the other direction is problematic. Other suggestions such as the derivations of *grm* from Arabic, "to lack" (Keller, 206) or from Akkadian *karāmu,* "to withhold" (Van der Woude, 126) are not convincing.

[8]The Hebrew root *pḥz* carries the connotations of "haughty, puffed up, arrogant, impudent, undisciplined." Regarding prophets, it probably implies that they were speaking their own notions without waiting for a word from Yahweh (Jer. 23:32). LXX's *pneumatophoroi* probably does not mean "inspired" in a positive sense here, but something like "windbags, blowhards." Aquila's *thambeutai* does not mean "puffed up" (so Rudolph, 286), but "terrifying persons." Neither V's *vesani,* "insane, raging," nor T's "evil" catch the sense of the Hebrew participle.

[9]Hebrew *bōg^{e}dôt* is an abstract noun that serves as the *nomen rectum* in the construct chain *'anšê bōg^{e}dôt,* "men of treachery." None of the versions preserve the syntactical construction, but V's "faithless men"

and T's "lying men" are not bad translations, since the treachery is to be associated with the false prophecies these prophets were giving. S, however, introduces an additional group when it renders "and the men are wicked," and LXX's *kataphronētai,* "contemptuous men," though it presupposes the same Hebrew text (see Hab. 1:5; 2:5) does not capture the sense of the Hebrew.

[10]The expression *lā'ôr* clearly means "twilight" or "nightfall" in Job 24:14 (see Robert Gordis, *The Book of Job* [New York: Jewish Theological Seminary of America, 1978], 268). Zephaniah's thought is that Yahweh is constant and reliable; the natural order of the world, the regular succession of night and day, depends upon Yahweh's royal command, but one can count on it every morning and evening (cf. Gen. 8:22; Isa. 40:26; Jer. 33:19; Job 38:12; Ps. 104:19–20). Rudolph's emendation to *kā'ôr,* "like the sunlight" (p. 286), is unnecessary. V and some texts of LXX have "morning after morning he gives his judgment in the light, and it is not hidden." S also has the conjunction before the negative, but it renders "in the light, and it does not tarry." Other texts of LXX omit this whole line by haplography, skipping from *l'*[*wr*] to *wl'*.

[11]LXX also has a double rendering of this last line. The original reading *kai ouk eis nikos adikian,* "and not unto victory unrighteousness," is difficult. LXX uses *eis nikos* to translate *lnṣḥ,* "forever" (Jer. 3:5; Amos 1:11; 8:7; Job 36:7; Lam. 5:20). Since *lā'ad* sometimes occurs as a synonym for *lnṣḥ,* LXX may have misread *ywd'* as *lā'ad,* and then may have interpreted this reading in the light of its understanding of *lnṣḥ* (so Rudolph, 286). A second translation of the Hebrew was apparently added when the preceding line, originally omitted by haplography, was inserted. *Kai egnō adikian en apaitēsei,* "and he did not know unrighteousness in reclaiming," misreads *'awwāl,* "a wicked person," as *'āwel,* "unrighteousness," and apparently misreads *bōšet,* "shame," as *bᵉšē't,* "in taking away" (Rudolph, 286). LXX's initial expression in v. 6, *en diaphthorai,* "in destruction," was probably LXX's original translation of *bōšet,* which it took with the following sentence and read as *bᵉšē't,* "in devastation."

[12]MT has *gôyīm,* "nations," and V, S, and T all support its reading. This reading does not fit the context, however, since the following verse shows that Zephaniah is talking about punishments that had come upon Jerusalem and its land, not upon some foreign country. LXX's *hyperēphanous,* "the proud ones," apparently reading *gē'îm* instead of *gôyīm,* is probably a response to this exegetical difficulty, but it is hardly correct, since the expression "the proud ones" does not go well with "towers," "streets," and "towns." Read *gôyām,* "their nation." Though suffixed forms of *gôy* are relatively rare, they are attested (Gen. 10:5, 20, 31–32; Ezek. 36:13–15; Zeph. 2:9; Ps. 106:5), and one should note that Zepha-

niah is one of the writers who uses such a form to refer to God's people (2:9). Both *gôyām,* "their nation," and *gôyîm,* "nations," would have been written *gwym* in the original consonantal orthography; thus, given the infrequent usage of suffixed forms of the noun, it is not at all surprising that the unusual suffixed form of the singular was soon misread as the very common plural form.

[13]S's *dwyt',* "the miserable one," is an intra-Syriac corruption of *zwyt',* "the corner."

[14]These two parallel expressions raise the suspicion that they are variant readings, only one of which is original.

[15]The second-person verb forms are supported by all the versions and should not be emended away. They show that the original vocative address of the rebellious city in the *hôy*-oracle had not totally been lost from sight.

[16]LXX's second-person form here is a mistake caused by attraction to the two preceding verb forms. The idiom *hikkārēt mē'ênē-,* "to be cut off from the eyes of . . . ," apparently means the same as the more common idioms *hissātēr* or **hē'ālēm mē'ênē-,* "to be hidden from the eyes of . . . ," and the use of this somewhat unusual verb in the idiom is probably to be attributed to a desire to play on the same root used in v. 6 to express the punishment.

[17]Reading *m'ynyh* with LXX in place of MT's *m'wnh,* "her abode." The various attempts to preserve the MT have difficulty construing the following line.

[18]The idiom *pāqad 'al,* "to visit upon," is normally used in the negative sense "to punish," and that is the way the idiom is used elsewhere in Zephaniah (1:8, 9, 12). The positive sense is attested in only one passage (Ezra 1:2 = 2 Chron. 36:23). The interpretation of the idiom as "everything that I have commanded regarding her" is quite problematic despite Rudolph's assertion to the contrary (p. 286); the idiom *pqd 't* + person + *'l* + task, "to command someone concerning something," is common, but the idiom *pqd* + acc. rei + *'l* + person, "to command something upon someone," is hardly attested at all. The reference must be to punishment that has come upon Jerusalem and her land as discipline, but that means that the preceding verse must refer to disasters that had previously overtaken Jerusalem and Judah, not other nations.

[19]LXX misread *'ākēn,* a strong adversative, as a causative imperative, perhaps an *'aphel,* from *kwn,* "make ready!" and S also perpetuates this error. That error in turn led LXX and S to also misconstrue *hškymw,* "they rose early," as an imperative.

[20]Reading *l^e'ēd* with LXX and S in place of MT's *l^e'ad.* V's *in futurum,* "in the future," interprets MT's reading as containing *'ad,* "forever." Gerleman takes the expression to contain the word *'ad,* "booty"

(p. 55), and Sabottka assumes the meaning "throne" suggested by Dahood (pp. 113–114). Sabottka also assumes the meaning "from" for the preposition and translates "from the throne" (pp. 110, 113). None of these suggestions based on the MT reading carries conviction.

[21]Rudolph emends MT's *ʿᵃlêhem,* "upon them," to *ʿᵃlêkem,* "upon you," because in the context of a judgment oracle against Jerusalem, a sudden shift to a judgment on the nations does not fit (p. 287). The emendation is not necessary, however, for the antecedent of "them" is not the nations and kingdoms, but the more remote 3 m. pl. forms at the end of v. 7 that refer to the people of Jerusalem, whose behavior became ever more corrupt. See the commentary.

[22]LXX omits *zaʿmî.*

[23]MT and the versions read *ʿammîm,* "the peoples," but the context suggests that the reference should be to the people of Judah. Elliger proposed the correction to *ʿammî,* "my people" *(BHS),* which would give an acceptable sense, though it would probably require that one posit an intentional scribal correction to the simple plural. I suggest an original reading *ʿammām,* "their people," the suffix referring to the sinful leaders of Judah upon whom God's wrath was poured out. In the preexilic orthography of Zephaniah's time, which did not use internal matres, both *ʿammām* and *ʿammîm* would have been written as *ʿmm.* Thus an early misreading of the form as the simple plural of the noun would be quite understandable. For further discussion, see the commentary section.

[24]LXX misread *bᵉrûrāh* as *bᵉdôrāh,* "in its generation." V and S have "an elect lip," and T interprets the expression as the return of a common language, "one chosen speech."

[25]LXX and S omit this line. The rendering of *ʿᵃtāray* as "my supplicants" is supported by V's *supplices mei* and by the Greek texts that have *iketeuontas me.* The Greek texts with *prosdechomai,* "I will receive, undertake, await," apparently read *ʾittadtî* (Rudolph, 292). The form *pûṣay* is analyzed as the qal passive participle of *pûṣ,* "to scatter." One could also consider reading *battᵉpûṣāh,* "in the dispersion."

[26]This line does not go with v. 13 as the MT's punctuation suggests, but as the stichometry suggests, it provides the subject for the last line of v. 12.

Commentary

Zephaniah 3:1–13 has a fairly clear compositional unity even if it is composed of originally disparate elements. The introduction of the *hôy*-oracle against Jerusalem in 3:1 clearly separates this material from the immediately preceding material against Nineveh in 2:13–15. Apart from the last line of v. 5, which some critics take as a late gloss, Zeph. 3:1–5 is generally regarded as a single unit. At v. 6, however, there is a shift to direct address by God in the first person, a feature that continues through v. 13. That might suggest the beginning of a new unit, but v. 6 could hardly serve as the original introduction for an independent oracle; it begins too abruptly, without any introductory formula. J. M. Powis Smith regarded this verse and v. 7 as isolated fragments (ICC, 241). But even if v. 6 was originally a part of a more extended independent oracle, it is now certainly related to the preceding material, since v. 6 explicates the theme of Jerusalem's refusal to accept discipline introduced in Zeph. 3:1–2. Moreover, the thought is clearly continued in v. 7, which, contrary to Smith, must have always gone with v. 6. The original introduction to v. 6 may have been dropped to facilitate the use of vs. 6–7 as a continuation of Zeph. 3:1–5. Since v. 8 requires vs. 6–7 as the grounds for its announcement of the future judgment, the literary unit cannot end with v. 7, and v. 9 provides a positive reason for carrying out God's command to wait in v. 8, so the unit cannot end at v. 8. The first logical conclusion for the unit is v. 13.

[3:1] The placement of this *hôy*-oracle immediately following the oracle against Nineveh in 2:13–15 has misled some interpreters, including the ancient translator of the Peshiṭta, into also identifying the rebellious city in 3:1 as Nineveh. That is clearly wrong, however, and simply illustrates the danger of a careless reading across the boundary between two separate oracles. Contiguity in a collection of prophetic oracles is no guarantee that the juxtaposed oracles have any relationship to one another except for physical proximity in the collection and perhaps common authorship. The rebellious city attacked in Zeph. 3:1 is not named, but the things said about it in the following four verses make it clear that Jerusalem is the city intended. It is a city that should have learned from God's discipline, that should have trusted in Yahweh and drawn near to him as her God (3:2). Though her political leaders were oppressors, her prophets were treacherous, and her priests defiled the holy and did violence to priestly instruction (3:3–4), Yahweh remained righteous within her midst (3:5). A Judean prophet would hardly say such things about Nineveh, but they were recurring motifs in the prophetic critique of Jerusalem.

The three participles following the particle "hey" give an unflattering characterization of Jerusalem, and they are more closely related than they appear at first glance. If the form *mōr*ᵉ*'āh* is correctly analyzed as a qal f. s. active participle from *mārāh,* "to rebel," it portrays the city as stubbornly disobedient and rebellious. Isaiah had already used the same verb (Isa. 3:8) and an adjective derived from this verb (Isa. 30:9) to characterize the stubborn refusal of Jerusalem and Judah to obey Yahweh's commands, and the root was later used in the same way by Jeremiah, Ezekiel, and Third Isaiah (Jer. 4:17; 5:23; Ezek. 5:6; Isa. 63:10; for the adjective, Ezek. 2:5, 6;

3:9, 26, 27 passim). The second participle portrays the city as being polluted through that rebellion. Since the verb *gāʾal* is used especially of soiling one's hands or clothes with blood while committing an act of violence (Isa. 59:3; 63:3; Lam. 4:14), one should probably associate this pollution of Jerusalem with unjust violence against the poor and powerless. The third participle supports this conclusion with its specific characterization of the city as an oppressor.

An oppressor requires someone to oppress, and since the following verses speak of the violent abuses of the ruling classes in Jerusalem, one should understand the oppressed to be the less favored citizens of the city whom the authorities exploited and sometimes killed in their corrupt administration of the city. Isaiah had earlier issued a similar attack on Jerusalem's ruling classes for their oppression of their own people (3:13–15), and, while Isaiah's characterization of Jerusalem and its inhabitants uses different vocabulary than Zeph. 3:1, Isa. 1:2–20 contains all these same motifs of a city marked by stubborn disobedience (1:2–9), polluted through violence (1:15), and characterized by oppression (1:16–17; cf. also Isa. 1:21–23). Micah referred to such oppressive government as one that "builds Zion with criminal bloodshed" (Micah 3:10), and Jeremiah's later characterization of Jehoiakim's rule gives a good picture of what such government was like (Jer. 22:13–17). If one may judge from the Deuteronomistic Historian's account of the reigns of Manasseh and Amon (2 Kings 21:1–26, esp. v. 16), the practices condemned by Isaiah, Micah, and Jeremiah were even more pervasive in Zephaniah's time prior to Josiah's reform.

[2] Verse 2 explicates the city's first epithet in v. 1, while vs. 3–4 explicate the last two epithets. Jerusalem's stubborn rebellion is seen first of all in her refusal to listen to any voice or to accept any discipline. The refusal to hear any voice probably refers to the ruling classes' rejection of prophetic critiques of their behavior (Isa. 30:8–12; Micah 2:6; Jer. 7:23–28; 22:21), while the refusal to accept any discipline refers to the leaders' unwillingness to learn from the disasters that had overtaken them in history, disasters that the prophets interpreted as God's punishment of his people, intended to bring them back to obedience (Isa. 1:5–9; 9:7–20 [8–21]; 5:25–30; cf. Amos 4:6–11). The last two lines of v. 2 indicate that this rebellion arose out of Jerusalem's unwillingness to trust in Yahweh. It was Jerusalem's attempt to find her security in wealth, in military power, in foreign alliances, or even in other gods—in short, in almost anything other than Yahweh himself—that led her to reject God's demands. Rather than draw near to her God in trust, she sought to establish her own security, and in so doing she refused God's offer of life (Isa. 1:19) and turned from justice to trust in oppression (Isa. 28:12; 30:12, 15–16).

[3] Zephaniah places the blame for the violence and oppression that has polluted Jerusalem on the ruling classes. Following a well-attested pro-

phetic convention (Micah 3:1–12; Jer. 2:8; 5:31; 23:1–32; Ezek. 22:23–31), he singles out specific leadership groups for criticism. He likens the royal officials to roaring lions and Jerusalem's judges to wolves of the steppe. That is, both groups are fierce, carnivorous animals that prey on those who are under their authority. This negative use of animal names to characterize elements of the nobility represents an ironic reversal of a positive use of the same names to glorify an individual's or a group's courage, strength, or cunning over against the enemy. Thus Judah is a lion (Gen. 49:9), Dan a serpent (Gen. 49:17), and Benjamin a ravenous wolf (Gen. 49:27). Some such animal names were also used positively as indication of status in the nobility (see Patrick Miller, "Animal Names as Designations in Ugaritic and Hebrew," *UF* 2 [1970]: 177–178). Shema', a royal official of Jeroboam II, actually owned a seal with a roaring lion depicted upon it (*ANEP,* no. 276). Zephaniah's reversal of this positive use of animal names suggests a radical perversion of government; these leaders' courage and strength are no longer turned outward toward Jerusalem's enemies, but inward to devour the city's own citizens. The last line of the verse gives a further characterization of the wolves of the steppe, but its precise meaning remains somewhat obscure. It may mean that they are so ravenous that they devour their prey, bones and all, before the break of morning. If this is the sense, the comparison may imply something concrete about the nature of the abuses in the city's judicial system. The courts normally opened in the morning (Jer. 21:12), but the outcome of the cases may have already been decided the night before by bribery and corruption of the judges.

[4] Zephaniah moves from the political officials to the religious. The order may reflect Isaiah's negative judgment that the elder and prominent man was the head, while the lying prophet was the tail (Isa. 9:14 [15]). At any rate Zephaniah condemns the prophets as impudent and treacherous. He probably characterizes them as impudent because they brazenly give their own opinion as the word of Yahweh (cf. Ezek. 22:28). His characterization of them as treacherous probably implies both that the prophets' words deceive and mislead the people (cf. Jer. 23:32) and that they are willing to shape their prophetic word to suit whoever is paying for it (cf. Micah 2:11; 3:5).

Zephaniah then condemns the priests for profaning the holy things and doing violence to instruction. The first complaint probably deals with their failure to maintain the appropriate cultic distinctions between the holy and profane (cf. Ezek. 22:26), a failure that points to a lack of respect for Yahweh (cf. Mal. 1:6–9). Their violent treatment of *tôrāh,* the priestly instruction or rulings given primarily in regard to cultic questions, is probably related and refers to the bending of the normal rulings to show partiality to the influential and powerful (cf. Mal. 1:9). It could also refer to excessive or oppressive cultic levies or fines imposed on the less influential (cf. Amos

2:8). The priests issued the rulings as to what sacrifices were acceptable in different situations, and their control of the means of propitiation and reintegration of an offender back into the cultic community gave them ample opportunity to abuse their authority for their own gain (cf. 1 Sam. 2:12–17; Hos. 4:4–8; Micah 3:11). On the other hand, the priests were also involved in resolving difficult cases outside the strictly cultic realm, cases of homicide, civil law, and assault, and their rulings in such cases are also referred to as *tôrāh* (Deut. 17:8–13). Obviously, such cases as these would also present them with the opportunity to treat the *tôrāh* violently, to bend their rulings to favor the powerful.

[**5**] This corrupt behavior of Jerusalem's political and religious leaders stands in sharp contrast to the righteous behavior of Yahweh, Israel's God who lives in Jerusalem. He is a God of faithfulness who does no wrong (cf. Deut. 32:4). His faithfulness is evident in the regularity of the natural order day after day and night after night (cf. Gen. 9:21–22; Jer. 33:20). The expression *mišpāṭô yittēn,* "he gives his judgment," presumably refers to Yahweh's continuing care over and ordering of nature, to his commands that bring forth the morning, call the stars out by name, and dictate the rhythms of nature (Job 38:12, 31–33; Isa. 40:26; Ps. 104:28–30). Yet this glaring contrast between God's faithfulness and the crooked perversity of his human officials leaves those wicked officials unfazed. They are simply too brazen to know shame (cf. Isa. 3:8–9; Jer. 3:3).

[**6**] Somewhat abruptly, the prophet switches from third-person address about Yahweh to direct quotation of Yahweh's words in the first person. Despite the abruptness of this switch, however, Yahweh's speech in vs. 6–7 is clearly tied to the preceding verses by the common theme of Jerusalem's refusal to accept discipline (vs. 1–2). Yahweh first narrates the judgment he had sent against Jerusalem and her people. That judgment is summarized in God's statement, "I cut off their nation," but he goes on to explicate the meaning of that statement by a series of images that all reflect the same historical reality—the destruction of Judah's major fortified cities. The desolate, fortified towers, the rubble-strewn streets through which no one passed, and the ruined cities lying empty of human inhabitants all point back to the Assyrian devastation of Judah in the time of Hezekiah. According to Sennacherib's account of that campaign, the Assyrian king destroyed forty-six of Hezekiah's fortified cities, deported over 200,000 people, and cut off a significant portion of Judean territory, which he reassigned to Philistine rule (see John Bright, *A History of Israel,* 3rd ed. [Philadelphia: Westminster Press, 1981], 286). Isaiah paints a similar portrait of that devastation in his complaint about Judah's refusal to learn from her punishment (Isa. 1:5–9), and nothing comparable had befallen Judah in the interval down to the time of Zephaniah.

[7] Then Zephaniah has Yahweh continue his speech in a way that

echoes this earlier passage of Isaiah. After narrating his judgment on Judah, Yahweh reflects on Jerusalem's failure to learn from it. Slipping briefly back into the direct address with which the oracle opened, God says to Jerusalem, "I thought surely you will accept this discipline and learn to fear me." Then falling back into the use of the third person in reference to the city, God continues to state his expectations: "Surely her eyes cannot miss the significance of all the punishment that I brought upon her." But Yahweh has to admit he was sadly mistaken. Far from learning from this disaster in Hezekiah's day, the people of Jerusalem quickly made their behavior even more corrupt. This appraisal corresponds to that of the Deuteronomistic Historian, who also portrays the situation in Jerusalem under Hezekiah's successor Manasseh as far more corrupt than in the preceding period.

[8] In view of Jerusalem's failure to learn from past punishment and her increasing wickedness, one could only expect from Yahweh a threat of new judgment to come. Verse 8 fulfills that expectation, but it does more than that. It opens with *lākēn,* "therefore," a word which the prophets normally use, after the statement of grounds, to introduce a divine declaration or command (BDB, 486). In this case, it is a command to wait for Yahweh until the day when he would rise up to witness against his people. The verb *hakkēh,* "to wait for," normally implies a waiting for a favorable intervention of Yahweh, but Rudolph argues that the context here rules out such a reading (p. 290). Since the preceding context gives good grounds for a fierce judgment on Jerusalem but no grounds for any judgment on the other nations, the judgment must be against Jerusalem, and thus the command to wait must be taken in an unusual threatening sense. One may agree with Rudolph's premise, however, without accepting his conclusion. He does not consider the possibility that the command is addressed to a particular group in the land. This is the first 2 m. pl. form in the unit, however; given the similar forms in 2:1–3, where the prophet urges a particular group to seek to escape the coming judgment, one must ask whether the prophet again had such a group in mind. One should note that the indictment in the preceding verses was directed against the ruling classes, not against the poor and oppressed of his people. Note, moreover, the contrast between the 3 m. pl. references to the sinners (v. 7c) upon whom God's wrath will be poured (v. 8c) and the 2 m. pl. reference to those who are to wait for Yahweh's intervention. Rudolph destroyed that contrast by too quickly emending the 3 m. pl. suffix in v. 8c to a 2 m. pl. Yahweh's command to wait for him should be understood as addressed to the same oppressed followers of Yahweh mentioned in Zeph. 2:3; their relief could only come when Yahweh had refined Jerusalem by judgment. Note the very similar use of the verb *hakkēh* when Isaiah is waiting out the threatened judgment on Israel (Isa. 8:16).

The oppressed followers of Yahweh are to wait for him to rise up as a witness against Jerusalem and its people. Yahweh obviously has a lawsuit against his people, and he has decided to gather together the nations as his agents to execute his punishment upon Jerusalem (cf. Jer. 1:15–16). The antecedent of the pronoun in the expression "to pour upon them" is not the nations and kingdoms mentioned in the preceding two lines, but the people of Jerusalem, whose corrupt actions are cited as the grounds for the judgment at the end of v. 7. Grammatically, the antecedent is ambiguous, and the fact that "nations" and "kingdom" offered the nearest 3 m. pl. nouns that could serve as an antecedent for the suffix has led to exegetical confusion. Nevertheless, the more distant 3 m. pl. forms at the end of v. 7 are exegetically the only appropriate antecedent. As noted above, the context gives good grounds for Yahweh pouring out his wrath on Jerusalem, but none at all for punishing the other nations. Moreover, Ezekiel, who seems to have been dependent on this passage in Zephaniah, clearly interprets Yahweh's wrath as being poured out on the people of Jerusalem (Ezek. 22:23–31; Rudolph, 290). One could paraphrase the sense of the passage, then, as follows:

> Therefore wait for me, you oppressed ones who follow me,
> Until I rise up as a witness against your wicked rulers,
> Because it is my judgment to gather up nations,
> And assemble kingdoms as my agents of destruction,
> To pour upon your oppressive rulers my anger. . . .

Rudolph considers the last two lines of v. 8 as a later gloss that extended the judgment originally restricted to Jerusalem to the whole land of Judah (p. 290), but his argument seems quite strained (cf. the discussion on 1:18). A judgment on Jerusalem would inevitably affect the inhabitants of its larger territory outside the city, and Zephaniah's admonition to the "poor of the land" in Zeph. 2:3 shows that the prophet had no illusions about that fact.

[9] Verse 9 is introduced by the causal conjunction *kî* and followed by the temporal adverb *'āz,* which refers back to the day of Yahweh's rising mentioned in v. 8. The clause so introduced gives a positive reason for the pious to wait on Yahweh's intervention. Judgment is not the final word; it is simply a means to bring the people of Judah and Jerusalem back to an uncorrupted devotion to Yahweh.

The received text reads "to the peoples," which would suggest that God is promising to give the foreign nations pure lips so that they can all worship Yahweh along with Judah. This reading would make the verse parallel to the thought in Zeph. 2:11. The context in Zephaniah 3 makes this reading problematic, however. The preceding verses speak of the sin and corruption of Jerusalem and her leaders; it says nothing about the sins of the nations. Moreover, the following verses, apart from the somewhat obscure v. 10, speak exclusively of God's purifying work as directed to his own people. Verse 11 speaks of the removal of the haughty officials of Jerusalem, and v. 12 speaks of the poor and humble people Yahweh would leave in the city as the remnant of Israel. Finally, v. 13 picks up and explicates the meaning of v. 9's reference to the pure lip by explaining how this remnant, unlike the previous occupants of Jerusalem, will no longer sin and speak deceitfully. Given this exclusive attention in the larger context to Jerusalem's present wickedness and future transformation, one should probably read "to their people" or "to my people." If one reads "their people," the pronominal suffix would refer to the sinful leaders of Jerusalem upon whom God's judgment would fall (v. 8). If one reads "my people," the suffix would obviously refer to Yahweh. The reading of the received text may have arisen through a simple scribal error, but it is one of a number of features in the text of Zephaniah 3 that tend to give the chapter both a more universalistic scope and, at the same time, to shift God's judgment away from Jerusalem and onto the foreign nations.

The promise that God would restore to the people a pure lip recalls the cleansing of Isaiah's lips in his famous call passage (Isa. 6:4). Isaiah's reference to the uncleanness of his and his people's lips in that passage is probably to be understood in the light of his complaint that the people drew near to God with their mouth and honored him with their lips, but their heart was far from him (Isa. 29:13); that is, their actions belied their words. Zephaniah promises a correction of this situation so that all the people can worship and serve God appropriately. The expression "to call upon Yahweh" refers specifically to the invoking of God's name in praise and prayer, but it is often used as a general expression for worship. The word "serve" can be used in the sense of cultic service or worship, but it can also be used in the broader sense of a life of obedience to God's demands. The phrase "with one shoulder" is an idiomatic expression derived from the realm of the draft animals, which were yoked together and with their shoulders shared the weight of their common work (cf. Isa. 9:3 [4]; 10:27; 14:25). This phrase and the preceding "all" emphasizes that in the restored Jerusalem, all the people will serve Yahweh. The oppressive rulers and judges, and the impious prophets and priests (vs. 3–4), not to mention the servants of Baal and other foreign deities (Zeph. 1:4–6), will all be gone, and the remnant will all be devoted to Yahweh (cf. vs. 11–12 below).

[10] Verse 10 presents the interpreter with a crux, because of textual and translational difficulties with the two key expressions in the second line of the verse. The expression *ʿᵃtāray* is probably correctly rendered as "my supplicants," but the translation of *bat-pûṣay* as "daughter of my dispersed ones" is less certain. Both this rendering of the expression and the correction of the expression to *battᵉpûṣāh,* "in the dispersion," would imply that God's supplicants from Ethiopia were not foreigners but Judeans who had been exiled there. So understood, the verse would introduce the theme of the return of Judean exiles from Ethiopia or Nubia. The region referred to is the region of the Blue and White Niles (cf. Isa. 18:1–2), the southernmost area ruled by the Ethiopian or Nubian kings of the XXV (Ethiopian) dynasty (ca. 716–663 B.C.). There is little reason to believe that there were many Judean exiles so far south of Egypt in Zephaniah's time, however, so it is doubtful whether such a thought could be attributed to Zephaniah or his time. The theme of a return from Assyria and the lands of the north might be possible this early (Isa. 11:11–12, 15–16; Jer. 31:8), but specific reference to the exiles in Egypt or Ethiopia probably presupposes the enormous dislocation of Judean population in the period from about 601–580 B.C., the period associated with the beginning of the Babylonian exile. Thus, the verse is probably a later addition to the text, just as Zeph. 2:11 is.

Other treatments of the verse find a reference to foreign worshipers of Yahweh. Some scholars have assumed that the expression *bat-pûṣay* conceals the name of a foreign people. Keller, who corrects the expression to *bitᵉpûṣāh,* which he takes to mean "in abundance," translates the verse as "From beyond the rivers of Cush come my worshippers, in abundance they bring me offerings" (CAT, 210). Both these treatments would identify the supplicants as foreigners. Others achieve the same results by deleting one or both of the troublesome expressions. Rudolph deletes *bat-pûṣay* (p. 292) and Van der Woude deletes both *ʿᵃtāray* and *bat-pûṣay* as a gloss inserted by a later, postexilic Judean particularist who attempted to undercut the original universalism of the passage by turning the foreigners into Judean exiles (p. 132). Neither Rudolph's nor Van der Woude's explanation of the text is convincing, however, because the tendency in later readings of the text is toward highlighting the role of the nations and increasing the universalism. If the verse does refer to foreign worshipers, however, its resemblance to Zeph. 2:11 would be even more striking, and that would only confirm the judgment that it is a later insertion in the text.

[11] Verse 11 opens with a temporal expression that refers back to the day when God will have purified the speech of his people through judgment (v. 9). Prior to the judgment, the wicked officials in Jerusalem were too brazen to feel shame at their behavior, though it turned Jerusalem into a rebellious, polluted, and oppressive city (vs. 1–5), but, after this purifying judgment, there will be no need for the city to be ashamed of those rebellious deeds, for their perpetrators will be gone. God will remove Jerusalem's arrogant officials from the city, and their haughty abuse of power will no longer characterize the life of Jerusalem, the city built on God's holy mountain.

[12] Instead, the population that will remain in Jerusalem will be a poor and humble people, the pious who obeyed God and pursued righteousness (Zeph. 2:3). This remnant of Israel will seek their security in the person of

Yahweh. Their trust will be in the power of God, not in human power, wealth, or prestige.

[13] Thus they will have no need to repeat the earlier abuses of Jerusalem's inhabitants. Because they trust in God for meaning and security in life, they will not commit iniquity or oppression; lying, deceitfulness, or cheating will be absent from their lives. The specific mention of the absence of a deceitful tongue in their mouth is clearly intended to pick up and explicate what is meant by a pure lip in v. 9.

Finally, such trust in God will not be in vain. The future Jerusalem of this humble remnant will find the security that eluded the rebellious Jerusalem of the arrogant officials of Zephaniah's day. Like a well-pastured flock securely protected from all predators, the inhabitants of this purified Jerusalem will enjoy an abundant, peaceful existence free from nagging fear or sudden terror.

2. Rejoice! 3:14–20

3:14 Cry out for joy, daughter Zion!
Give a shout, O Israel!
Rejoice and exult with all your heart,
Daughter Jerusalem!
15 Yahweh has turned aside your judgments,
He has turned away your enemies.[1]
The king of Israel, Yahweh, is in your midst,
You will not see[2] evil again.
16 In that day it will be said to Jerusalem,
Do not be afraid, Zion,
Let not your hands droop down.
17 Yahweh, your God, is in your midst,
A warrior who saves.
He will rejoice[3] over you with joy,
He will shout over you with jubilation.
He will soothe in his love[4]
18 Those grieving[5] far from the festival.
I will gather up from you the "Hey you!"[6]
So that one will not raise[7] a reproach over you.[8]
19 I will make an end[9]
Of all your oppressors at that time.
I will save the lame,
And the scattered I will gather.
I will make them renowned and famous
In every land of their shame.[10]
20 At that time when I bring you,[11]
And at the time[12] of my gathering you,
I will make you famous and renowned

Among all the peoples of the earth,
When I restore your fortunes
Before their[13] eyes, says Yahweh.

Textual Notes

[1]The plural should probably be read with a number of manuscripts, LXX, S, and T.

[2]Reading *tir'î* with LXX and S. MT has *tîrā'î,* "you will not fear," but its reading has probably been influenced by the *yr'* in v. 16. The common idiom *r'h r',* "to see evil," supports the correction.

[3]LXX's *epaxei,* "he will bring in," may presuppose the reading *yāšîb,* "he will bring back," rather than MT's *yāśîś,* but the MT is clearly the superior reading.

[4]This line comes between the two preceding lines in MT and all the versions, but in so doing it splits apart two parallel lines that speak of God's rejoicing with shouting and jubilation. It goes with the first line of v. 19, and the verb *yaḥ*ᵃ*rîš* should be understood as transitive, "he will bring to silence," i.e., "he will soothe" those who are crying in anguish. Once the line was transposed, the object was no longer available for correct construal, and the intransitive rendering, "he will keep silence," made no sense between two lines that speak of God shouting with joy. This resulted in further textual corruption that tried to bring this line into agreement with the parallel lines that bracket it. LXX and S read *y*ᵉ*ḥadd*ᵉ*šēk,* "he will renew you." T has "he will suppress your guilt in his love." Note that all these variants presuppose a suffix on the verb in agreement with the suffixed preposition in the two parallel lines. A more recent proposal of Rudolph and others suggests reading *yirḥaš,* "he is stirred up," (Rudolph, 293; cf. Ps. 45:2 [1]), but the line would still be out of place between the two parallel lines reflecting God's joy.

[5]MT's *nûgê* is the m. pl. construct niphal participle from *yāgāh,* "to grieve" (cf. Lam. 1:4). The transposition of the preceding line left this object without a verb, and, as a result, it has suffered corruption in some textual traditions. LXX apparently read either *k*ᵉ*yôm,* "as the day," or *kîmê,* "as the days," and construed it as the conclusion of the preceding line: "he will rejoice over you in joy as in the day of a feast." S followed LXX in this reading. T apparently connected the participle with *yāgāh* II, "to remove, be distant": "Anyone among you who holds himself away at the times of your festivals I will remove from your midst." V's *nugas,* "silly ones," was presumably chosen for its similarity in sound to the Hebrew participle. Its interpretation, "the silly ones who turn back from the law I will gather," has some similarity to that of T.

[6]This line is a very difficult crux. I emend MT's *hyw* to *hôy* with LXX

and understand it as a brief way of referring to a taunt or reproach by citing only the opening expression (see Hab. 2:6, where one raises up [*nāśā'*] a taunt [*māšāl*] by reciting *hôy*-sayings). Rudolph's emendation of *mimmēk,* "from you," to *mimmakkêhem,* "from those who smite them" (p. 294), may have weak support from LXX's *syntetrimmenous,* "those who are crushed," but his reading breaks down because he has not recognized the transposition in v. 17.

[7]Reading *miśśē't,* privative *min* + the infinitive of *nāśā',* "from the raising of." S offers a rather free translation, but it gets the general sense of the passage right: "And I will remove from you those who spoke reproach against you." LXX apparently read *hôy mî yiśśā' 'ᵃlêhā ḥerpāh,* "Hey, whoever raises reproach against her," but this does not fit well with the rest of the verse.

[8]MT has the third-person suffix, but the context calls for the second person found in both S and T.

[9]Restoring *kālāh,* "an end," after the participle *'ōśeh* (cf. Isa. 10:23). The word was lost by haplography due to the similarity with *kol,* "all," in the following phrase. T's translation either reflects such a Hebrew text or supplies the missing *kālāh* as an obvious ellipsis. One can defend MT's absolute use of the verb *'āśāh* (see Ezek. 22:14; 23:25; Rudolph, 294), though the stichometry is less balanced with that reading: "I will deal with all your oppressors at that time." The suggestion that one correct MT's *'t-kl-m'nyk,* "with all your oppressors," by a transposition to *klh 't m'nyk,* "an end with your oppressors," is doubtful, since the versions, despite their quite different translations, all seem to reflect basically the consonantal text of MT. LXX misdivided the MT as *'tk lm'nk,* "with you for your sake." S read the participle as a passive, "I will deal with all of them when they are oppressed among you at that time."

[10]Reading *bkl 'rṣ bštm* with V, S, and T. MT has to be corrected, or the word "their shame" will stand in total syntactical isolation. An alternative correction involves deleting the suffix on *wśmty⟨m⟩* to produce the translation "I will turn their shame into praise and fame in all the earth" (Rudolph, 294). This is a bit awkward, however, because the direct object, "their shame," occurs at the very end of the verse, after the objects of the prepositions *l,* and this is against the idiom's normal order: *śwm* + acc. + *l.* LXX's alternative of turning the isolated word into a verb and reading it with the next line, "they shall be ashamed at that time," is clearly erroneous.

[11]MT must be read as an unmarked relative clause since it is in parallel with a temporal construction using an infinitive construct. LXX apparently reads *'ēṭîb,* "I will do (you) good," for MT's *'ābî',* "I will bring."

[12]Read *bᵉ'ēt,* the construct form without the article.

[13]So S and some Lucianic texts. MT, LXX, V, and T have "your eyes,"

which would imply "in your lifetime." The context, however, which speaks of Israel's fame among all the nations, suggests that this will happen when God restores Israel's fortunes before the eyes of these nations. They will see God's salvation of Israel and form a new opinion about these formerly oppressed people (cf. Isa. 52:10–15). The corruption from *-hem* to *-kem* is easily explained by the influence of the 2 m. pl. suffix on *šᵉbûtê-kem,* "your fortunes," in the preceding line.

Commentary

A new unit begins in v. 14 and runs through v. 20, but this new unit is intimately connected to the preceding, since the transformation of Jerusalem mentioned in vs. 9–13 provides the grounds for v. 14's command to Jerusalem to rejoice. The clear, logical connection between the two units makes it unclear whether this larger unity is the remnant of an original rhetorical unity or whether it is part of the secondary compositional unity imposed on the whole chapter.

[3:14] The command to Jerusalem to rejoice has clear parallels at the beginning of new oracles (Isa. 54:1; Zech. 2:14 [10]; 9:9), but similar commands are also found in rhetorical transitions of thought within the same oracle (Isa. 12:6; 44:23; 49:13; Joel 2:21). If one may judge from Isa. 52:7–10, the original *Sitz im Leben* for such commands was the cry of heralds calling for public rejoicing because of the arrival of messengers bringing good news of victory or deliverance to the city. The command prophetically presupposes that the day of Jerusalem's purification and restoration predicted in vs. 9–13 has now arrived. The parallel command to Israel picks up the thought in v. 12 that the humble inhabitants of the purified Jerusalem are the remnant of Israel, used here not as a designation for the northern kingdom but more inclusively as a designation for all God's chosen people.

[15] Verse 15 bases the command to rejoice on the good news that the judgments mentioned in v. 8 have ended. "Your judgments" refers to the judgments imposed on Jerusalem by Yahweh, who announced in v. 8 his decision ("my judgment") to send the foreign nations against the city to punish it. Those are the enemies that Yahweh has now removed from his city. Because Yahweh is in Jerusalem as Israel's king, the city will no longer see such disasters. One should note the contrast to v. 5, where Yahweh was also said to be in Jerusalem, but his earlier presence in the city brought destruction because the corruption of the city's officials made Yahweh hostile to it. A holy God will not live comfortably in a moral slum. In the future, however, Yahweh's presence in Jerusalem will be salvific, not destructive, for then the remnant inhabiting Zion will be righteous, fit to enjoy God's company (cf. Isa. 33:13–19).

[16] In that day, Jerusalem will receive prophetic oracles of salvation and encouragement, not prophetic indictments and threats of impending judgment. "Do not be afraid" is a very common element in oracles of salvation, and it is often used to introduce them (2 Kings 19:6; Isa. 7:4; 10:24; 35:4; 40:9; 41:10; passim). The parallel expression, "let not your hands droop down," is not as common, but it (2 Chron. 15:7) and its positive reformulation, "strengthen your hands" (Zech. 8:13), are attested in such oracles.

[17] The reason given for this encouraging word is once more the reassurance that Yahweh, Jerusalem's God, dwells within her. He is a warrior who is capable of saving his city. If evil overtook it in the past, it was because Yahweh himself declared war against it (v. 8), but, with Jerusalem's purification, those days when God's anger burned against his own city are gone. In the future, Yahweh will be so proud of Jerusalem that he will rejoice over his city with a public display of jubilation. In his love, he will comfort those who are grieving because they are too far away to attend her festivals. The thought in this last line of v. 17 and the first line of v. 18 may be an oblique reference to God's promise to gather in the exiles of Judah (vs. 19–20).

[18] Because God will be pleased with Jerusalem, his prophets will no longer pronounce *hôy*-oracles against the city (cf. v. 1), and no one will raise a reproach against her.

[19] God will do away with all of Jerusalem's oppressors at that time. The oppressors here probably include both the arrogant Judean officials who formerly dominated and oppressed the city (vs. 1–5, 11) and the foreign nations whom Yahweh used to purge the city of these officials (v. 8). Having done away with the oppressors, Yahweh will gather up and save those who had been oppressed and scattered by these enemies. The imagery here is that of a shepherd who gathers together a flock that has been scattered by predators and who doctors the sheep that were injured in the attack. This was a very popular metaphor to describe the role of the king in ancient Near Eastern society, however, so its use here is simply continuing the royal metaphor of Yahweh as Jerusalem's warrior king. The last two lines of the verse suggest that these former exiles will now be held in honor in the very lands where they once lived in shame as exiles. For the thought, compare the nations' reevaluation of Israel in Isa. 52:13–53:6.

[20] Verse 20 simply expands on the thought of the preceding verse and emphasizes that God's salvation and glorification of his people will be evident to all the nations of the world (cf. Isa. 52:10).